Not Yet

Not Yet

Reconsidering Ernst Bloch

Edited by
Jamie Owen Daniel and Tom Moylan

VERSO
London · New York

First published by Verso 1997
© in the collection Jamie Owen Daniel and Tom Moylan 1997
© in individual contributions the contributors 1997
© in *Spuren* (pp. 215–23 this volume) Ernst Bloch, *Spuren*, pp. 11–25,
© Suhrkamp Verlag, Frankfurt am Main 1969

The rights of Jamie Owen Daniel and Tom Moylan
to be identified as the editors of this work
have been asserted by them in accordance with
the Copyright, Designs and Patents Act 1988

Verso
UK: 6 Meard Street, London W1V 3HR
USA: 180 Varick Street, New York NY 10014–4606

Verso is the imprint of New Left Books

ISBN 0–86091–439–9
ISBN 0–86091–683–9 (pbk)

British Library Cataloguing in Publication Data
A catalogue record for this book is available from the British Library

Library of Congress Cataloging-in-Publication Data
A catalog record for this book is available from the Library of Congress

Typeset by CentraCet Ltd, Cambridge
Printed by Biddles Ltd, Kings Lynn and Guildford

Contents

CONTENTS

Why *Not Yet,* Now?

Jamie Owen Daniel and Tom Moylan

Several of the essays in this volume allude to the possibility that a reconsideration of the utopian Marxist project of Ernst Bloch might seem, just now, to be audaciously inappropriate. After all, we presently take for granted, in ways that would have been unthinkable a decade ago, the absorption of the former German Democratic Republic into the market economy of the Federal Republic, the dissolution of the Soviet Union into paralyzed ethnic nations without economies, and the re-emergence of vicious expressions of chauvinism and xenophobia around the globe. Marxism has been pronounced dead and its project labeled irrelevant by many who wonder about the value of historical materialism at the so-called "end of history." In such a context, it might be asked what any of us could gain from the work of a thinker who sought so consistently to contribute to and reinforce the critical vision of twentieth century Marxism – especially now, when "utopia" has been both buried and colonized by transnational capitalism. A call to reconsider the thought of the man whom Oskar Negt has called "the German philosopher of the October Revolution" might thus appear to be little more than a nostalgic look backward on the part of leftist academics to a time when Bloch's unsettling utopian project did not seem so quaintly idealistic.

This book, however, is just such a call for reconsideration, since the editors believe that a closer look at the aftermath of the events described above will help to bring other perspectives and other possibilities into focus: a focus which will resolve more sharply as the emerging conditions of local and transnational realities at the end of the century are more fully grasped. Exploitation, suffering, and destruction continue around the world, and yet we continue to hear expressions of a stubborn hope for a better life by a diverse range of people who increasingly find little in the current situation to celebrate. This better life is one that many do *not* define solely in terms of access to personal wealth or to brand-name commodities or services. Rather, they seek, in a variety of ways, what Theodor Adorno once called, within the context of a conversation with Bloch, "the capacity to imagine the totality as something completely different." It is this capacity, we believe, which can be fortified and expanded by a reconsideration of the work of Ernst Bloch.

In putting together a collection of essays which respond in differing ways to this work, we want to provide evidence that Bloch's version of "warm" utopian Marxist critique is neither outdated nor out of place. Rather, we hold that it still suggests strategies for imagining "the totality" as a viable alternative to the seemingly ubiquitous "new world order" initiated under the Reagan/Bush and Thatcher administrations in the 1980s, and which continue with a vengeance in the 104th Congress and elsewhere in the 1990s. In so doing, we do not want to resurrect Bloch's work without a critical consideration of its strengths and weaknesses in relation to the contemporary moment, without acknowledging that the older discourses of historical materialism and utopian anticipation upon which Bloch builds have benefitted from various poststructuralist critiques. Such critical challenges have provoked the sort of rethinking of Marxist discourses that is absolutely essential if these theoretical practices are to prove adequate to the task of meeting contemporary political needs, needs that can not be met by resuscitating the agendas of either the old left or the new left. We thus want to emphasize, and to illustrate by the example of the essays collected here, that a third-generation rereading and, to use Brecht's term, refunctioning of these discourses can provide a humane, imaginative, and enabling alternative to the paralyzing cynicism of those whom Peter Sloterdijk has referred to as "voyeurs of the decline," those disillusioned academics and intellectuals on the right (and, indeed, on the disillusioned left) who seem all too ready to accept the "new world order" as an inevitability.

Our own engagement with Marxism, utopianism, and Bloch began some twenty years ago, when both of us were students involved in the intellectual community that developed around the journal *New German Critique*, in Milwaukee, Wisconsin. While our work has moved in various directions since then, we have each consistently returned in our writing and our teaching to Bloch's insistence on a utopian standpoint, a utopian epistemology, as expressed in an eclectic array of writings that were clearly intended to function as provocations and irritants rather than as any kind of dogmatic foundation or program. Through its insistence on tracking the traces of utopia in the smallest details of everyday life, Bloch's work provided us with an early model for cultural studies that could recognize and value popular cultural expressions. Through its unyielding optimism, it provided us with a counter-balance to the necessary pessimism of the cultural criticism of the Frankfurt School.

*

Five essays in this volume were first published in a special issue of *Utopian Studies*, the journal of the Society for Utopian Studies. Others developed out of a special session on Ernst Bloch at the 1991 meeting of the Modern Language Association in San Francisco, which we organized with the help of the Marxist Literary Group. We would like to thank both these organizations for their support of this project in its initial stages. Most of all, we want to thank each of our contributors for their insights and their persistence.

We also want to thank several others for their help in this long journey. Jack Zipes has been there all along, both in the dialogue with Bloch that has been a constant subtext in his own work, and through his important translation of Bloch's writings on art and literature. Andreas Huyssen and Lyman Tower Sargent, in their own, very different ways, moved our individual work along. Peter Fitting, Fred Pfeil, Mary Layoun, and Paul Smith each gave challenging support at key moments. Michael Sprinker recognized the value of the project for Verso, and Malcolm Imrie saw the project through to completion with his easygoing manner and his patience with endless transatlantic faxes. Val Bogan's extraordinary cover art has given Bloch's hope a concrete image that print cannot match, and Áine O'Brien has shared with us her suspicious faith in our collaboration on utopian discourse. And special thanks to Jane Hindle and Judith Ravenscroft for their work on the final manuscript.

The essays by Vincent Geoghegan (chapter 2), Ruth Levitas (chapter 5), Tom Moylan (chapter 7), Darko Suvin (chapter 8), and Ze'ev Levy (chapter 11) all appeared first in *Utopian Studies*, 1: 2 (1990), and are reprinted here with permission of the editors. David Kaufmann's essay (chapter 3) was published in the *Yale Journal of Criticism* and is reprinted here by permission of Blackwell Publishers. Klaus Berghahn's essay (chapter 13) was first published in *Modernity and the Text: Revisions of German Modernism*, ed. Andreas Huyssen and David Bathrick (New York: Columbia University Press, 1989), reprinted here by permission of Columbia University Press.

Finally, we want to thank our respective daughters, Katy and Sarah Moylan and Caitlin Daniel-McCarter, for providing the most tangible traces of utopia in our everyday lives.

November 1996

Traces of Hope:
The Non-synchronicity of Ernst Bloch

Jack Zipes

The reputation and reception of Ernst Bloch, the political philosopher of hope, have undergone so many changes in Europe and the United States during the last thirty years that it is difficult to follow the different debates about the meaning and impact of his works. These debates are also complicated by the fact that both critics and defenders often refuse to separate the man from his philosophy, especially since he played such an active role in politics. Ernst Bloch was always out of step with his totalitarian times, though in step with Stalinism, in step with unorthodox Marxist philosophy, and out of step with vulgar Marxism. Wherever he went, he stirred up trouble because he refused to accept the status quo of existing social and political conditions. His philosophy urged people to search for every possible clue and trace in the past and present so that they could go beyond their times. Bloch, like his heroes, Moses, Jesus Christ, Thomas Münzer, and Karl Marx, was a rabble-rouser.

Even well after his death, Bloch remains a figure of controversy. In Germany many critics reject his thought because of his allegiance to the East German government which, they believe, undermined the sincerity and integrity of his philosophical project. In the United States several writers have taken him to task because of his contradictory defense of Stalinism and critique of the fascist tendencies of capitalism, which are difficult to reconcile.

Throughout his life – and it was a very long ninety years which spanned two world wars, fascism, Stalinism, various revolutions, the Cold War, the Korean and Vietnam wars – it seemed that Bloch was somehow way ahead of his times or trying to co-ordinate his thinking with the "proper" position of a real-possible communism that would prepare the way for the classless society, a utopian world which we have glimpsed but not seen. At the onset of the First World War, he broke with the sociologist Max Weber because of the latter's nationalist inclinations, opposed the German militarists, went to Switzerland and participated in anarchist-pacifist groups while writing essays against the war. Though detested by many Germans, he returned to Germany after the war to write *Geist der Utopie* (1918) and *Thomas Münzer as Theologian of Revolution* (1921), two radical books that celebrated the apocalyptic potential in the world that could foster the classless society. Branded a political enemy by the Nazis in 1933, he escaped to Switzerland to write *Heritage of Our Times* (1934), in which he elaborated his important category of non-synchronicity and critiqued the Communists and Social Democrats for failing the proletariat, peasants, and middle class. He also appalled many of his friends by supporting the Moscow Show Trials in 1936/37 because he believed that the Soviet Union was the last bastion of hope against Nazism. In 1938, after working for the anti-fascist resistance in France and Czechoslovakia and supporting the Soviet Union, Bloch decided to emigrate to the United States, where he ironically was safer with his unorthodox Marxist ideas than in the Soviet Union. Bloch was even granted US citizenship, though he could never adapt to the "American way of life" and was fiercely critical of the manner in which American capitalism concealed class struggle and displayed tendencies that he associated with fascism, a political critique that he shared with the Frankfurt School. By 1949, with the anti-communist repression in full swing throughout the United States and an offer to direct the Institute for Philosophy in Leipzig, Bloch left for the German Democratic Republic, ironically after having completed most of *The Principle of Hope* in the land of capitalism par excellence. Although he was permitted to publish the three volumes of *The Principle of Hope* (1952, 1954, 1959) in the German Democratic Republic, he soon became disenchanted with the doctrinaire policies of the East German state and the hostile working conditions in Leipzig. He frequently tried to make compromises with the SED (the Social Unity Party) so he could offer an alternative to vulgar Marxism in his Institute, but he was forced to leave his post in 1956, because he allegedly aided various groups of dissenters and was betraying communism with his "bourgeois ideology." Excluded from the university and virtually silenced in the public realm, Bloch's only writing and speaking outlet was in West Germany. Therefore, when he was on vacation in Tübingen during the building of the Berlin Wall in the summer of 1961, he finally decided to abandon East Germany and stop making compromises with the government. But he did not stop speaking out in the name of his Marxist principle of hope. Until his death in 1977, Bloch taught at the University of Tübingen and became involved in many different political struggles. He supported the Social Democrats in West Germany, criticized censorship and the professional proscription of civil servants, and worked actively against nuclear armament, German anti-Semitism, the Vietnam War, the Soviet invasion of Prague, and the terrorism of the Baader-Meinhof group.

Venerated as the Marxist philosopher of revolutionary hope, his works were seriously discussed and used throughout West Germany until the late 1980s. But since the tearing down of the Berlin Wall and also since the translation of many of his works into English and French, he has fallen almost into disrepute and neglect. Almost but not quite.

As Marxism and communism have become suspect in the 1990s, so have all those thinkers who were committed either to so-called communist governments or who sought to appropriate and elaborate dimensions of Marx's thought to bring about radical social and political change in the late twentieth century. In particular, many German intellectuals have turned away from Bloch because of his compromising relations with the East German government. Or, they have rejected Bloch because of his idealism: how can one speak about hope and utopia when millions of people are unemployed in Germany and when violent xenophobia has erupted, not only in Germany, but throughout most of Europe? (It seems almost obscene to read Bloch's optimistic writings and critiques of western capitalism, when it appears that a regulated but dynamic use of market forces may be the only means to save the world from destruction.) Of course, in the United States and Great Britain, Bloch has never really been taken all that seriously anyway. With the exception of American theologians during the 1970s and some exceptional but isolated studies by Fredric Jameson, Wayne Hudson, Anson Rabinbach, and Douglas Kellner, among others, Bloch has never received the critical attention that the Frankfurt School has received, even though he shared many things in common with them, especially with Walter Benjamin. It is as if Bloch were too orthodox and too idealistic in his Marxist philosophy despite his "heretical" thinking, or perhaps too esoteric and arcane to be comprehended. Finally, there is a great deal of fear nowadays on the Left about associating one's thinking with a philosopher like Bloch, who was scrupulously dedicated to Marxism and sought to anticipate the meanings of class struggle in his writings with a religious fervor.

Yet, it is exactly because of this fear and because of Bloch's present non-synchronicity, I believe, that his work demands our attention today. Against despair and against fashionable postmodernist thinking, Bloch's philosophy of hope provides a sober perspective for, and useful categories to grasp and move out of, the dark morass of present-day world politics. Moreover, many of his philosophical principles can provide an important impetus in radical cultural work, even as they need to be elaborated and applied in concrete situations. Certainly, there is a great deal to do in the American and British context of Bloch reception, and the present collection of essays is one of the first major efforts to appreciate why Bloch, though always out of step with his times, is so important for our times.

In the first section of this book, "Bloch and History", Vince Geoghegan,

David Kaufmann, and Jamie Owen Daniel discuss Bloch's radical
concept of memory, each one providing an illuminating perspective on
his notions of recollection, recognition, and reminiscence. Geoghegan's
essay "Remembering the Future" raises the question whether memory
can have a utopian function, and after citing examples from Plato and
Proust, he argues that memory has a built-in utopian and ethical
dimension. Moreover, he maintains that the individual memory can
only be validated in a social context, and thus collective memory as
history assumes an important role in our private lives. In short, what we
make out of memory has great social and political ramifications for the
future, and here is where, Geoghegan believes, the work of Bloch and
Herbert Marcuse can help us appreciate how we can make a utopian
use out of memory. Bloch made a very clear distinction between
anamnesis (recollection) and *anagnorisis* (recognition), whereby he
criticized *anamnesis* for being too static and conservative and holding
onto the past. On the other hand, *anagnorisis* is like *déjà vu*, a shock of
recognition; it brings back a trace or fragment from the past in such a
new way that it can be reactivated and transformed for future action.
Geoghegan criticizes Bloch for his dualistic approach to recollection
and recognition, and he seeks to overcome the dualism by linking
Bloch's thought to Marcuse's important work on memory as a source of
both rootedness and differentiation. Through his explication and
amplification of Marcuse's notions of memory, Geoghegan is able to
show that Bloch's category of recognition and *Novum* depended on
recollection "as a repository of experience and value in an inauthentic,
capitalist world," which must be re-utilized as historicized memory that
anticipates and guides political action.

    David Kaufmann takes another approach to Bloch's concept of
anagnorisis in "Thanks for the Memory: Bloch, Benjamin, and the
Philosophy of History," and he, too, uses a member of the Frankfurt
School, namely Benjamin, to highlight the unusual components in
Bloch's thought. Like Geoghegan, Kaufmann focuses on Bloch's emphasis of the shock value of recognition, and he discusses how Bloch and
Benjamin employed *déjà vu* within memory to present a way for reading
and redeeming the past: as a series of intentional claims whose normativity is witnessed by the emotions felt in the memory of neglect.
Kaufmann is most interested in Bloch's orientation with regard to
cultural artifacts, and he perceptively demonstrates how Bloch's method
enables him to locate past ciphers of hope in social representations as
surplus production that forms a cultural heritage which surges forward.
That is, there is a latent utopian potential in every cultural product that
must be mined if we are to intervene adequately in contemporary
political struggles and keep the process open-ended. Unlike many critics
of Bloch, Kaufmann argues in an illuminating reading of *Natural Law
and Human Dignity* against *The Principle of Hope* that Bloch's philosophy

did not have a limiting teleological orientation. Rather, Bloch kept pointing to the gaps in our heritage that still have not been filled and the autonomous choices that individuals must make if history is to come into its own. But history can only come into its own if human beings perceive the contradictions in society and politics and take charge of their own destiny. For Kaufmann, Bloch is highly relevant today because he is the self-reflexive Marxist philosopher who militantly insists that we continue to look for utopian signs in our heritage and do not tolerate the abandonment of hope in overcoming the alienating conditions of capitalism.

It is the abandonment of hope that concerns Jamie Owen Daniel in her essay "Reclaiming the 'Terrain of Fantasy': Speculations on Ernst Bloch, Memory, and the Resurgence of Nationalism." Her focus is on the present political situation and the rise of reactionary nationalism in Europe, and she uses Bloch's *Heritage of Our Times* to demonstrate that there is a strong tendency among Europeans to deny memory and to *forget* what fascism accomplished in the 1920s and 1930s. Moreover, the left is apparently vacating a terrain of need in the imagination which the fascists filled. In times of crisis, Daniel argues, there is a hunger for heritage and national identity in most European countries, and if it is neglected, it will be filled by the right with distorted views of the past that foster ethnic warfare. Though Daniel does not provide a Blochian blueprint for dealing with right-wing nationalism, she does effectively point to how Bloch's categories in *Heritage of Our Times* can expose the underlying meanings of the "new" national identities so that meaningful Marxist alternatives can claim a share of the terrain of fantasy and develop meaningful oppositional alternatives.

The second part of the book, "Concrete Utopias: The Big Picture," moves away from the theoretical consideration of memory and the past to examine specific ways in which Bloch's thought can be made more concrete in Marxist praxis. Ruth Levitas's essay, "Educated Hope: Ernst Bloch on Abstract and Concrete Utopia," is an insightful study of the distinction between abstract and concrete utopia. For Levitas, Bloch's idea of abstract utopia concerns the desire for a better world and is compensatory, whereas concrete utopia is anticipatory and involves willfull thinking about a real possible future. She discusses this distinction in relation to Mannheim's dichotomy between ideology and utopia and Edward Thompson's notions of Marxism and utopia in his book, *William Morris: Romantic to Revolutionary,* with the purpose of clarifying Bloch's category of *docta spes,* or educated hope, which concerns the process of education and political consciousness by which one gains a sense of what concrete utopia is vis-à-vis abstract utopia. However, she convincingly points out that Bloch's distinction between abstract and concrete utopia is epistemologically untenable and must be qualified. The value of educated hope arises out of the *political* commitment to the realization of utopia through Marxism, and its rehabilitation, and cannot be defended on epistemological grounds. If the world is to be changed and not simply interpreted, Levitas argues, then value-based choices must be made, and it is here that Bloch's work is invaluable because he constantly compels us to assume what he called the "upright gait" by ethical/moral action guided by principles of educated hope.

In "Ernst Bloch, Utopia, and Ideology Critique," Douglas Kellner continues Levitas's discussion by demonstrating how Bloch's practice of ideological criticism discerns emancipatory utopian dimensions even in ideological products, ferreting out those aspects that might be useful for radical theory and practice. What interests Kellner most is Bloch's focus on the emancipatory-utopian elements in all living ideologies that enables him to overcome a narrow dismissal of bourgeois culture. As Kellner perceptively demonstrates, Bloch was interested in the revelations of unrealized dreams, lost possibilities, and abortive hopes in all kinds of cultural artifacts, and in preserving them as the basis of a socialist cultural heritage. In this respect, Bloch is a model for the praxis of a socialist cultural critic, who can learn from his work how to discern the utopian surplus and potential in high and low culture and relate it to the struggles and possibilities of the present.

Whereas Kellner shows how Bloch's method of uncovering traces of surplus value in art and literature can be useful for cultural critics, Tom Moylan demonstrates the significance that Bloch's ideas have for liberation theology in "Bloch against Bloch: The Theological Reception of *Das Prinzip Hoffnung* and the Liberation of the Utopian Function." Moylan explains that Bloch's approach to religion consisted of an atheistic yet messianic re-utilization of the history of religions, for Bloch maintained that the tendency of such revolutionary bringers of light from Moses to Jesus was to bring God down to earth and to humanize religious principles in such a way that the transcendental God would no longer be needed and could be dismissed. Important in Bloch's philosophy is his reconception of religious discourse as a privileged place of awe and mystery, which is for Bloch the site of the Utterly Different. According to Moylan, Bloch secularized the Utterly Different to show how it functioned within the realm of a human anticipation which is itself constantly open to that which has not yet been realized. In the process of this secularization, Bloch conceived a creative atheism that negates the idolatrous god figure yet retains and transforms the space of religion so that "the kingdom, even in secularized form, and all the more so in its utopian-tal form, *remains as a messianic Front-space even without any theism.*" In the rest of his essay, Moylan provides a comprehensive analysis of how Bloch influenced liberal and left theology in the 1960s and enabled theologians such as Harvey Cox, Thomas Altizer, Leslie Stewart, Jürgen Moltmann, Johannes Metz, Gustavo Gutiérrez, and Franz Hinkelammert to break out of inherited religious discourses and to pursue an agenda of hope without becoming trapped in the compensations promised by a supernatural deity or a technocratic society. In his comprehensive analysis of their work, Moylan makes careful distinctions among the theologians and concludes by arguing that the great impact of liberation theology is indicative of how the utopian function in Bloch's philosophy prevents itself from becoming ideologically hypostatized and how it can be radically used to challenge present-day anti-communism and transnational capitalism, drawing on the best of both Christian and Marxist practice.

Moylan is clearly concerned with how Bloch's categories can be put to practical use in the area of religion, and Darko Suvin picks up on this concern in "Locus, Horizon, and Orientation: The Concept of Possible Worlds as a Key to Utopian Studies," but his focus is more on academics. Suvin maintains that there are two distinct wings to the growing field of utopian studies, the literary (or fictional) and the sociological (or factual), and since there is a danger that the "discipline" of utopian studies might become too disparate and nebulous, he argues for some common and centrally significant tools of inquiry to guarantee common lines of investigation. There are, however, two paradoxical obstacles that one must overcome in trying to bring about some commonality in the field: (1) many critics treat utopian works and utopias as if they were closed systems; (2) there is an unhealthy ambiguity between objectors to utopian orientation as such and objectors to closed utopias, bringing about a strange alliance between bourgeois conservatives and anti-Stalinist leftists. For Suvin, Bloch's work is valuable because he provides the basis for understanding how the Marxist orientation of the utopian can provide direction in the field and keep the notion of utopia open. Indeed, Bloch noted that utopian location is only seemingly spatial, that the actual place focused upon is not to be taken literally and is less significant than the orientation toward a better place somewhere in front of the orienter. By using notions such as locus, horizon, and orientation and relating them to Bloch's final theses on the concept of progress in his Tübingen lectures, Suvin concludes by proposing, with Bloch in mind, that the field of utopian studies should keep an orientation toward the open ocean of possibility that surrounds the actual and is immeasurably larger than the actual short-range goals of the academic field.

It is evident from Suvin's remarks that he is disturbed by the de-politicization of utopian studies at the university level, and his essay is an endeavor to intervene in that area. On the other hand, in "Paulo Freire, Postmodernism, and the Utopian Imagination: A Blochian Reading," Henry A. Giroux and Peter McLaren go beyond the university and address educators on all levels by re-evaluating the work of the radical educator Paulo Freire in light of Bloch's utopian politics of hope. Their purpose is to demonstrate how Freire and Bloch can counter the challenges of postmodernist theory which has undermined the agency of the subject and political action. Instead of simply dismissing postmodernism, Giroux and McClaren discuss the different types of postmodernist thought as posing problems and providing critical perspectives that could be appropriated and used for expanding the possibilities of critical pedagogy and cultural resistance. Here is where the work of Freire and Bloch is important. In discussing Freire's *The Politics of Education* and Bloch's *The Principle of Hope*, they note that both thinkers come dangerously close to relying on essentialist definitions of human needs and human nature and to setting up a fixed teleological framework in the name of the working classes within which social change should occur. Nevertheless, these "communist" tendencies do not invalidate their key utopian concepts and radical approaches to emancipatory praxis. By relating their ideas to Teresa Ebert's notion of *resistance postmodernism*, they demonstrate that Bloch and Freire's utopian hope is at the basis of self-transcending action and militant optimism that contest consumer capitalism and postmodern nihilism. By diminishing the boundary between actuality and possibility and by positing the utopian impulse not as a fixed human essence but as one of existential necessity for bringing about social transformation, Bloch and Freire create the conditions that would make cultural workers less likely to repress their own histories or confuse the act of knowing with passing over into the totalizing realm of explanatory certainty. Therefore, Giroux and McLaren conclude that the ideas of Bloch and Freire ultimately lead to the positing of critical utopias that emanate from continuous struggle within specific pedagogical sites and among competing theoretical frameworks. In the final analysis, these critical utopias enable educators to clearly see how the real-possible conditions for the utopian function can take root in the concrete materiality of daily struggle.

In the third part of the present anthology, "Imagining the Totality: Smaller Pictures," the writers shift their focus from the debates within large fields and academic disciplines to analyses of Bloch's contributions to specific issues and cases. In "Utopian Projections," however, Stephen Eric Bronner begins this section by outlining the general relevance of Bloch's work within the context of the political struggles during his lifetime. While critiquing the idealistic components of Bloch's thought, Bronner also contends that his philosophy presents something startlingly new that militates against provincialism and against the status quo in many different domains. Indeed, Bronner suggests that, by embracing it and qualifying it, we can recognize that the potential for emancipation in Bloch's thought breaks the constraints of every fixed and finished system, and the essays that follow his analysis are examples of how Bloch can serve to keep critical philosophical discourse open and to maintain its political relevance.

In "Utopia and Reality in the Philosophy of Ernst Bloch," Ze'ev Levy argues that Bloch's concept of utopia is chiefly an outcome of his general philosophical outlook which seizes the whole of reality as a mediation between subject and object. The major focus of his essay is *The Principle of Hope* and how Bloch developed certain categories to break with Freud and focus on the drive of hunger, which embodies an involved energy to ensure a human being's existence, as key to grasping the logical category of possibility. Hope is not merely a projection of reason but an expression of what is really possible, and Levy explains that there are four levels of possibility in Bloch's philosophy (the formal, the cognitive, the objective, and the dialectical) that he carefully elaborates. Utopia represents the projection of ideal possibilities against which the existing social realities are measured. It is, according to Levy, hope as a real force emanating from the hunger and desire to fulfill these possibilities that forms the link between theory and praxis and makes Bloch's philosophy a key method of exposing different types of ideologies.

Whereas Levy focuses on a limited number of key categories in Bloch's major work, *The Principle of Hope*, Tim Dayton's essay, "The Mystery of Pre-history: Ernst Bloch and Crime Fiction," concentrates on a much shorter work by Bloch, "A Philosophical View of the Detective Novel", to show its broader relation to Bloch's open system and how this essay can take on even a greater meaning when related to *The Principle of Hope*. For Dayton, Bloch's key category in his analysis of the detective novel is the "un-narrated factor and its reconstruction." That which is not narrated is the mystery that must be disclosed if we are to understand the crime, and Dayton perceptively shows that the unnarrated factor is related to Bloch's notion of the darkness of the lived moment which cannot be wholly known but serves as the driving force to fill the void in our lives. The past can only be known in the future, and thus the detective novel which focuses on a past crime or event is actually future-oriented and keeps the future open so that the past can find fulfillment. However, as Dayton points out, some critics, like Franco Moretti, have argued that most crime fiction denies the utopian tendencies of crime fiction because such fiction allays the anxiety of bourgeois society about the effect of the forces it unleashes. It fixes the limits of social mobility, making the intrusion of the working class into active social agency a crime, and displaces criminality outward from the bourgeois social order to the unruly sectors in time and space. Despite the appeal of this argument, Dayton believes that it is too functionalist, and after discussing a variety of contemporary detective novels, particularly with hard-boiled detectives, he depicts how Bloch's notion of hope can enable us to see that the hope of this genre is to be found in its despair at the fate suffered by hope at the hands of the present. Indeed, like other forms of popular literature, which Bloch also took most seriously, there are utopian traces in detective fiction that arise from the darkness and point in the direction of the home that we have all sensed but never seen.

Klaus L. Berghahn, too, is particularly interested in these traces in his essay "A View through the Red Window: Ernst Bloch's *Spuren*." He begins his article by situating Bloch's fascinating collection of "traces" (*Spuren*) in its cultural context (an excerpt from which follows his essay, in English translation for the first time). By the end of the 1920s, there were a number of remarkable authors like Walter Benjamin, Bertolt Brecht, Siegfried Kracauer, and Robert Musil, who wrote epigrammatic stories, more like terse observations, without plots. All these writers, like Bloch, were concerned with finding the exceptional in our ordinary quotidien experiences, and Berghahn thoroughly analyzes how Bloch wrought his tiny narratives into *Denkbilder* (thought-images), a term coined by Benjamin. A thought-image is a description of an everyday *modern* experience that includes a reflection and commentary. At its best, Berghahn maintains, it is a "dialectical image," which presents, analyzes, and grasps a situation in order to change it. The most distinctive characteristic of Bloch's "traces," which can be found throughout his philosophical work, is their montage technique. As Berghahn demonstrates in his conclusion, Bloch's *Spuren* reveal his exceptional quality as an avant-garde writer, who used image and thought to decipher the contradictions of reality and to provoke a commitment to action or responsible reaction from his readers.

Such a response can be seen in Mary N. Layoun's essay, "A Small Reflection on a Dream Thrice Removed of Hope from a Refugee Camp." This politically poetic essay seeks to understand the dream of a young Palestinian refugee in Lebanon, who has seemingly internalized the system of domination of the refugee camps and therefore appears to be afraid of returning home to Palestine. Such is the official interpretation of his dream at a conference of Palestinian refugees that was held in France. However, by relating the boy's dream to Bloch's theory of home as developed in *The Principle of Hope*, Layoun is able to reveal that this dream is all about understanding traces of home and community that are not explicitly enunciated in forms recognized by official ideological standards. Basically, as Layoun explains, though the boy is afraid of leaving the camp, he still desires a type of solidarity that he gleaned in the camps and is necessary for his future struggles. By re-utilizing Bloch's notion of hope and utopia, Layoun shows that it is possible to see more in the dream of the boy than the internalization of a system of domination. Indeed, she suggests at the end of her essay that Bloch's focus on *Vor-Schein* (anticipatory illumination) and *Heimat* (home) can help us uncover the disruptive and illuminative power of imagining the future; it enables us to realize that, even when a dream appears to indicate conservative nostalgia, we must pay attention to its forward-looking gestus that offers *more* than the simple desire to stay at home. Home is always more than a return to the past.

In the final analysis, it is this *more* as surplus in Bloch's very own works that concerns the writers of this volume, and they have assembled the utopian traces in Bloch's philosophy to propose a unique cultural heritage. It is a Marxist cultural heritage that can provide hints and clues of how one can intervene in actual political struggles. We must not forget – and these essays do not allow us to forget – that Bloch focused on indelible signs of cultural production, whether pre-bourgeois, bourgeois or proletarian, to show how the future can be illuminated by the past. So it is with the "past" works of Ernst Bloch which are still waiting for the fulfillment that they demand and provoke.

Three years before his death Bloch delivered a remarkable and provocative talk over the radio that demonstrates just how timely his works still are and how they will continue to transcend his time. The talk was entitled "Abschied von der Utopie?" or "Farewell to Utopia?"[1] The word *Abschied* can also mean dismissal, departure, or separation. It implies a taking leave of somebody or something, and in 1974, Bloch was posing the question, after the end of the student movement in Germany and the splintering of the left, whether we should give up utopia. He asked whether utopia had any force or meaning anymore, especially since the Social Democrats in West Germany had attained power and were apparently moving ahead with change, to be sure at a snail's pace, but change nevertheless.

For Bloch, the question mark in the title of his talk was intended to be provocative, for there was no question in his mind that utopia would always be needed, and always there. The question mark was intended to question all those people on the left and right who were calling for an end to utopia, dismissing it as foolish talk, talk of dreamers. "But what was behind all this?" Bloch asked.

At the beginning of his talk he makes a distinction between false and genuine future to analyze the motives of those calling for a farewell to utopia. The false future is all that which repeats itself a hundred or a thousand times in the future. It is indeed future but there is nothing really new in it. On the other hand, genuine future contains a *Novum*, which always has a tendency, a possibility, or a probability that opens up the horizon. We are safe with the false future, for it is like looking forward to going to sleep in a bed that we know is there. But the genuine future involves risk, because we are not certain what lies out there beyond us. We must imagine, grasp the tendency of the *Novum*, and dare to move ahead with it. However, most people are afraid to do this, and as Bloch argues:

> The call for farewell to utopia becomes therefore a call for an ideology which one does not at all want to articulate, namely the ideology of fear, at least of uneasiness, of strangeness in face of the Left, and consequently it is the expression of the condition of homelessness, in which the Left finds itself in our Parliament and in our party structure. [77]

If this is true, that is, if the call for farewell to utopia is ideological and also reveals that the left is without a "home," then what can be done to expose this call as ideological and also to move forward toward the *Novum*? Bloch maintains that the ideological talk about farewell to utopia can be readily recognized as fear of the uncertain and the fantastic and can be overcome, just as the pettiness of petty talk about utopia as mere dream can be identified for what it is and readily surmounted. Nevertheless, there is also a farewell to genuine utopia that is necessary and must be taken if we are to proceed toward utopia with *Novum*. Bloch cites the cases of More, Campenella, Proudhon, Fourier, Owen, and Saint-Simon and points out that they all conceived "genuine utopias," but they all had a common failing which we must recognize so that we can take leave of them:

> These utopian thinkers were indeed deficient because they jumped over the connecting links which they did not know sufficiently and therefore did not think how the opposite, the bourgeois society, could originate out of the best utopian will for a classless society full of freedom, equality, and brotherhood. [79]

In contrast, Bloch insists that the connecting links must be established, and they were indeed established by Marx and Engels. Marxism itself is not utopia but rather the *Novum* of concrete utopia. By this, Bloch means that nothing meaningful and concrete can be accomplished in the short term without having a distant goal on the horizon, which is not fixed or teleologically closed. The *Novum* is never closed, just as Marxism can never be closed. And yet, it is the illuminating orientation that exposes all that is false in our experiences. Therefore, without the grasping of the tendencies of Marxism in the possibilities of the present, that is, without the introduction of Marxist terms, principles, ethics, and praxis, we cannot move forward toward utopia.

Bloch believed that we could never have enough of concrete utopias in our lives because they were the stepping stones to the ultimate utopia. They were the traces that we had to detect and follow if our lives were not to be lies. His philosophical work and his personal struggles constitute a sort of concrete utopia, a lesson in Marxism, a lesson for the present that will continue to have political ramifications for the future. To read Bloch and try to concretize his principles today may mean for some critics to be out of step with our times and too idealistic, but as the essays in this volume show, Bloch is more in step with the beat of utopia than we want to admit but perhaps need to admit.

Note

1. See *Abschied von der Utopie?*, ed. Hanna Gekle (Frankfurt am Main: Suhrkamp, 1980).

Part I
Bloch and History

Remembering the Future
Vincent Geoghegan

The best moment of love is when one is climbing the stairs.
Casanova

The best moment of love is when the lover leaves in the taxi.
Michel Foucault

The subject of this essay is memory.[1] As should become clear, the word "memory" covers a range of phenomena. It is best conceived of, not as a thing, or place, or object, but as a varied set of systems and practices.[2] Scientists disagree about the precise nature of the memory, but it can perhaps be divided into three basic aspects. First, there are the various processes whereby material is collected or "memorized." Secondly, there is the complex and constantly changing body of data, the memory "itself." Finally, there are a variety of conscious and unconscious processes where material is "remembered." The underlying complexity of these processes and systems is partly reflected in the proliferation of terms denoting memory in common use: recollection, recognition, reminiscence, and so on.

The purpose of this essay is to explore the relationship between memory and utopianism. The term "utopianism" will be deployed in a broader sense than is perhaps usual. It is commonly used as a pejorative term to describe hankerings after the impossible. Such a definition is too narrow, robbing the word of a richer content, and signally a failing to register the actual, and complex, manifestations of utopianism. This limited definition is also often used in the service of highly subjective definitions of realism, where interests and ideologies determine what, supposedly, can or cannot be achieved. Utopias, in short, *can* be both rational and feasible. "Utopianism" will be used here, therefore, in a broader and less value-laden way, to describe the human need and capacity to create a desirable environment; a conscious and unconscious rearranging of reality, usually involving an imagined future. In this sense, utopianism can be benign or malign, plausible or implausible, possible or impossible.[3]

The assumption made throughout is that utopianism can adhere to diverse objects. Two bizarre cases can perhaps serve to demonstrate this initially. Leo Lowenthal, for example, considered "anti-Semitism a perverted and suppressed form of utopia. The Jews represent something that others would like to be." Thus the various jibes directed against Jews conceal real desire; for "clannishness" read "community," for "exploiting others" read "the elimination of heavy physical labour," and for "lascivious" read "they enjoy their lives fully."[4] In a similar vein, Klaus Theweleit, on the basis of an analysis of *Freikorps* literature (the men's memoirs and letters, and the literature produced by and about them), has unearthed the ugly fantasy world of these proto-fascists.[5] Distorted images of women abound, such as those of the "White Nurse," angelic, aristocratic, pure, and the "Red Nurse," wicked, working-class, lascivious, underlying which is an ultimately genocidal interplay of fear and desire. In both cases there is a complex interaction between fantasy and reality, where an external source attracts and feeds the desire and its imagery, but is itself transformed and distorted in the relationship.

Can memory have a utopian function? The negative "common sense" view is given by Aristotle in *De Memoria et Reminiscentia*: "Now to remember the future is not possible" (607). In Plato, however, we find more promising territory. For Plato, memory was, in a sense, the source of all creativity. Thus in the *Theaetetus*, Socrates speaks of "Memory, the mother of the Muses" (78). Plato could assert this because of his epistemological theory of timeless universal forms, where remembering was the royal road to the pre-existing essences of all things. He could therefore say in the *Meno* that "seeking and learning are in fact nothing but recollection" (130). The price to be paid, however, was the loss of genuine novelty. The authentic future was merely a return to an authentic past. History was rendered circular and backward-looking; real, positive newness was precluded. Nonetheless, Plato had pointed to the potentiality of memory as a location of powerful images and concepts, standing against the debilitating forgetfulness of everyday life.

The immense pull of the personal past has long been recognized. The term "nostalgia," although it has come to be used to refer to time, was originally coined to refer to place, for it meant the agony of being separated from home. The word, as its ending suggests, was used to describe the *illness* of desire for one's own homeland, quite literally home*sickness*. The temporal dimension was, however, implicit, since it was the depressed state brought on by the *memory* of (recollection of) home. "By the rivers of Babylon, there we sat down, yea, we wept, when we remembered Zion." The German word *Heimweh* conveys the same meaning and points to that evocative word *Heimat*, with its connotations of home, belonging, place of origin kept alive in the memory. Proust's

A la recherche du temps perdu is a famed literary example of the powerful ingression of memory into the present, where the dipping of a madeleine cake in tea stimulates idyllic memories (albeit with some somber tones) of childhood in the village of Combray (based on Proust's own experience with a more prosaic piece of dried toast). In this form of remembering the glance back is not to the Platonic world of universal forms, but to a type of personal golden age. As in Plato, the claim is that the memory traces evoke something valuable which has been lost. Unlike Plato this "something" is personal and therefore both historical and particular: "I remember and it is of value to me."

These special memories are notoriously inaccurate. Although usually based in fact, the material tends to be heavily massaged – a process that can be both conscious or unconscious. We are all familiar with the phenomenon of the crafted anecdote becoming reality for the raconteur. The element of self-deception involved suggests some quite strong needs are being met. This might help explain the person who, paradoxically, combines a perennially dreary present with wonderful memories. Andy Warhol, in a revealing moment, wrote that "your own life while it is happening to you never has any atmosphere until it's memory."[6] This is one aspect of the complicated relationship between memorizing, memory, and remembering. Psychologists disagree on how much of our experience is memorized, but clearly the form this process takes is going to structure the resulting data. How and why we memorize will obviously affect the memory. The memory is a changing and unstable source where, for example, new memories can overlay and interfere with old memories (retroactive interference), and old memories can eclipse the new (proactive inhibition).[7] Similarly, the act of remembering is a far from innocent act. Thus, a sense of the future can have a constitutive role in these processes. What we desire will play a role in the act of memorizing. A very obvious example of this is dealt with by Frances Yates in her fine *The Art of Memory*, where she describes the various memory-training techniques invented in antiquity to assist the ambitious lawyer and orator. These structurings are also present at far less conscious levels. In the case of remembering, hopes and anticipations will play an important role in the invention, distortion, selection, and framing of memory. What is most desired is missing in the often uncontrollable present but can be present in a controllable, if, in varying degrees, mythic, past. Harmony, warmth, and belonging can live in the supposed golden days of long ago. Thus the question "Can memory have a utopian function?" must take on board the fact that for many people memory has a built-in utopian function.

There is also a sense in which the term "remembering the future" is immediately appropriate. My past memories will have a constitutive role in the forging of my present and future perceptions. Since I am not a blank sheet or piece of blotting paper, but rather a dynamic, constructive perceiver, I enter the future with a body of assumptions and preoccupations located in memory. The infinite range of possible futures is winnowed down to my possible futures through this interactive process. In this sense I can be said to be "remembering the future."

The availability of memory is a further factor to be considered. Some memories seem to be much more in evidence than others. They appear to be persistent visitors bobbing in and out of consciousness. Augustine in the *Confessions* speaks of memories which "come spilling from the memory, thrusting themselves upon us when what we want is something quite different, as much as to say 'Perhaps we are what you want to remember?'" (214). Very pleasant experiences, with the intensity of the past moment, do appear to aid, or even invite, recollection – though it is present needs which initiate the process. We can be "re-minded" of things, and, as in a sudden meeting, "recognize" something. Cues of various sorts will activate memories, as we saw in the case of Proust. Context is also important, where one context, a particular configuration of furniture in a room, for example, can induce the memories associated with a similar configuration in the past. State of mind can also be significant; psychologists have found that, in general, material memorized when drunk is best remembered when drunk![8] The unlocking of memory, therefore, though uneven, is not unsystematic.

The memories least manageable, the ones most stark in their facticity, tend to be of an unpleasant nature. These can be of such a searing magnitude as to permanently disable – in the case of childhood sexual abuse, for example, where the memory of hurt and betrayal determines the future by undermining the possibility of fulfilling interpersonal relationships (though some experiences can be of such a traumatic nature that they are repressed into the unconscious). The reluctance to forget, the sense that this would be a betrayal, amongst many with traumatic memories testifies to the ethical dimension in memory. The constant reliving of these experiences, as with the experience of many who have been incarcerated in concentration camps, involves a visceral outrage. Memory is a window on our most basic values. The cry of "Never Again!" in the wake of the First World War was the forward-looking aspect of outraged memory (though the words "Lest We Forget" engraved on war memorials reveal the ever-present danger of widespread amnesia!). Similarly, the memory of shared adversity, of solidarity in danger, the positive aspect of the negative can bequeath new patterns of living to the present. When miners' wives say that they will never forget the great British coal strike of 1984–85, part of this is a triumphant memory of their new-found autonomy as organizers and militants. This is a memory component in praxis, where the memories, though possibly cooling and fading, can long outlive the initial actions.

Individuals can, of course, remember more than just direct personal experience. One can remember a vast array of information and facts, rules and procedures, of which one has had no direct personal experience. We say, for example, that we can remember information about the Bolshevik Revolution, or that we recall that $12 \times 12 = 144$ (relying on past rote learning, not working it out afresh). This form of memory both adds to personal experience and is itself partly illuminated by that experience (proper understanding of a historical experience, for example, is assisted by the input of similar personal experiences). It is also possible to experience the memories of others, via personal acquaintance or through various media, and add these to our own. In short, the individual memory can only be understood if its social dimension is recognized.

The utopian use of memory is clearly facilitated by two phenomena. First, and obviously, both past and future can only be experienced in the present – both are current mental states. Secondly, philosophers have been hard-pressed to distinguish memory from imagination. Hobbes in *Leviathan*, for example, considered that imagination and memory were both "decaying sense" (10). The problem arises because both memory and imagination may be using the same material, images, which appear to be adrift from any validating "reality." This prompts A. J. Ayer to argue "that no noncircular justification of memory can be given."[9] David Hume in *A Treatise of Human Nature* examines, and rejects, a couple of attempts to distinguish memory from imagination. His own attempt to distinguish is false, but false for an interesting reason. He argues "that the difference betwixt it [the memory] and the imagination lies in its superior force and vivacity" (133). This is empirically false as a generalization, since I might have very vivid sexual fantasies but remember very little of my second day at school, but it does register an intuitive feeling of the emotional power of memory. This reveals the problems in trying to separate absolutely the two realms, for my fantasies feed on memories and my memories may contain elements of pure fantasy. Furthermore, *contra* Hume, not all memories are image-based (e.g. the mathematical memory described earlier). Nonetheless, Hume's work is valuable in its recognition, albeit flawed, of the similarities between the realms of imagination and memory and their difference. He thus points to the source of the creative tension out of which can grow remembrance of the future. At any given point in time, the interpenetrating resources of memory and imagination are available for both conscious and unconscious use.

It is a testimony to the intense particularity of memory that those possessed of phenomenal memories experience difficulties in abstraction. The Soviet neuro-psychologist Luria studied the remarkable mnemonic powers of 'S' (Shereshevskii) and reproduced the latter's response to the phrase "the work got under way normally":

As for *work*, I see that work is going on ... there's a factory ... but there's that word *normally*. What I see is a big ruddy-cheeked woman, a *normal*

woman ... Then the expression *get under way.* Who? What is all this? You
have industry ... that is a factory, and this normal woman – but how does all
this fit together? How much have I to get rid of just to get the simple idea of
the thing![10]

In a similar vein Borges, in his short story "Funes the Memorious,"
imagines the difficulties of a character with an immense capacity for
remembering:

He was ... almost incapable of ideas of a general Platonic sort. Not only was
it difficult for him to comprehend that the generic symbol "dog" embraces
so many unlike individuals of diverse size and form; it bothered him that the
dog at three fourteen (seen from the aide) should have the same name as
the dog at three fifteen (seen from the front).[11]

So far the discussion has been of *individual* memories. Can one speak
of a *collective* memory? Jungian theory infers a "collective unconscious,"
the sedimented experience of the distant past, which manifests itself in
various archetypes (Mother, Rebirth, Spirit, Trickster) in, for example,
myth, religion, and folklore. This however requires both ahistorical
generalizations and some implausible cross-cultural comparisons – it can
also lend itself to fascist talk of folk and racial memories with its invitation
to regress to the exclusivist primitivism of "Blood and Soil." A more
plausible defense of the existence of collective memory would involve
recognizing the effect of a shared culture on the shared experience of
individuals, and would not make the grandiose universal claims of the
Jungians. In historic and contemporary societies where oral rather than
literary traditions prevail, the communal memory is transmitted in a
number of ways: by, for example, training specific people to be the
"remembrancers" (e.g. genealogists, memorialists, and rhapsodists
amongst the Rwanda) or by controlling the process of recital through
sanctions (death for mistaken recital in New Zealand!) or rewards (gifts
amongst the Rwanda).[12] David Middleton and Derek Edwards in *Collective
Remembering* demonstrate how a family builds up a shared set of memories, which then become the basis for future reminiscence:

It is an interactive environment, in which the parent takes pains to elicit
perceptions, memories and judgements from the children, to examine and
elaborate upon them, to contextualize and assign significance to them, in
terms of a shared past in which personal identity, family relationships and
the landmarks of development can be reconstructed. [41]

Paul Connerton, in *How Societies Remember,* focuses on the role of
"commemorative ceremonies" and "bodily practices" in the formation
of social memory. Krinka Petrov has asserted that "culture is memory,"
and that the totalitarian fear of such memories was manifested in 1941
when, in a Nazi bombing raid on Petrov's home town, Belgrade, "one

of the main targets was the National Library" (78). Similarly, Milan Kundera, in *The Book of Laughter and Forgetting*, notes the words of his friend Milan Hubl, one of 145 historians sacked in the wake of the suppressed Prague Spring: "The first step in liquidating a people is to erase its memory. Destroy its books, its culture, its history" (159). We might also recall the party slogan in that novel of memory, Orwell's *Nineteen Eighty-Four*: "Who controls the past controls the future: who controls the present controls the past" (37). A "collective" memory would consist of the complex memories of past generations embodied (refracted?) in cultural forms, interacting with personal memory. Factors such as class, ethnicity, gender, etc. would clearly tend to differentiate and preclude any simplistic abstraction such as "national memory" – a nation's memory, insofar as it exists at all, will necessarily be a complicated coalition of memories. Just as with individual memory, the resulting collective memory may have only a tangential link with historical fact. In short, to totally reject any notion of the collective would be to ignore the vital role of the social in the construction of the individual. Such a stance would be unable to explain the links between individuals and between generations, and would, in the case of the latter, fail to account for the phenomenon of transgenerational historical struggle, as in the case of the labor movement. Walter Benjamin recognized (in a rather one-sided fashion) the importance of historical memory when he condemned the Social Democratic training away of political memory: "This training made the working class forget both its hatred and its spirit of sacrifice, for both are nourished by the image of enslaved ancestors rather than of liberated grandchildren."[13] Christian Lenhardt has argued that a future socialist society which forgot the struggles of its forbears would be both guilty of rank ingratitude and still lacking true emancipation: "The evils of prehistory may have been overcome, but they will linger on in the collective *anamnesis* of liberated mankind. They must so linger, or else the achievement of true solidarity is just another form of one-dimensional experience."[14]

In the work of Ernst Bloch and Herbert Marcuse, we can find two valuable Marxist approaches to the utopian use of memory. Bloch's most direct approach to the issue can be found in a discussion with Michael Landmann at the *Praxis* summer school in Korcula, Yugoslavia in 1968. Bloch distinguished *anamnesis* (recollection) from *anagnorisis* (recognition). *Anamnesis* is defined as the Platonic remembering discussed earlier in this essay. Bloch sees it as epistemologically conservative, precluding new knowledge since all knowledge lies in the past. There is no shock of the new, all is soothingly familiar:

> The doctrine of *anamnesis* claims that we have knowledge only because we formerly knew. But then there could be no fundamentally new knowledge ... *Anamnesis* provides the reassuring evidence of complete similarity ...

> *Anamnesis* has an element of attenuation about it, it makes everything a gigantic *deja vu*.[15]

Elsewhere he makes the point that Hegel's philosophy is corrupted by *anamnesis*. Although the Hegelian system appears to be open to change and novelty, the underlying assumption is that the later development is merely the expression of a pre-existing potential.[16] Similarly, in *The Principle of Hope*, Bloch's critique of Freud involves an implicit charge of *anamnesis* in the claim that "there is nothing new in the Freudian unconscious" (56).

Anagnorisis, in contrast, involves recognition, not recollection. In *anagnorisis* memory traces are reactivated in the present, but there is never simple correspondence between past and present, because of all the intervening novelty. The power of the past resides in its complicated relationship of similarity/dissimilarity to the present. The tension thus created helps shape the new. The experience is therefore creatively shocking:

> the new is never completely new for us because we bring with us something to measure it by. We always relate what we find to earlier experience or to an image we have of it. As a result it often happens that we misjudge it upward or downward, but still it becomes richer for us, and is colored with history. It approaches us from our own past and must prove that it is genuine …; *anagnorisis* … is linked with reality by only a thin thread; it is therefore alarming.[17]

Bloch cites the biblical story of Joseph and his brothers to illustrate this theory. Joseph is cast into a pit and sold into slavery by his brothers who envy their father's love for him. Joseph eventually becomes an important official in Egypt where he encounters his brothers who have come in search of food. He recognizes them but they do not recognize him. Eventually Joseph reveals himself to the utter astonishment (and shame) of his brothers. Bloch comments:

> *anagnorisis* is a shock: he whom they cast into a pit suddenly stands there, powerful and handsome before them … [H]is brothers have not seen [Joseph] for 20 years. First he has changed, and second, they can no longer remember exactly after so long a time – as often happens with witnesses in court – and thirdly, they are not expecting to meet him as Pharaoh's deputy … In *anagnorisis* there must always be a distance between the former and present reality, otherwise it would not be so difficult and astonishing.[18]

Some insight into Bloch's concept of *anagnorisis* can, perhaps, be achieved if we consider a similar notion in Orwell's *Nineteen Eighty-Four*. The central character, Winston Smith, has a dream of what he terms "the Golden Country," an inviting rural environment, in which he meets a woman whose "grace and carelessness" directly challenge the totalitarian structures of Big Brother and the Party. Later in the book he arranges to meet the character Julia in the countryside. In the course of this tryst, "Winston looked out into the field beyond, and underwent a curious, slow shock of recognition ... 'It's the Golden Country – almost,' he murmured" (129). This proves to be an important step in Smith's move to total opposition to the regime. It is that word "almost" which suggests *anagnorisis* rather than *anamnesis*.

One can certainly take issue with Bloch's desire to establish a hard and fast dualism of these two processes. Certainly if *anamnesis* is as Bloch defines it, then it is rightly rejected. However, it would be worrying if this implied that *recollection* had no legitimate part to play. Recollection is a much broader phenomenon than Bloch's rather restrictive definition. It is surely the very basis of recognition. *Anagnorisis* rightly historicizes memory but is an implausible theory without a complimentary recollection. It may be that Bloch thinks that *anagnorisis* itself contains the progressive aspects of *anamnesis*, which would be acceptable, but since this is not spelt out, the basis for confusion remains.

Bloch's value lies in his attempt to reconcile the claims of the past and the future. He recognizes the importance of memory as a repository of experience and value in an inauthentic, capitalist world. His fear is, however, that it will act as a drag on progress. There has to be room for novelty if the world is to progress, and history is not to be cyclical. However, it is not a desire to have novelty for novelty's sake, for novelty can take many disagreeable forms. The function of recognition in memory is a means of achieving this – a historicized memory guides but does not control.

Another Marxist who has had pertinent thoughts on the role of memory is Herbert Marcuse. To put his work in some kind of framework, it might be useful to make an initial distinction between a personal and a social golden age. A personal golden age, as we saw in the case of Proust, is an individual recollection of a happy past, often located in childhood. A social golden age refers to a whole society or culture; it is usually located in the past, and consequently can only be experienced indirectly via various cultural forms. Examples of the latter occur throughout history: Eden to the medieval world; the Anglo-Saxon constitution to seventeenth-century radicalism; ancient Greece to nineteenth-century Hellenophiles; historic matriarchy to some feminists. Social golden ages, like their personal counterparts, often play fast and loose with historic fact, and lend themselves to utopian co-option. Thus, in the case of ancient Greece, Martin Bernal, in *Black Athena*, speaks of the "fabrication of ancient Greece" since 1789. He argues that an "Aryan Model" emerged in which the Greeks were viewed as northern Europeans in the sun, and where the classical Greeks' own opinion, that they owed much of their civilization to the Egyptians and Phoenicians, was simply dismissed (for the great Greeks could owe nothing to "inferior" races). The most notable example of golden-ageism in the socialist

tradition was the vogue for primitive communism in the time of the
Second International. Stimulated by Engels's transformation of Mor-
gan's anthropological speculations, many writers lovingly dwelt on the
classless harmony of this earliest period of human history, and looked
to the return of these conditions in the more developed context of
future communism. The attraction lay, not simply in the fact that it
disproved arguments about the supposed "unnaturalness" of communism, or that it provided clues to the shape of future society, but also
because in the context of "scientific socialism," with its taboo of "utopian
socialism," one could think about the future by talking about the past –
the safe "scientific" past could become the focus for all those unfulfilled
utopian longings.[19]

In Marcuse's work on memory, both personal and social golden ages
appear. This is achieved by his radical appropriation of the work of
Freud. Memory and forgetfulness are central to Freud's work. Forgetting
defends against the intolerable, and memory overcomes the resulting
neurosis. He denied that forgetting involved the destruction of memory
traces, and argued that the imperishable primitive mind continued its
existence in contemporary individuals.[20] For Marcuse, memory is the
means to recapture earlier experiences of freedom and happiness. It is
highly subversive of any reconciliation between humanity and its present, and, by showing that happiness once obtained, it also raises the
possibility of, and the desire for, future satisfaction. This is the truth-
value of memory. Marcuse develops his theory of the revolutionary
function of memory by using, in his own special way, both personal and
social golden ages. He wishes to link "the origin of the repressed
individual" (ontogenesis) to "the origin of repressive civilization" (phy-
logenesis) and provide a theoretical basis for a fantasy which "preserves
the archetypes of the genus, the perpetual but repressed ideas of the
collective and individual memory, the tabooed images of freedom."[21]

Marcuse resisted recourse to the language of golden ages, though his
1972 comment, "Recollection . . . is not remembrance of a Golden Past
(which never existed), of childhood innocence, primitive man, et
cetera" (Counter-Revolution and Revolt, 70), perhaps reflects a sensitivity
to interpretations of his earlier work in these terms. Use is made in Eros
and Civilization of a type of social golden age. In this work he utilizes
Freud's depiction of pre-historic society, which he accepts cannot be
factually corroborated, but argues that "the alleged consequences of
these events are historical facts" (57). Freud's hypothesis has "symbolic"
value through dramatizing and explaining the basis of human history. It
is essentially a story of paternal domination giving way to paternal
liberation, only to be itself overthrown by a new paternalist domination.
The primal father's monopoly of sexual pleasure provokes an act of
patricide by his sons, but the moment of liberation rapidly gives way to
a new restrictive order as a response to the emergence of guilt. And yet

the memory of gratification will not go away, it has perennially reappeared throughout history, as an indictment of, and target for, the forces of repression. Marcuse posits a reappearance in the individual of an archaic heritage in which domination confronts liberation and that this is "awakened" by experiences such as the Oedipus complex which parallel ancient experiences. This coexists with the personal experience of infantile bliss, of undifferentiated polymorphous perversity. Such memory is a spur to chance, a powerful goad to re-create the lost conditions of happiness, for "the past continues to claim the future; it generates the wish that the paradise be re-created on the basis of the achievements of civilization" (33).

The corollary to this is that forgetfulness, amnesia, can be a powerful weapon in the armory of existing society. "The ability to forget," says Marcuse, "is the mental faculty which sustains submissiveness and renunciation" (163). By forgetting one both loses the imagery of liberation and forgives that which should not be forgiven. In *One-Dimensional Man* he cites Adorno's fear of "[t]he spectre of man without memory" (89) as bourgeois society seems to neutralize history. Insofar as memory is cultivated, it is in the repressive form of memorizing the requirements of the capitalist order – what Marcuse calls "the one-sidedness of memory-training in civilization" where "the faculty was chiefly directed toward remembering duties rather than pleasures; memory was linked with bad conscience, guilt and sin. Unhappiness and the threat of punishment, not happiness and the promise of freedom, linger in memory" (*Eros and Civilization*, 163). Memory triumphs over repression's greatest ally, time, by not allowing it to conceal either the dark or the light: "Time loses its power when remembrance redeems the past" (164). In this respect Marcuse was particularly struck by Benjamin's claim that, in the July Revolution in France, a number of the revolutionaries shot at the public clocks.

Martin Jay has argued that, to some extent, Marcuse falls foul of Bloch's strictures on *anamnesis*, that "he did not entirely escape the reproach that recollection is too close to repetition."[22] Jay has a point – there is the whiff of timeless essences from some of the above remarks. Also, recalling Bloch's remarks on the *anamnesis* of potentiality in the Hegelian system, we might note that Marcuse's ontogenetic and phylogenetic parallelism has a degree of affinity with Hegel's dialectical model of historical and social processes. This should not be pushed too far, however. From his early days, Marcuse had been at pains to stress the *historic*, including historic novelty, in human development. In a discussion of the concept of essence in the 1930s he rejected talk of timeless essences, and argued for what one might call "historical apriorism", where value emerges from the historical process: "In truth, an a priori element is at work here, but one confirming the historicity of the concept of essence. It leads back into history rather than out of it" (*Negations*, 75).[23] Novelty does emerge to enrich humanity, but this is quite compatible with a belief in the longevity of historic values and experiences. To say, for example, that all subsequent philosophy is a footnote to the work of Plato and Aristotle, insofar as it is true, is a testimony to the stature of these two thinkers, not a resigned acceptance of the circularity of history. Thus, when Marcuse discusses the new utopian world he is quite clear that the "regression" is based upon an advancing civilization.

The phenomenon of "postmodernism" is of some interest in this context. There has been a great deal of nonsense written by and about this amorphous "movement". When discussing artistic and intellectual trends, one should be suspicious of the prefix "post-," for it often precedes a caricature. In this case the absurd confection of "modernism" is used to denounce a most extraordinary collection of ideas and cultural forms from the Renaissance onwards. As a result, there has been a lot of hostile commentary on postmodernism, much of which makes valuable points. Thus, postmodernism is seen, variously, as relativism, conservatism, populism, eclecticism, and so forth. It can, for example, serve as a cover for pressing the claims of a reactionary golden age – of some supposed "organic" society "destroyed" by the "evils" of socialism, welfareism, planning, etc. (see Patrick Wright). Yet valuable elements have emerged in the debates over, and the practices of, postmodernism. Now it might be the case, if we look at "architectural postmodernism," that a whole series of socio-economic vested interests have good grounds for promoting this development, but to see this as a reason for outright rejection is to succumb to reductionism. What is of value? First, there is the critique of a naive conception of "the new" and a related sensitivity to the continuing validity of the perceived past (though with the ever-present danger of Disneyland eclecticism and pastiche). Thus, in the case of the former, attention has been focused, for example, on the shallow architectural futurism of the followers of Le Corbusier. The horrid tower blocks they spawned have a direct relevance to the question of memory. Based, to some extent, on a "meta-narrative" of progress and "the new," the keynote was a kind of one-dimensional forward-looking. In a sense these buildings embodied the implicit assumption of a people without a memory, or of a people with only a memory of the hardships of the old living conditions. The falsity of these premises (pardon the awful pun!) was rapidly revealed when the memories of community and human scale helped generate immense dissatisfaction. The concept of "the new" involved here was that of a radical break with the past, of an impossible Year Zero, where the attempt to totally sweep away the old ways destroyed much of value, and merely let in even nastier atavistic currents – the red brick of the Victorian house gave way to the concrete of the new cave. (The "modernist" really new has its place, so long as it is good and in the right place – ugly housing schemes and the skyline of Manhattan cannot be simplistically equated – there are no good or bad forms, only good or bad uses of form.) In contrast, architectural postmodernism at its best can be sensitive to individual and collective memories. Its pluralism gives it the potential at least for community roots. It can draw on individual memories of what is human, either directly or indirectly, and playfully appropriate significant cultural forms from earlier ages. The fact that some of this architecture is garbage (buildings one assumes are in the first stage of demolition turn out to be in the final stage of construction!), built for a comparatively narrow, affluent social base, is immaterial (if, unfortunately, "material" in other senses).

One should note the conservatism involved in many forms of the political use of memory, and its use by the right. Historically, fascism thrived on the politics of memory. Rural experiences of modernization, discontent with urbanism, the collapse of the prewar imperial world were but a few of the factors which generated a mass of memories that National Socialism was able to both reflect and develop. In the contemporary world, an organization like *Pamyat'* (*Memory*) exploited Soviet *glasnost* to break up election meetings in pursuit of an anti-Semitic, anti-industrial Russian nationalism. In a television interview, the leader of this "National Patriotic Front," Dimitri Vassiliev, against the background of a study lined with the iconography of "Old Russia," called for a "constitutional monarchy . . . unity of a single will, power in one pair of hands, exercised through the collective soul," and asserted: "How can there be anti-Semitism in Moscow with Karl Marx Avenue, Sverdlov Square? They were all Jews." In the United Kingdom, both "the good old days" and "the bad old days" have been used to conservative effect. In the case of the former, the appeal to "Victorian values," driven by prime-ministerial memories of a small-town, *petit bourgeois* childhood, has been a central plank of Thatcherism; yet, somewhat paradoxically, a Conservative minister has also claimed that, compared with the poverty of Victorian times, the poor in Britain had virtually disappeared, and that the left were confusing poverty with inequality. In the furor which followed this comment, a number of old people, wielding their memories like hatchets, backed up the minister on the basis of their own experience of "real" poverty in the 1930s.

A more complicated case, in Yugoslavia, is that of the Slovenian cultural movement *Neue Slowenische Kunst* (New Slovenian Art). The use of German in its title reflects the attempt to use both the old hegemonic language of the Austro-Hungarian Empire and, even more controversially, the iconography, aesthetics, and language of fascism. Thus, its most famous manifestation, the rock group Laibach (the German name for their home, the Slovenian capital Ljubljana), seemed to be deliberately evoking the fascist past in the style and presentation of their music. In fact, the group (and the movement) reject this type of interpretation of their work and vigorously deny any hankerings after National

Socialism. They say that they use a variety of cultural quotes drawn from many styles and cultures and that their goal is *Gesamtkunstwerk* (total art, or synthesis of the arts). They seem to wish to express, via eclectic mimesis, the contradictory historical experience of the Slovenian people. The lyrics of Laibach, when using the linguistic forms of fascist prose, do not express that ideology or do so in a documentary, ironic or parodied fashion. They draw on a complex range of symbolism in their transformation of pop material. Thus, Queen's song "One Vision" becomes "Geburt einer Nation" ("The Birth of a Nation"), with a clear association with Nazi expansionism. Clyde Joyce has also read into this title an evocation of the Ku Klux Klan imagery of D.W. Griffiths's silent epic film *Birth of a Nation*. The martial rhythms of the music, and the imagery of the accompanying video are suggestive of the Third Reich, as are the subtly reworked Queen lyrics: "Ein Mensch, ein Ziel, und eine Weisung. / Ein Herz, ein Geist, nur eine Lösung ... Ein Fleisch, ein Blut, / ein wahrer Glaube. / Eine Rasse und ein Traum, / ein starker Wille" (One Man, one goal, and one direction. / One heart, one spirit, only one solution ... One flesh, one blood, / one true religion. / One race and one dream, one strong will).[24] Their use, and apparent endorsement, of the imagery of the total state, seems to have as its goal the stimulation of analysis and redefinition – an attempt, perhaps, to create a new language and imagery out of the old, in a society where the official political and cultural language, including the local variant of Marxism, is bankrupt. The recourse to fascist symbolism, by co-opting the most tabooed of imagery, the most extreme of memories, and the tempting cultural resonances of Slovenia's German heritage, might be seen as a way of breaking through this dead language. If this is what they are doing, it is a dangerous path to tread and can easily be misunderstood. Thus in England, for example, they gained a cult following amongst young supporters of various neo-Nazi parties.

Even "progressive" memories can act as barriers. Old experiences can prevent the formation of new strategies, as with the case of the generals who fought the Second World War on memories of the First. Direct or indirect memories of the French Revolution of 1789 intruded into much nineteenth-century radicalism. Engels, for example, cited this revolution in his formulation of the "dictatorship of the proletariat," and recalled how Marx and himself had been, in 1848, "under the spell" of the French revolutions of 1789 and 1830. The tendency to look for Jacobins and Girondins in the last century parallels the search for Bolsheviks and Mensheviks in this. The problem is compounded by the mythic and utopian invention involved in the memories of these revolutions. As the bicentennial celebrations exemplified, the French Revolution has always served as a utopian canvas for current, and conflicting, perspectives. The net effect has been that the left has often destroyed genuine initiatives, or has been looking in one direction whilst change comes from quite another. One of Marx and Engels's principal objections to utopianism was precisely that it could foreclose the future by substituting past and present obsessions for the creative novelty of the proletariat.

Clearly, therefore, some people have memories which I might consider inappropriate, partial, unbalanced, self-indulgent, or just plain wrong. What is to be my response, given that they may be issuing forth in unacceptable political forms? Even leaving to one side the philosophical problems associated with the validity of memory, formulating a response is no easy task. The presentation of contrary historical evidence can help, but the problems connected with this should be obvious. Quite apart from the methodological problems associated with historical analysis, there is the psychological (and in some cases actual) capital invested in false, meaningful memories. All societies have far more people claiming, with varying degrees of sincerity, that they were present at significant historical events than the historical record allows. In Ireland it was the legions of people who must have been jammed like sardines in the General Post Office if they had all been participants in the Easter Rising of 1916. Attacking this type of memory head-on is probably unproductive. Memory configurations do, however, clearly undergo significant shifts. Major historical events can lead to widespread restructuring of memory. One suspects, for instance, that the experience of the Second World War caused major restructuring of the memories of many Germans – repressing some memories, highlighting and reinterpreting others, adding new potent imagery, and inventing where necessary. Since present concerns and future hopes do have such a structuring role in memory, contestation at these levels will feed back into the memory. Thus, paradoxically, talking about the future may be one way to come to terms with the past.

Implicit in all of this is the assumption that I and my memories stand in judgement on others. How is this to be fitted into a politics which is concrete without being relativist, and universal without being authoritarian?

A theory of the political power of memory should take on broad aspects of the postmodernist critique of grand, totalizing, universal visions, without succumbing to the self-contradiction and relativism of a thinker like Lyotard. Thus Lyotard rightly rejects the imperial edifice of scientific Marxism, along with other "grand narratives of legitimation," but seemingly bases this rejection on a further rejection of systematic thought itself, thereby precluding the very basis of his own critique, and opening the door to helpless relativism.[25] He is of value in his pluralistic stress on the importance of the local, the actual, the practical, and the different. Likewise, the "anti-foundationalism" of Richard Rorty has something to offer.[26] Rorty rejects philosophical attempts to ground reality in some absolutely secure foundation. Such comfort is simply not available. Universal philosophy must give way to particular "conversations" between finite individuals, rooted in distinct cultures. There is nothing above or beneath contingent human projects. As with Lyotard, the danger of throwing the baby out with the bath water is clear. A number of critics have argued that Rorty's thorough rejection of universalist philosophy undermines the possibility of any kind of critical reflection, thereby surrendering the individual to the status quo.[27] Certainly some of his remarks are chilling, as in the description of his desired "post-philosophical culture":

> This means that when the secret police come, when the torturers violate the innocent, there is nothing to be said to them of the form "There is something within you which you are betraying. Though you embody the practices of a totalitarian society which will endure forever, there is something beyond those practices which condemns you." This thought is hard to live with.[28]

Indeed! In short, any appropriation of postmodernism and anti-foundationalism must combine sensitivity to the particular and the possibility of universality. Alasdair MacIntyre's recent work seeks to do this by focusing on the nature of historic communities. He argues that specific communities are bounded by their own forms of rationality, but this does not involve relativism, "for it is a crucial and integral aspect of each of these standpoints that it involves a claim to rational hegemony." A relativist, by denying the possibility of such rational hegemony, is effectively rendered homeless: "The adherent of a perspectivist relativism, who for a moment seemed to be free to inhabit all and any of these standpoints, is in fact excluded from them all."[29] Furthermore, relativism requires an abstracted rootlessness at variance with the communal nature of individuality. MacIntyre discusses the relativist individual thus:

> It can only be an individual whose distinctive identity consists in key part in the ability to escape social identification, by always being able to abstract him or herself from any role whatsoever; it is the individual who is potentially many things, but actually in and for him or herself nothing.[30]

Memory is at the very heart of rootedness. Many people will be familiar with the experience of awakening from sleep, and not knowing where they are, or even who they are (or possibly what they are?), and then have memory provide the necessary information. Proust provides a marvelous evocation of this phenomenon:

> when I awoke in the middle of the night, not knowing where I was, I could not even be sure at first who I was; I had only the most rudimentary sense of existence, such as may lurk and flicker in the depths of an animal's consciousness; I was more destitute than the cave-dweller; but then the memory – not yet of the place in which I was, but of various other places where I had lived and might now very possibly be – would come like a rope let down from heaven to draw me up out of the abyss of not-being, from

which I could never have escaped by myself: in a flash I would traverse centuries of civilization, and out of a blurred glimpse of oil-lamps, then of shirts with turned-down collars, would gradually piece together the original components of my ego. [5–6]

The neurologist Oliver Sacks, in *The Man Who Mistook His Wife for a Hat*, tells the moving story of an elderly woman who, due to a physiological disorder, began to hear Irish songs in her waking hours. Amidst her alarm and annoyance there was also the sense of a door opening on a lost childhood. Orphaned at five, the woman had been sent from Ireland to a "forbidding" aunt in America, where, much to her subsequent regret, the memories of Ireland had faded away. The songs reawakened these memories, and brought her an emotionally satisfying sense of grounding and completedness. Sacks recorded her response: "I know you're there, Dr Sacks. I know I'm an old woman with a stroke in an old people's home, but I feel I'm a child in Ireland again – I feel my mother's arms, I see her, I hear her voice singing" (137). As the repository of individual and social data and value, memory is the very basis of belonging.

Memory is also the basis for differentiation. One should be careful of assertions of racial memory or the memory of the *polis*. A given society is a complex intersection of memories, not all compatible. It is, however, far from chaotic – social and historical structures generate clusters (admittedly complex) of memory-bearing actors. Much political contestation is already driven by group and individual memories, and these memories fuel the various alternatives proposed. Working-class groups operate with the negative memories of personal and historic exploitation and the positive memories of co-operative behavior (trades unions, communities, etc.). Women's groups likewise combine the experiencing of patriarchy with the experience of sisterhood. These memories provide much of the raw material for the vital utopian dimension of their politics. To the extent that these memories reveal shared values and experiences, the basis is established for the assertion of historical universals. It thus opens the door for a utopianism which is grounded in the historically evolving memories of groups of individuals. The future, in this conception, is not a return to the past but draws sustenance from this past. Memory is the means in the present to ground the future in the past. Ernst Bloch ends his epic *The Principle of Hope* with this remark on a person in future society:

Once man has established his own domain in real democracy, without depersonalization and alienation, something arises in the world which all men have glimpsed in childhood: a place and a state in which no one has yet been. And the name of this something is home [*Heimat*].

[1,376]

Unless one subscribes to a Sorelian concept of myth, where analysis of motivational belief can destroy its potency, there is much to be gained by a more self-conscious politics of memory. Sensitivity to personal and social memories can both enrich the resulting utopian imagery, and increase tolerance for the motivating memories of others. If this does happen, then we are also getting closer to an understanding of that *frisson* caused by the words, "I remember."

Notes

1. I would like to thank the following for their valuable comments on earlier drafts: John Le Juen, Bob Eccleshall, Mick Cox, Richard Jay, Rick Wilford, Ruth Levitas, Peter Lassman, Hoda Zaki, Helen Kuryllo, Erika Gottlieb, Csaba Toth, and Aharon Ben Ze'ev.

2. See Alan D. Baddeley, *Your Memory: A User's Guide* (Harmondsworth: Penguin, 1983), and Kenneth Higbee, *Your Memory* (London: Pitakus, 1989).

3. See my *Utopianism and Marxism* (London: Methuen, 1987).

4. Leo Lowenthal, *An Unmastered Past: The Autobiographical Reflections of Leo Lowenthal* (Berkeley: University of California Press), pp. 32–3.

5. Klaus Theweleit, *Male Fantasies*, I: *Women, Floods, Bodies, History* (Cambridge: Polity Press, 1987).

6. Victor Bockris, *Warhol: The Biography* (London: Frederick Muller, 1989), p. 58.

7. See Baddeley, *Your Memory*, pp. 60–62.

8. See Baddeley, *Your Memory*.

9. A. J. Ayer, *Bertrand Russell* (Chicago: University of Chicago Press, 1988), p. 90.

10. Baddeley, *Your Memory*, p. 45.

11. In *Labyrinths* (London: Penguin, 1970), p. 18.

12. J. Vansina, *Oral Tradition: A Study in Historical Methodology* (London: Routledge & Kegan Paul, 1965).

13. Walter Benjamin, *Illuminations* (London: Collins, 1973), p. 262. Compare Christian Lenhardt, "Anamnestic Solidarity: The Proletariat and its *Manes*," *Telos*, 25 (Fall 1975), pp. 133–54.

14. Lenhardt, "Anamnestic Solidarity," p. 138.

15. Michael Landmann, "Talking with Ernst Bloch: Korcula, 1968," *Telos*, 25 (Fall 1975), p. 178.

16. Wayne Hudson, *The Marxist Philosophy of Ernst Bloch* (London: Macmillan, 1982), pp. 78–9.

17. Landmann, "Talking with Ernst Bloch," p. 178.

18. Ibid., pp. 178–9.

19. See my *Utopianism and Marxism*, ch. 4.

20. Herbert Marcuse, *Eros and Civilization* (London: Sphere, 1972), pp. 73, 256.

21. Ibid., p. 108.

22. Martin Jay, *Marxism and Totality* (Cambridge: Polity Press, 1984), p. 237.

23. See also my *Reason and Eros: The Social Theory of Herbert Marcuse* (London: Pluto Press, 1981), esp. ch. 2.

24. Laibach, *Opus Dei* (Mute Records, 1987), my translation.

25. See Douglas Kellner, "Postmodernism as Social Theory: Some Challenges and Problems," *Theory, Culture and Society*, 5: 2–3 (June 1988), pp. 239–69; Nancy Fraser and Linda Nicholson, "Social Criticism without Philosophy: An Encounter between Feminism and Postmodernism," *Theory, Culture and Society*, 5: 2–3 (June 1988), pp. 373–94; and Andrew Benjamin, ed., *The Lyotard Reader* (Oxford: Basil Blackwell, 1989).

26. Richard Rorty, *Philosophy and the Mirror of Nature* (Oxford: Basil Blackwell, 1980).

27. See Richard J. Bernstein, "One Step Forward, Two Steps Backward: Richard Rorty on Liberal Democracy and Philosophy," *Political Theory*, 15:4 (1987), pp. 538–63.

28. Richard Rorty, *Consequences of Pragmatism* (Brighton: Harvester, 1982), p. xlii.

29. Alasdair MacIntyre, "Practical Rationalities as Forms of Social Structure," *Irish Philosophical Journal*, 4: 1–2 (1987), p. 18.

30. Ibid., pp. 18–19.

Thanks for the Memory:
Bloch, Benjamin, and the Philosophy
of History

David Kaufmann

As they themselves hope for the Messianic age, the Prophets
make hope the basic affect of politics, history, and religion.
What others refer to as faith, they refer to as hope. This
turning away from the actually given, this forward-thrust of
the present into the future, this liberation of man's mind
from the overpowering grip of reality – all this constitutes
their idealism.

Hermann Cohen

Contemporaries and rather uncomfortable friends,[1] Walter Benjamin
and Ernst Bloch seem to come to us from different epochs. Bloch died
quite recently (in 1977), yet his philosophy, especially in *The Principle of
Hope*, appears to be fired by the peculiar intellectual passions of the first
decades of this century and presents itself as a somewhat antiquarian
curiosity. On the other hand, Benjamin's *Aktualität* – his relevance – has
been constantly renewed in the forty years since his *Schriften* were first
published. Benjamin, it seems, is *always* reborn, or rather, reclaimed,
refunctioned, and renewed.

Nevertheless, Bloch's work contains great strengths at the same time
that it comes as an uneasy reminder for the left. His major work
uncovers the utopian content of even the most desperately ideological
configurations. At the same time, it is incontestably riven by the most
suspect Stalinist commitments. On the credit side, Fredric Jameson has
found Bloch extraordinarily useful as a model of flexible and resilient
utopianism. Jameson's first attempt to align Marxist hermeneutics with
the fourfold interpretation of medieval exegetes was proposed in the
chapter devoted to Bloch in *Marxism and Form* and Bloch's influence is
quite visible in *The Political Unconscious*, in spite or because of the
Althusserian fireworks that illuminate that book. And Jameson's early

mediation of Bloch has been justly quite influential on a number of young literary critics for whom the category of utopia is less an embarrassment than a call to arms. But Jameson's account, though not by any means inaccurate, is indeed quite partial. Jameson's Bloch is mostly the Marxist theologian of *The Principle of Hope*, the drill sergeant of the visionary. Jameson rightly praises Bloch for his ability to find political value in conservative – even fascist – authors. But Jameson does not cite *Heritage of Our Times* which was written in the early 1930s as a remonstrance to German leftism. Rather, he relies on Bloch's more generalizing tendencies which he finds in the often remarkably ahistorical *The Principle of Hope*. To situate Bloch in terms of patristic hermeneutics is to see him as he is at his windiest, as the apostle for the Church of the Octoberist Marx. To read Bloch's work as integrated, of a piece, is to turn his thought into what it always threatened to be, the codex of utopian thought, the great consolidated work. It is to petrify Bloch according to his own most suspect desires; desires which are belied by the tendencies of his other works. In this essay, I want to play Bloch and Benjamin against and with each other, to situate Bloch in a more interesting way than as the faded philosopher of Stalinist hope.

Bloch (whose writings cry out for refunctioning) like Benjamin (who seems to be perpetually in the throes of rediscovery) thus poses the problem of inheritance, or to use a less top-heavy term, of reception. How to account for the odd temporality of these writers? One could begin to reckon their different affects and effects by ascribing to them that fine Blochian notion of *Ungleichzeitigkeit*, that is, of non-synchronicity. Bloch first explored this category in his study of fascism, *Heritage of Our Times*. Written in the mid-1930s (and the most recent of Bloch's books to be translated into English), *Heritage of Our Times* indicts the left for being partially responsible for the success of the National Socialists. In Bloch's account, the left misunderstood the appeal of the Nazis by dismissing all the atavisms and irrationality of the fascist movement as mere childish regression from the superior ratio of Marxism. Socialists and Communists failed to see that Nazism had a strong emotional appeal, a strong draw on archaic desires and cultural outcroppings:

> It is not the "theory" of the National Socialists but rather their energy which is serious, the fanatical-religious strain which does not merely stem from despair and stupidity, the strangely roused strength of faith.[2]

The Nazis could gain hegemony because they alone understood the peculiar historical configurations of German development, the unsatisfied needs of the archaic remnants that persist in the present. They were able to see that German reality was not reducible to a bipolar struggle between capital and labor, that the peculiar history of the nation had left a strong peasant class that was allied to neither one side nor the other. Furthermore, the Nazis were brilliant in seeing how the radically anti-industrial, reactionary but still proto-revolutionary impulses of various disenchanted groups whose formations preceded and survived the growth of capitalism could be mined to maintain capitalistic growth. In other words, fascism used the energy of non-synchronous elements of German society – the hold-outs from previous eras – to save the industrial state from its own contradictions and crush the leftist alternative. Revolutionary praxis, then, would require an appeal to the strong emotional claims of Germany's specific past and an elegant redirection of the investments of those claims. A successful revolution would have to put the power of the non-synchronous elements of the past to work for the future. Following Bloch's argument, then, we could say that he presents an example of the non-synchronous that is not easy to bring into fruitful contradiction with the present. There is perhaps too much Schelling in *The Principle of Hope*, and far too much Stalin. Benjamin, on the other hand, has to be born too late: he is truly non-synchronous, the theoretician of memory who can only have an effect when he himself is a memory.

But we give Bloch too little credit in this account even though we are using his categories. It might well be that we make a mistake if we reduce Bloch and Benjamin too much to the content of the tales they have to tell. If we follow the lead of Benjamin's later aesthetics we have to concede that the telling is as important as the narrative itself – how things are seen is as important for radical practice as what is seen. To become part of the community of the tale, we must be able to reproduce the story;[3] to become revolutionized spectators of film, we must be taught new habits of perception that we can take out into the world we must change.[4] So perhaps Bloch and Benjamin come to us with complicated trajectories: their careful negotiations might well present their most important legacy for our times.

In fact, an odd collaboration between Bloch and Benjamin provides us with a useful hint for such an understanding. In an essay from the early 1960s, Bloch remembers a conversation he had with Benjamin on Capri in 1924.[5] Although he cannot remember who said what (a problem they both seem to have suffered from in that each one felt that the other had stolen his ideas) Bloch does recall that they discussed the meaning of *déjà vu*, especially in Tieck's tale, "Der Blonde Eckbert." From the memory of this conversation a redemptive phenomenology of *déjà vu* is constructed. Bloch does not think that *déjà vu* is proof of Platonic anamnesis. Rather, *déjà vu* is an "act of intention":

> the actual "fausse reconnaisance" does not lead us back to real experience in a previously existing life . . . it reproduces an act of the self's own orientation [einen ichhaften Richtungsakt reproduziert].[6]

What has been "seen" before is not the point: one recovers an interrupted intention, an orientation to and in the world. The eerie sensation of shock – the sense that one has been here before – is quite real and quite accurate, but it registers an orientation that has been forgotten or repressed. To go further: in their discussion of Tieck, Bloch and Benjamin decide that the shock comes from this lived memory of a neglected intention and that attendant feelings of guilt come from precisely that realization of neglect. *Déjà vu*, then, has an odd structure. Shock marks the recognition of what has not been fulfilled, of an intention and self-orientation that have been actively displaced and disrupted. The scary revenant in the uncanny present is not the infinite repetition of the past – it is rather a reminder of what one had meant to do for the future. We can see then a strong structural relation between *déjà vu* and the non-synchronous. This becomes clear in Bloch's discussion of the Nazi ideology of *Blut und Boden*:

> Home, soil and nation are such *objectively* raised contradictions of the traditional to the capitalist Now, in which they have been increasingly destroyed and not replaced. They are contradictions of the traditional to the capitalist Now and elements of ancient society which have not yet died: they were contradictions even in their origin, namely to the past forms which never in fact wholly realized the intended contents of home, soil and nation. They are thus already contradictions of unfulfilled intentions ab ovo, ruptures with the past itself: not there and then, like the ruptures of contemporaneous contradictions, but throughout the whole of history as it were, so that here concealed contradictions even to history, namely still unrefurbished intentional contents of the past itself, possibly rebel as well.[7]

Déjà vu is to the individual what non-synchronous ideological formations are to the collective: memories of positions and orientations that were promised but have not yet come to be, ciphers of orientations that have yet to be fulfilled. They serve as the outstanding debts of personal and cultural history. Thus Bloch and Benjamin (for the remonstrance of guilt in the phenomenon of *déjà vu* is clearly Benjamin's touch) present a way for reading and redeeming the past: as a series of intentional claims whose normativity is witnessed by the emotions felt in the memory of neglect.

How then do we describe Bloch's orientation? Bloch is, especially in *The Principle of Hope*, a philosopher who locates the ciphers of hope in society's self-representations. He wants to save the past and ideology from themselves. He attempts "to preserve within the critique of ideology the tradition that is criticized."[8] Tradition can be liberated from its untruth because the excess of ideology contains the kernels of truth and salvation. Thus even the gross imaginings of false consciousness always overshoot the mark of the present they seek to describe or the future they hope to figure. This excess has the paradoxical effect of pointing quite directly to the necessary inadequacy of the present and its patterns of domination. Hence utopia is always latent in *every* cultural product, every work in which illusion competes with and completes reality: "Bloch's utopia settles into the empty space between [illusion] and what merely exists."[9] That gap between the corrective totalizations of illusion and the brute world they want to correct is the realm of utopia.

Bloch thus presents himself as a redemptive reader of what used to be called the superstructure. The strongly classicizing aesthetics of *The Principle of Hope* (different in emphasis than his defence of Expressionism) make art and mythology the projected completion of a world that continually seeks its predicate. Thus Bloch can claim that "Art is a laboratory and also a feast of implemented possibilities."[10] What saves this contention from sheer outrageousness is the assumption that imaginative representations of the world take as their material the as-yet-unseen tendencies of that world and drive them into an artistic pre-appearance. Art is thus not a reflection of the world but of what the world wants to become. It shows us not what has been but what could well be, what desires to be.[11] There is, Bloch asserts, "a driving in things." This flow of possibilities within the world serves as a material ground for the ongoing processes of history, and this horizon has a subjective correlate in urges, wishes, and dreams. In short there is "an open dimension in people" and an "open dimension in things": the former seeks the paths to its fulfillment in the latter.[12] There is thus a fine fit between the mind and the world:

> The concrete imagination and the imagery of its mediated anticipations are fermenting in the process of the real itself and are depicted in the concrete forward dream; anticipating elements are a component of reality itself.[13]

The imagination figures forth something that is already latent in reality; hence the seamless correlation between the imagination, the world, and the media through which the imagination bodies itself forth. The second nature of social immanence is treated as if it were Nature itself.

It is worth interrogating Bloch's rather capacious notion of "the world" which seems to encompass technological history, human history, and nature. The world does indeed world in Bloch's writing: it is always pregnant with itself and looks to man to bring it forth.[14] For Bloch, man and world are aligned so that artistic works serve as the alembic of the future. Hanna Gekle has rightly complained that Bloch asserts the correlation between subject and object, mind and world without working through the aporias this correlation presents.[15] We can extend Gekle's conclusions and the internal ambiguities of Bloch's philosophy, as expressed in *The Principle of Hope*, by noting that Bloch's adequation of subject and object returns the utopian to the realm of immanence. It does not break with the order of the social but continues it.

This critique would serve as a fatal blow to any utopian project. I therefore think it is worth applying as much pressure as possible to the tension between what Bloch calls "the subjective factor" (the strategic mobilization of contradiction against an inhumane order)[16] and the sense of closure that his Marxism provides. Marxism as science has "rescued the rational core of utopia and made it concrete as well as the core of the still idealistic tendency-dialectics."[17] Marxism has given the utopian moment its grounding and has provided it with the sublunary home of the future. But in thus using Marxism to rehabilitate utopia, Bloch closes the openness he claims Marxism has made concrete. He reduces "the concept of utopia to regulative ideas" and puts an end to the dialectical dissolution of categories.[18] Or, to quote Adorno's rather brisk summation:

> His philosophy conceives the end of the world as its ground, that which moves what exists, which, as its *telos*, it already inhabits. It makes the last first. That is Bloch's innermost antinomy, one that cannot be resolved.[19]

Hence the subjective insurrection against the badly existent only returns the existent to itself, helps the world on its way to the end it must necessarily reach. At the same time that Bloch wants to open the vista of an undetermined future, he is busily admitting impediments to such freedom. Against the subjective factor, the moment of utopian excess, he posits the telos at the end of the mind.

Thus Bloch at his most blustery – in the vast, windy expanses of *The Principle of Hope* – presents us with a deeply problematic legacy. There are a number of demerits by his name: his resolute obliteration of differences; his oddly joyless teleology which allows us to dream and then restricts those dreams in the name of the *docta spes* which is less an educated hope than a chastened one; his classicizing aesthetics and his pre-critical ideas about signification. But we should also be wary of such easy totalizations, of giving Bloch's thought a solid monumentality which its aspirations to be a "process philosophy" would seem to deny.[20]

In the second volume of *The Principle of Hope*, Bloch delivers a short eulogy on the utopian aspects of the natural-law tradition. In Bloch's narrative, the bourgeoisie of the eighteenth century was able to harness the orientation toward the future that this tradition provided and build revolutions from it. The energies inherent in natural law were not exhausted by these revolutions, nor was the pathos of the individual inherent in the tradition merely ideological.[21] Yet what Bloch gives, he is also willing to take away: he goes on to maintain that happiness is more urgent and more central a human concern than the natural law's emphasis on dignity.[22] Thus Bloch posits a hierarchy, not a dialectical relation, between these two aspirations, or rather between the two ideals of fulfillment and justice.[23]

The doctrine of rights, therefore, is merely a sideshow in the great circus of *The Principle of Hope*. Although Bloch treats it with some respect, he shares – at this moment – the early Marx's apparent distrust of the realm of rights.[24] It might be worth speculating that his experiences in the GDR in the 1950s made Bloch change his mind. (*The Principle of Hope*, while revised during this period, was the product of Bloch's American exile – hence its negative relation to the basis of US law.) Here is Bloch in *Natural Law and Human Dignity*, published in the year of his defection to the West:

> Liberation and dignity are not automatically born of the same act; rather they refer to each other reciprocally – with economic *priority* we find humanistic *primacy*. There can be no true installation of human rights without the end of exploitation, no true end of exploitation without the installation of human rights.[25]

Note that Bloch has established a dialectical, mutually determining relationship between justice and happiness, liberation and law. The redeployment of the term "dignity" signals a return to Kant, a return that Bloch is happy to acknowledge:

> This much is certain: There is just as little human dignity without the end of misery as there is happiness without the end of all old and new forms of subjugation. It is precisely at this point that the best contributions of the Enlightenment enter the picture in a way that does not permit them to be pushed aside again.[26]

The construction of the dialectical relation between rights and utopia – the dignification of dignity itself – is a part of a general strategy of historical recovery. For Bloch, the Enlightenment constellation of Kant, Rousseau, and the revolutionary Tricolor still contains unexhausted and unfulfilled semantic potential. Thus the Enlightenment is a task that is still before us:

> We are concerned with a peculiar heritage; its best remains in abeyance and is still to be appended. What is past does not return, especially not in an out-of-date way; but it can be taken at its word. It is just as urgent *suo modo* to raise the problem of a heritage of classical natural law as it is to speak of the heritage of social utopias.[27]

The past does not return. Bloch does not want the call to an unfinished tradition to sound like an incitement to historical regression, to a fumbling nostalgia. But the pastness of the past does not invalidate its claims on the present. Natural law remains a problem to be worked through, an intention to be respected, and a question to be answered. In fact, Bloch's form of ideological redemption, the salvation of the excessive moment of illusion from the limiting social relations it legitimates and criticizes at the same time, is designed precisely to make tradition a quarry of latent possibility once it has undergone the stringencies of dialectical analysis.

Tradition, of course, is a prickly and suspect term because of its own ideological overload. And one can see more than a trace of Bloch's interest in Heidegger in his appeal to heritage. But Bloch here is not quite like the Gadamer who equates our relation to a variegated tradition and with our relation to a single living Other. Gadamer maintains that the imperative openness to alterity "involves recognizing that I must accept some things that are against me, even though no one else forces me to do so."[28] Bloch's strong version of Benjamin's notion of the weak messianism of memory involves *not* accepting what is against me, but recovering that thought which will help me win freedom from a heteronomy.

Furthermore, the tradition that Bloch sketches in *Natural Law and Human Dignity* is not a unified transmission of hope from the past. Rather, it is a riven and dialectical affair, determined from the outside by its opposition to the established complacencies of custom and positive law:

> The unity of *physis* as a concept of value resides solely in its opposition to traditional institutions, to the law, to *nomos* . . . to normalized good behavior that has been reduced to breeding and mores. In opposition to this, the Sophists introduced the figure of the subject, of the naturally free and cunning individual.[29]

The human subject, therefore, is only a figure, a trope of resistance, like nature itself. Natural law creates the realm of the private – the domestic and the psychological interior[30] – as a way of fighting the falsely homogenizing primacy of the Athenian aristocracy.

As an ideology, however, classical natural law cannot help but suffer from the internal contradictions of its historical ground: under the Stoics, natural law found itself supporting both a commitment to universalizing necessity and a belief in private freedom; found itself proclaiming a cosmic rationality while celebrating the personal victory over private unreason. Nevertheless, from these divergent elements it was able to lay the conceptual basis for notions of equality, mutual aid, formal democracy, and the right to peace.[31]

In this story, rights and law which are born from an opposition to the class-driven distinctions of positive law are in turn opposed – and briefly overcome – by the containment strategies of Thomistic and Lutheran doctrine. These align natural law with positive law, legitimate domination, and allow justice to rain down from above.[32] The insurgent energies latent in the notion of "nature" are driven under ground, must wait until the rise of capitalism and the reappropriation of classical notions of natural law. Althaus, Hobbes, and Grotius – the natural-law theorists of the seventeenth century – leap over the middle ages and the Reformation, apply mathematics to the traditional logic of the natural law and reclaim the lost legacy of subjective right, of justice from below. In so doing, they bring into bright relief concepts, such as the social contract and the right to resistance, which had been undeveloped in their Greek and Roman incarnations.[33] The reactivation of natural law is, for Bloch, the utopian fuse that drives the bourgeois revolution. As the clear wind blowing against the edifice of feudalism, natural law becomes a progressive force again. Or perhaps it would be more accurate to say that it becomes a directly progressive force for the first time. Its social effects were indirect in the classical world.

The revival of natural law thus lends an odd quality to the doctrine's historical effectiveness, its effective history. The seventeenth century begins to redeem a past that was not ever present in itself, bodies forth in social reality moments that had until that point remained dormant in the margins of illusionary excess. The present reanimates the past but gives it a new configuration. Ideas that have no direct effect in their own time take on a revolutionary efficacy in a later period. Tradition is therefore a kind of deferred action, of the *Nachträglichkeit* that Freud discusses in his report on the "Wolfman."[34] In this non-linear conception of lived time, the past creates itself retro-actively. So it is in Bloch's thought that the central kernel of that of Locke and Hobbes was sown as a footnote to Epicurus. The imminent content of the past can only be recognized because it has been reformulated and refunctioned by its inheritors.

This mutual determination between the past and the present – their crystalization in what Benjamin calls "the now of recognizability" – runs through *Natural Law and Human Dignity*. Bloch shows how the traces of the most ancient law, the maternal law, though they maintained an underground existence in the Greek and Roman conceptions of natural law, did not come to consciousness until Bachofen excavated them in the nineteenth century to return them to the heart of jurisprudential thought.[35] The non-contemporaneity of the present moment, the historical tensions in the "now" that Bloch examines in *Heritage of Our Times*, show up in *Natural Law and Human Dignity* as the stratification of words, their temporal depth and emancipatory potential.[36] Bloch excavates "freedom" and reinstates autonomy as the first color of the revolutionary flag of the future.[37] Note, though, how deferred action acts in Bloch's text. The past is not an open treasure-trove. It has to be claimed. Progress is not the self-actualization of the world – it is, at best, a product of human choice and bravery in the face of terrible odds.

In *Natural Law and Human Dignity* we can therefore see a vision of human history that is not subordinated to the teleological machinery that drives *The Principle of Hope*. The signal moment in Bloch's historical reconstruction of the ruptures and reworkings of the natural-law tradition comes when he adamantly refuses to ontologize nature:

> It is not a tenable position that defends the idolization of external correlates, turning them into eternal man, that is, the idolization of a supposed *immutable and normative totality of nature*. In the Cynics, the Stoics, and Rousseauism, nature was constituted in different ways as the category that contrasted with societal relations, and this was powerfully conserved in the genuine and profound persistence of maternal law, and also . . . as a fetish against social defaults.[38]

Natural law pits an ever-shifting conception of "nature" against the frozen positivities of social relations. It is the subjective counter-move against the badly existent. It disrupts and offers counter-proposals, derived not from a hypostatized entity called "the world" but rather from the untapped semantic energies of a re-collected past. Natural law is "the element that resists, the insurgent element in all revolution."[39] Its negative grounding is in social relations as they are: its positive grounding is in a past which it calls forth and which, in so doing, it constitutes in a new way.

Human rights, then, are a force that resists and names oppression. They serve as a focal point for insurgency. In Bloch's own work, they disrupt the staunch utopian's all-too-ready deferral to the genius of world history, his Stalinist apologetics, his tub-thumping vision of solidarity. They retain the residue of difference as a political norm: "Even [the] pathos of the free individual seems like a warning against any confusion or mixing up of collectivity with the herd and herd character."[40] Natural law, then, is a necessary corrective to the abstractness that threatens to petrify Marxist thought. The doctrine of rights protects the concreteness of the particular against the homogenizing efforts of the universal. Bloch invokes the bourgeois Enlightenment to recover the revolutionary aspects of socialism against the orthodoxy of the Soviet state.[41] One could even argue that "natural law" and "the Enlightenment" are the names Bloch gives to the structural principle that in other texts he calls utopia. They all mark moments of personal inhibition and ideological excess that call for an improved existence. In *Natural Law and Human Dignity* autonomy is brought forth from the past to unsettle the present and to provide an orientation for the future.

Hence one can detect a more melancholy theme in this text, a more embattled note than one finds in *The Principle of Hope*. In Bloch's account of the fascist revival of Thomistic natural law, we can read a warning that human rights are always in danger, must always fight the powers of regression.[42] The struggle is precisely that, a fight whose result is not foreordained. The past might well contain norms we should act to fulfill, but the past also serves as a warning against an unqualified hope for success. Thus "progress" is modified in Bloch's own progressivist presentation. *Natural Law and Human Dignity* indicates that an emancipated future is a task to be won. It does not rest in the natural flow or the drive of things.

If Bloch seems to lack *Aktualität* it is perhaps because he has been all too readily reducible to a Marxist Schelling, because his apparent faith in an outdated philosophy of history seems to misrecognize in the greatest danger the most far-fetched hope. Bloch has been easy to dismiss.[43] By the same token, Benjamin's continuing relevance might arise from the pathos of his aristocratic despair, his deep distrust of the ideology of progress. Such a distrust is indeed common now. This despair finds its objective correlative in the violent regressions of recent history and is reinforced intellectually by critiques of teleology.

I have had occasion to note that Bloch seems to have a rather unproblematic – I called it a "pre-critical" view of language. While fascinated by representations, he is not at all bothered by representation itself. The same, of course, is not true of Benjamin. In fact, we would do well to see his famous testament, the "Theses on History," as a critique first and foremost of the representation of history, of historiography in its narrowest and broadest sense. The German title – "Über den Begriff der Geschichte" – points squarely to the fact that Benjamin addresses the concept of history, not history itself. Thus Tiedemann's complaint that the theses do not provide an ontology of historicity strikes me as uncharacteristically wide of the mark.[44] At stake for Benjamin in this text is less our historical being than how we conceptualize what is called "history."

We might well choose to see Benjamin's critique of conceptuality in the terms he establishes in *The Origin of German Tragic Drama* where he opposes knowledge to truth, concepts to ideas:

> Truth, bodied forth in the dance of represented ideas, resists being projected . . . into the realm of knowledge. Knowledge is possession. Its very object is determined by the fact that it must be taken possession of – even if in a transcendental sense – in the consciousness . . . For knowledge, method is a way of acquiring . . .; for truth it is self-representation, and is therefore immanent in it as form. Unlike the methodology of knowledge, this form does not derive from a coherence established in the consciousness, but from an essence . . . Whereas the concept is a spontaneous product of the intellect, ideas are simply given to be reflected on. Ideas are preexistent.[45]

The idealist language of Benjamin's exposition might well require some exposition of its own,[46] but his intent should be clear. Conceptuality is a

product of the mind: it marks the mediation of the particular through a
potentially false universal, discovers its knowledge through the pre-
existing categories of its own methodology. It thus sacrifices the alterity
of the phenomenon by yoking it, transforming it into psychic property.
Benjamin's invocation of the truth as the self-representing essence of
the phenomenon is designed to save the phenomenon from the
narcissistic hold of the epistemological subject.[47] Conceptuality, taken
as a necessary moment in the representation of ideas,[48] is nothing more
than a moment. If it is revered as an end in itself, it reveals nothing but
itself.

So, the "concept of history" does not discover the truth of history, at
least not directly. If we follow the tenor of *The Origin of German Tragic
Drama*, we can see that the concept of history will tell us nothing on its
own. Rather constellations of phenomena will reveal not the truth of
history per se but the truths that are the essence of historical periods,
the juxtapositions of extremes that point to the truths of those periods.
Thus history is not a conceptualizable entity that can be possessed but
"the object [*Gegenstand*] of a construction, whose site is not homogeneous and empty time; but it forms/depicts [*bildet*] a time that is filled
with Nowtime."[49] Proper historiography will not present us with the
image (*Bild*) of the empty temporal experience that rules our capitalist
modernity. Instead, it will provide us with a counter-image, where time
is distinguished not by quantity (any one minute is the same length as
any other – all minutes are lined up like soldiers) but by quality and
presence. The presence thus imaged forth by the historical work will be
a specifically *textual* space. Specific moments from the past will come
into a conjunction with the present (*Gegenwart*) in order to leap out of
the eternal recurrence of heteronomy into the plenitude of Nowtime
(*Jetztzeit*). In this space the threatened insurgent moments of the past
will be recovered and redeemed.

Benjamin is quite clear that this historiographic moment is nothing
more than an image:

> In this structure [the historical materialist] recognizes the sign of a messianic
> cessation of happening, or to put it differently, of a revolutionary chance in
> the fight for the suppressed/oppressed [*unterdrückte*] past.[50]

In the structure – not in single phenomena, but in their arrangement –
the materialist sees an image of the Messiah, or, to put it differently, a
figure for historical redemption. That sign of the cessation of happening
is like the rainbow: not the covenant itself, but a sign of the covenant, a
fore-image of the idea of hope.

For this reason, Benjamin summons up that other sign of lost hope –
the wizened dwarf of theology. It is safe to say that theological tropes
serve the same function in Benjamin's theses that the theory of ideas

served in *The Origin of German Tragic Drama*. A series of supposed outmoded figures (ideas, the Messiah) is summoned into a dialectical relation with the most modern modes of thought in order to break the universalizing reductions of that modernity, "to escape the trance-like captivity of bourgeois immanence."[51] Bourgeois immanence lies squarely at the heart of intellectual representations: philosophy dissolves all particulars in its imperial quest for systematization; historiography wants to reduce all struggle to the foreordained march of an alienated world process. Against these attempts to make the world safe for the badly existent, Benjamin marshals the arsenals of the past, ideas and essences which disrupt the hegemony of the forces of heteronomy. He attempts to save the particular from becoming a trophy in the ongoing triumph of other people's victories. Unlike Bloch who refuses (structurally) to see a difference between "second nature" and Nature, Benjamin wants to bestow on the discarded artifacts of second nature the respect and the pathos due to suffering Nature itself.

Thus in his famous theses Benjamin refunctions the attack on systematization he had launched in *The Origin of German Tragic Drama* so that he can attack the systematization of experience, of the particular, of time itself. Benjamin's theses have such a strong pathos because they argue that all hope is lodged in temporal consciousness and in memory. The decay of memory is the subjective index of the decay of a sense of time itself: to worship progress is to worship the lash of the reified thought that subjugates us in the first place. It is to forget the indications from the past that would teach us that such oppression might well be resisted, might be resisted well. These indications have a "retroactive force and will constantly call into question every victory, past and present of the rulers."[52] But they are caught in a continual state of siege:

> The danger affects both the content of the tradition and its receivers. The same threat hangs over both: that of becoming a tool of the ruling classes. In every era the attempt must be made anew to wrest tradition away from a conformism that is about to overpower it.[53]

Benjamin makes it quite clear that this attempt to win tradition back from the forces of illegitimate violence is the task of the materialist historian:

> The gift of fanning the spark of hope in the past will only attend that historian who is thoroughly convinced of this: even the dead will not be safe from the enemy if he wins. And he has never stopped winning.[54]

Thus the historian has the job of waking us up, of reminding us that the hope that has not yet been fulfilled might well be lost for ever: the semantic possibilities of the past are always in danger. This clarion call to battle is designed to shock one out of passivity. By making the present the custodian of the past, Benjamin asserts that history will *not* take care of itself. Oppression will not cancel itself out as if the world were studiously dialectical. So in a lucidly Blochian moment, Benjamin tries to redeem the discredited visions of Fourier. He points out that while the positivist adherents of progress see the exploitation of nature as value-neutral at worst, Fourier sees that all exploitation is finally human exploitation. The technology that subdues nature also subdues the workers.[55] Machines will not free people through enslavement. The destructive moment of historical materialist thought, the destructive character itself, must be taken on as a responsibility. And it all depends on the presentation of the past, on the intellectual and his texts.

Benjamin's revolutionary optics[56] conjure the spirits of theology to signal the break between immanence and transfiguration, between the existent and the true. Like Bloch, his account enacts what it describes: it creates a constellation where an "outmoded" form of thought – the theological – comes into contact with the most modern and provides ciphers of a fulfilled future. As Rainer Nägele has pointed out, *Nachträglichkeit* is the chief historical force for Benjamin.[57] Theology therefore lends momentum to historical materialism. But, as in the case of Bloch, Benjamin's version of *Nachträglichkeit* is an intellectual's counter-move against a homogenizing view of history. Benjamin, even more than Bloch, works from a dialectical notion of tradition.[58] In "Über den Begriff der Geschichte", he actually describes two kinds of tradition: the first is called culture and is the domain of the oppressors. The second is unnamed, and bears the traces of struggle and desire. It must be remembered, not as souvenir (*Andenken*) but as memoration (*Eingedenken*), which will heal in the present (in its textual manifestations) and in the future (in the messianic moment of revolution).[59] In Benjamin as in Bloch, counter-tradition – be it troped as Enlightenment or theology – only becomes powerful at the moment when it flashes *again*, when it is redeployed against a present that threatens to congeal into undesirable totalizations.

We can therefore argue that Bloch's "mistake" in *The Principle of Hope* lies in his assumption that the mid-nineteenth century's insurgent appropriation of the philosophy of history still had a revolutionary force, that it still could serve as a moment of intellectual opposition into the 1940s. While the philosophy of history provided important categories and presented important possibilities at a certain time, its semantic power withered when it became the official ideology of the institutionalized communist parties. Perhaps what dates Bloch's *magnum opus* is that it marks a revolt against the more dated aspects of Heidegger's, Jung's, and Freud's philosophies, and that it tends to forget that it itself constitutes a historical intervention and a historical representation. What makes *Natural Law and Human Dignity* a more interesting text is that it is a full revision in the light of history of a stance that Bloch had come to realize was no longer credible.

The importance of Benjamin and Bloch might best rest in their examples. The argument about Benjamin's provenance – is he a Jew or a Marxist? – is an odd one, fed by Cold War distrust and an odd opposition of categories. In Benjamin's work as in Bloch's, religion and Marxism function in similar ways: they are meant to disrupt the cool surfaces of established discourses, to break the thrall of the everyday and to recall the reader to those hopes that have almost been lost. And these interventions are specific: Judaism comes into conflict with *Germanistik* and a scientistic Marxist economism to restore them to the scattered truths of the particular; Marxism comes into conflict with Judaism to redeem the historical nature of the religion's utopian hopes.[60] Bloch sought to restore the irrational to Communism and then used the lance of the Enlightenment to tilt against the irrationalism of the Eastern bloc. In their individual texts and in that spectral totality we call their "text," Bloch and Benjamin disrupt the workings of the dominant discourse within which they are writing and in so doing provide formal ciphers of eschatological rupture.

In this essay therefore, I have argued that the interconnected figures of *déjà vu* and *Nachträglichkeit,* the odd temporality of lost and recovered intention, help explain both the themes and the structures of Bloch's and Benjamin's work and help us redeem Bloch's *opus* for our time. In an earlier published version of this piece, I wondered about the motivation for such a purely textual basis for political hope and I engaged in a rather lacerating self-critique. In the two years that have passed since I finished that version, I have come to wonder about my own reservations. I want to ask myself whether my sense of the inefficacy of textual mediations within our educational institutions does not betray a distrust of all institutions, that is, *a rather regressive desire for immediacy.* But hope of all kinds needs to take place, needs places to happen. Historical hope, hope based on history, can only happen in those places in which history is reconstructed, taught, and argued. The problem does not lie with the existence of institutions, but with their lack and with the lack of flexibility always inherent in institutionalization. The utopian despair of Benjamin's theses is not that far from the grim and beautiful anti-organicism of Horkheimer's famous "Traditional and Critical Theory":

> The circle of transmitters of this tradition [critical theory] is neither limited nor renewed by organic or sociological laws. It is constituted and maintained not by biological or testamentary inheritance, but by a knowledge which brings its own obligations with it.[61]

Horkheimer wrote this essay in German in a journal published in France in the hope that it would find German readers in spite of Nazism. Similarly, Benjamin wrote his theses in the face of the Nazis' destruction of discursive institutions and sent two copies back to the world. It would therefore be a sin – a *Schande* – against their memories if we argued that we live under similar conditions. Rather, we have to take their break with the organic seriously by working with and from this insight.

In order to do this, though, we have to deal with the problem of verification presented so cogently by Horkheimer in the essay I have cited above. The break with the philosophy of history, with the notion of the intelligibility of the "historical process," shakes the certainty out of hope and opens it to its full utopian fragility. To derive a notion of historical verification in the face of the openness of the future, we would probably have to resort to a thinker important for Benjamin and close in many intellectual ways to Bloch – Franz Rosenzweig, who could be called, with a certain degree of playful irony, the Jewish Bloch. (Bloch of course was a Jew, but the Christology of *Der Geist der Utopie* annoyed both Benjamin and Scholem.) If we returned to Rosenzweig (and to Hermann Cohen, Rosenzweig's mentor and the man against whose thought Rosenzweig and the younger Benjamin frequently define themselves), we could then begin to remedy an ill that this present essay is still heir to – its postmodern tendency to reduce the category of redemption, so important to Bloch, Benjamin, Rosenzweig, and Cohen, to a "mere" figure, a chastened reduction which also betrays a weird nostalgia for the immediate and the immediately effective.

This impatient nostalgia and its repeated historical chastening might however signal the very ground and sustenance – dare I call it the very dialectic? – which maintain and constitute redemptive hope. The Talmud displays this rhythm in Rabbi Tarfon's neat antiphon:

> R. Tarfon said: – The day is short and the work is great and the laborers are sluggish and the wages are high and the householder is urgent.

> He used to say: – The work is not upon thee to finish, nor art thou free to desist from it.[62]

The first teaching stresses the urgency and the enormity of the sheer labor of righteousness: the second emphasizes patience and the acceptance of both human finitude and human responsibility. And if we project this uneven rhythm of hope onto history, we come to the Messiah about whom Rosenzweig writes in a commentary on the medieval poet Judah ha-Levi:

> The expectation of the coming of the Messiah, by which and because of which Judaism lives, would be a meaningless theologumenon, a mere "idea"

in the philosophical sense, empty prattle, if the appearance again and again of a "false Messiah" did not render it reality and unreality, illusion and disillusion. The false Messiah is as old as the hope for the true Messiah. He is the changing form of this changeless hope. He separates every Jewish generation into those whose faith is strong enough to give themselves up to an illusion, and those whose hope is so strong that they do not allow themselves to be deluded ... And this goes on until the day when all will be reversed, when the belief of the believers will become truth, and the hope of the hoping a lie. Then – and no one knows whether this "then" will not be this very day – the task of the hoping will come to an end.[63]

Bloch might warn us against the false Messiah and thus argue for the importance of the "docta spes," the hope that accommodates itself to the reality principle. I would prefer to see him (or her) as the product of the conflict between the historical moment and the dreams it produces, dreams that only history – that is, the future that could be this very day itself – can redeem.

Notes

1. See Ernst Bloch, "Recollections of Walter Benjamin," in *On Walter Benjamin*, ed. Gary Smith (Cambridge, Mass.: MIT Press, 1988), pp. 338–45.

2. Ernst Bloch, *Heritage of Our Times*, trans. Neville and Stephen Plaice (Berkeley and Los Angeles: University of California Press, 1991), p. 60.

3. Walter Benjamin, *Illuminations*, trans. Harry Zohn (New York: Schocken, 1968), pp. 98–101.

4. *Illuminations*, pp. 239–40.

5. Ernst Bloch, "Bilder des Deja Vu," *Verfremdungen I* (Frankfurt am Main: Suhrkamp, 1962), pp. 24–36. Actually Bloch does not recall the date. Judging from the details he does give, the conversation had to have taken place during the summer of 1924. See Gershom Scholem, *Walter Benjamin: The Story of a Friendship*, trans. Harry Zohn (New York: Schocken, 1981), pp. 121–3; see also Walter Benjamin, *Briefe* (Frankfurt: Suhrkamp, 1966), 2 vols., I, p. 353. Benjamin, unfortunately, does not record the dialogue.

6. "Bilder des Deja Vu," p. 127.

7. *Heritage of Our Times*, pp. 108–9.

8. Jürgen Habermas, *Theory and Practice*, trans. John Viertel (Boston: Beacon Press, 1974), p. 240. As this essay is an attempt to recover Bloch for an American audience, I will always cite readily available US editions.

9. Theodor Adorno, *Notes to Literature*, trans. Shierry Weber Nicholsen (New York: Columbia University Press, 1991), 2 vols., I, p. 204. Adorno goes on to complain that because Bloch sees utopian traces everywhere, they are really nowhere (I, p. 210).

10. Ernst Bloch, *The Principle of Hope*, trans. Stephen Plaice, Neville Plaice, and Paul Knight (Cambridge, Mass.: MIT Press, 1986), p. 216. Hereafter this work will be abbreviated as *PH*.

11. *PH*, pp. 214–15.

12. *PH*, p. 288.

13. *PH*, p. 197.

14. *PH*, pp. 247–8. See also Jürgen Habermas, *Philosophical-Political Profiles*, trans. Frederick G. Lawrence (Cambridge, Mass: MIT Press, 1983), pp. 71–3.

15. Hanna Gekle, "The Phenomenology of the Wish in *The Principle of Hope*," *New German Critique*, 45 (1988), pp. 71, 78–80.

16. *PH*, pp. 147–8.

17. *PH*, p. 141.

18. Habermas, *Philosophical-Political Profiles*, pp. 77–8.

19. Adorno, *Notes to Literature,* I, p. 213.

20. See Wayne Hudson, *The Marxist Philosophy of Ernst Bloch* (New York: St Martin's Press, 1982).

21. *PH,* pp. 540–47.

22. *PH,* p. 548.

23. Particularly disturbing in this regard is the following Stalinist apologia:

> Ideals relate to this supreme hope-content, possible world-content, as a means to an end; there is therefore a hierarchy of ideals, and a lower one can be sacrificed to a higher one, because it is resurrected anyway in the realization of the higher one. For example, the supreme variation of the highest good in the socio-political sphere is the classless society; consequently, ideals like freedom and also equality act as means to this end, and derive their value-content ... from the highest good in socio-political terms. In such a way that it does not merely determine the content of the ideals as means, but also varies them according to the requirements of the supreme end-content, and where necessary temporarily justifies the deviations.
>
> *PH,* p. 173

Theoretically, then, the means will be sublated in an end that will retain them and bring them out of their isolation. The great chuffing engine of the dialectic will therefore bring to perfection what it has in the meantime destroyed. The theoretical consistency of Bloch's position seems remarkably blind to its own political implications. By relegating terms that belong to the sphere of justice to the final aim of a classless society, Bloch is willing to sacrifice the safeguards of autonomy in the name of overcoming heteronomy.

24. Thus Marx:

> None of the supposed rights of man, therefore, go beyond the egoistic man, man as he is, as a member of civil society; that is, an individual separated from the community, withdrawn into himself, wholly preoccupied with his private interest and acting in accordance with his private caprice.

Karl Marx, *Early Writings,* trans. T.B. Bottomore (New York: McGraw-Hill, 1964), p. 64.

25. Ernst Bloch, *Natural Law and Human Dignity,* trans. Dennis J. Schmidt (Cambridge, Mass.: MIT Press, 1986), p. xxix. Hereafter the title of this book will be abbreviated as *NL.*

26. *NL,* p. xxx.

27. *NL,* p. xxix.

28. Hans-Georg Gadamer, *Truth and Method* (2nd rev. edn., New York: Crossroad, 1990), p. 361.

29. *NL,* pp. 8–9.

30. *NL,* pp. 10–11.

31. *NL,* pp. 15–16.

32. *NL,* pp. 25–44.

33. *NL,* pp. 45–60.

34. Sigmund Freud, *Three Case Histories* (New York: Macmillan, 1963), pp. 226–32, 281–96, 303–6. See also J. Laplanche and J.-B. Pontalis, *The Language of Psychoanalysis,* trans. Donald Nicholson-Smith (New York: Norton, 1973), pp. 111–14.

35. *NL,* pp. 110–19.

36. *NL,* p. 154. There is therefore a strong relation between *Nachträglichkeit* and *Ungleichzeitigkeit:* the *Ungleichzeitigkeit* which Nazi propaganda is able to mine becomes effective (*nachträglich*) precisely because it was never fulfilled, brought into the present.

37. *NL,* pp. 154–63.

38. *NL,* p. 192.

39. *NL,* p. 275.

40. *PH,* p. 547.

41. "No constitutional state in prosperity can in the long run conceal the true catastrophic essence of capitalism, nor can any Stalin ... conceal the most humane of all victories: socialism" (*NL,* p. 275).

42. Regression is a dangerous term here, of course, for it smacks precisely of the teleology I am trying to defend against. In my account, regression signals the return to the exhausted semantic potentials of the past.

43. Habermas has been quick to dismiss him: his attack on the Marxist Schelling is positively Adorno-esque in its edge and finality. (The fine satire of this relatively early

essay makes one wish that Habermas had pursued this vein of vituperation.) Nevertheless, it might be interesting to note that in his essay on Benjamin, Habermas goes out of his way to praise *Natural Law and Human Dignity* for its important redirection of the notion of "progress" from physical need to emancipation.

A similar ambivalence can be seen in a fascinating interview Habermas gave in 1983 in which he concedes to Bloch the need for emancipatory images and utopian figures, but then wants to maintain a firm distinction between theory and utopia: he maintains, as much as is possible, Adorno's injunction against positive images of future redemption. Nevertheless, Habermas makes a beautiful case for Benjamin's reversal of the poles of history:

> Utopias are important ... but memory is just as important ... We need a symbolic form of representation for those things for which we have fought, for which a collective effort was required. What is terrifying about material progress, even about political and constitutional progress ... is this traceless disappearance of the historical past. It is terrifying both for past suffering and past sacrifice ... and for the identity of those who come later ...

Habermas, perhaps too influenced by the early sections of *The Principle of Hope*, does not seem to want to grant utopian potential to memory. We can, I would like to argue, see a strong internal relation between memory and utopia and save them both from a theoretical disdain they do not deserve and that Habermas, in his own theoretical accounts, does not want to bestow on them. See Habermas, *Philosophical-Political Profiles*, pp. 63–78, 158; "Conservative Politics, Work, Socialism and Utopia Today," *Habermas: Autonomy and Solidarity*, ed. Peter Dews (London: Verso, 1986), pp. 131–47 (quotation, pp. 139–40).

44. Rolf Tiedemann, "Historical Materialism or Political Messianism," *Benjamin: Philosophy, Aesthetics, History*, ed. Gary Smith (Chicago: University of Chicago Press, 1989), p. 294.

45. Walter Benjamin, *The Origin of German Tragic Drama*, trans. John Osborne (London: New Left Books, 1977), pp. 39–40.

46. See Charles Rosen's elegant account, "The Ruins of Walter Benjamin," *On Walter Benjamin*, ed. Smith, pp. 152–60.

47. I here defer to Adorno. See T.W. Adorno, "A Portrait of Walter Benjamin," *Prisms*, trans. Samuel and Shierry Weber (Cambridge, Mass.: MIT Press, 1984), p. 235.

48. *Origin of German Tragic Drama*, p. 35.

49. Walter Benjamin, "Theses on the Philosophy of History," *Illuminations*, trans. Harry Zohn (New York: Schocken, 1969) p. 261. I have altered the translations against the German where I have felt that Zohn's versions have not been adequate. The footnotes will refer the reader to Zohn's text.

50. *Illuminations*, p. 263.

51. Adorno, *Prisms*, p. 236.

52. *Illuminations*, p. 255.

53. Ibid.

54. Ibid.

55. *Illuminations*, p. 259.

56. My account here owes much to Susan Buck-Morss, *The Dialectics of Seeing* (Cambridge, Mass.: MIT Press, 1989), pp. 205–330.

57. Rainer Nägele, *Theater, Theory, Speculation: Walter Benjamin and the Scenes of Modernity* (Baltimore: Johns Hopkins University Press, 1991), p. 76.

58. A note here: it might well be argued that my homogenizing view of Bloch and Benjamin tactfully ignores Bloch's fierce attack on anamnesis in the first sections of *The Principle of Hope* and Benjamin's fierce anamnetic solidarity. A resolution might lie in the realm of dialectics: the past and the future are not mutually exclusive categories. A more accurate, but perhaps less satisfying answer to this problem might lie in Bloch's attempt to create a science of the future from the materials he claims are at hand. These materials are, on the most part, historical and historically determined: a point he would readily concede. The science of the future is a critical form of knowledge that is not limited to static categories that other forms of science want to ontologize. Its raw materials are the present, but as he shows in his other works, that present is never present: it is a conjunction of differing tendencies.

59. See Walter Benjamin, "Central Park," *New German Critique*, 34 (1985), pp. 48–55; Irving Wohlfarth, "On the Messianic Structure of Walter Benjamin's Last Reflections," *Glyph*, 3 (1978), pp. 156–8.

60. See Irving Wohlfarth, "On Some Jewish Motifs in Benjamin," in *The Problem of Modernity*, ed. Andrew Benjamin (New York: Routledge, 1989), pp. 165–6.

61. Max Horkheimer, *Critical Theory* (New York: Seabury Press, 1972), p. 241.

62. *Pirke Avot*, II, p. 20.

63. Franz Rosenzweig, *Franz Rosenzweig: His Life and Thought*, ed. Nahum Glatzer (New York: Schocken, 1961), pp. 350–51; the translation has been very slightly modified.

Reclaiming the "Terrain of Fantasy": Speculations on Ernst Bloch, Memory, and the Resurgence of Nationalism

Jamie Owen Daniel

> Two world wars and continuing nationalism have ... shown that the imaginary element of the nation is more enduring than any reality.
>
> Carlos Castoriadis

> Not everything that is irrational can be dismissed as stupidity.
>
> Ernst Bloch

In his 1982 study of *The Marxist Philosophy of Ernst Bloch*, Wayne Hudson concluded that Bloch's work remained "doubly anachronistic" in that he was both "non- and over-contemporaneous in his relationship to the present" (19). Now, more than a decade later, we might assume that his work has become *triply* anachronistic in light of the trajectory of events that extends from the so-called "fall" of the Berlin Wall, through German unification, the official dissolution of the Soviet Union, and the collapse of Yugoslavia. What could possibly be stood to gain at this point, we might wonder, by resuscitating the wildly eclectic corpus of a pre Frankfurt School Marxist theoretician of utopia whose writing style often seems to oscillate between the hallucinatory and the incoherent? What, if anything, remains to be salvaged of the work of a philosopher whose humanist agenda allowed him to support the Stalinist show trials that sent thousands of political dissidents to their deaths? To what extent is the "German philosopher of the October Revolution," as Oskar Negt referred to him, still a living part of our post Soviet Union and post Cold War heritage? My response to these questions in what follows will be suggestive rather than exhaustive, and is made in the cautiously hopeful spirit of Bloch's typically awkward assertion, formulated in 1962 even as the Berlin Wall was being built, that "[t]he paths in the midst of collapse are layable" (*Heritage of Our Times*, p. 8).

*

Within the context of the West German *Historikerstreit* or "historians'
debate" of the 1980s that laid the foundation for German unification in
1990, the historian Michael Stürmer wrote that, "in a land without
memory, anything is possible."[1] Obviously, this "anything" could include
the only initially exuberant "reconciliation" of the socialist German
Democratic Republic with the Federal Republic and its capitalist economy and thus, implicitly, with the heritage of the Third Reich, in
opposition to which the GDR had always defined itself. This rhetoric of
reconciliation is doubly ironic when we consider that the unification has
been officially and rather insistently understood as a marker of the
Federal Republic's laying to rest of its fascist past, of which the Berlin
Wall had always been, quite literally, a concrete reminder. As Monika
Maron put it, with the unification, "the Germans announced to the
world their victory over their own history."[2]

Had he lived to witness this extraordinary sequence of events, Ernst
Bloch would surely have had much to say about the feasibility of laying
to rest a past which, whether or not this was ever acknowledged, had
played such a crucial role in the definition of both German national
identities since 1945. For, as Anson Rabinbach was the first to point out,
Bloch concerned himself explicitly with the continued presence of the
past in the present, especially when that present believed itself to have
most radically broken with and overcome the past. Bloch consistently
sought to expose, and, to use Benjamin's term, to redeem "those
ideological remnants of past epochs that have been appropriated by
fascism."[3] He did this most pointedly in the 1934 book, *Erbschaft dieser
Zeit* (translated as *Heritage of Our Times*), a complex collection of
fragmented texts in which he attempted to work out why, during the
period of economic and political crisis that preceded the election of
Hitler in 1933, it was not communism or even socialism, but fascism that
proved to be the most popularly appealing social movement. Bloch was
indeed one of very few intellectuals on the left who were able before
the war to recognize the "authenticity" (a term I use cautiously, of
course) of fascism as a cultural synthesis, as well as to acknowledge the
paucity of the leftist response to the fascist organization, through a
mythic vision of heroic nationalism, of the energies and hopes that
could be invested in national identity more generally. As he puts it in
Heritage of Our Times, Marxism did not respond to the German people's
need for a stable image of themselves: "Marxist propaganda [has failed
because it] lacks an opposite land to myth . . . Large masses in Germany
. . . were able to become National Socialist precisely because the
Marxism which presents them does not also 'represent' them at the
same time" (60). Bloch makes a compelling case for taking seriously the
response of fascism to complex human needs that were unrecognized,
and thus unmet, by the left's call to an *internationalist* common identity
based in class; the problem in the left's response to fascism is that it

cannot acknowledge that "fascism was not simply an instrument of deception," but rather the miscarried manifestation of hopes and dreams not taken into account and addressed by Weimar society and its leftist theoreticians. As Rabinbach argues, "Bloch is able to understand the appeal of fascism because he discovers in it the iconography of satisfaction."[4] His theory of the appeal of fascism is thus both "an indictment of the Left for abandoning the terrain of fantasy to fascist colonization,"[5] and, in retrospect, a demand that the unmet needs that fascism was willing and able, at least initially, to address be recognized and addressed by the left, even when, and perhaps *especially* when, these needs seemed to contradict an idealized image of what might constitute the popular agenda.

I want to argue that we on the left today risk replicating the error of Bloch's contemporaries in Weimar if we too blithely assume, as have many analysts, that the East Germans who stormed across the Invaliden-strasse to spend their money in West German shops were motivated primarily by a blind compulsion to consume any and all available Western commodities, rather than by a more complex configuration of unmet needs. Stefan Heym provided a typical example of this perspective in late 1989, when he lamented, with an extraordinary degree of contempt, that

> [t]he very same people who had risen up and taken their fate into their own hands ... who had only recently seemed to be marching nobly into a promising future became suddenly a horde of frenzied shoppers, backs pressed into stomachs, marching only to the Hertie and Bilka department stores and on the hunt for glitzy trash. What expressions on their faces as, with cannibalistic lust, they rooted like pigs through display tables intentionally placed in their paths by Western shopkeepers; and what bovine humility ... when, with the patience and obedience they had been taught at home, they stood in line for the hand-outs called deceptively and with psychological treachery "welcome money" by the strategists of the Cold War.[6]

With Bloch's analysis of Weimar in mind, we should resist coming to the too simple conclusion that has been voiced by both dismayed leftist intellectuals like Heym and smugly self-righteous conservatives in the United States, i.e. that the Berlin Wall fell because East Germans simply couldn't go on any longer without the VCRs and microwaves and Disney products to which they had been denied access for so long. His analysis might instead provide us with a model for a more tempered response than this smug cynicism, which condescendingly figures the East Germans who had just changed history as shallow and mindless consumers. For just as it has been argued that Germany's fascist past cannot and should not ever be fully laid to rest (Elie Wiesel cautioned on US television that the removal of the Wall could contribute to the collective forgetting of the events that led to its having been erected), neither can nor should the "new past" be dismissed, the socialist past that was the legacy of the radical German socialist and communist traditions of Bloch's Weimar and that had provided the ideological and moral foundation for the GDR in the first place. Bloch's often quoted remarks within the context of the German popular embrace of National Social- ism during the materially impoverished 1930s, that "man does not live by bread alone, especially when he has none," is particularly resonant here in that it suggests that the GDR did not fail simply because it so often failed to provide basic material needs (not to mention Heym's "glitzy trash"), but rather because it ultimately failed to provide a coherent cultural synthesis that met the equally essential and concrete needs of the imagination. It could not provide sufficient space for the free flow and satisfaction of what he calls "the undercurrent of very old dreams" (*Heritage of Our Times*, p. 57).

Among these "very old dreams," of course, is the dream of a German nation. What is often emphasized in more thoughtful responses to the seemingly overnight disintegration of the GDR is the central role played in the logic of unification by a previously unmet need to claim, or reclaim, and then assert a national identity. This line of reasoning usually assumes the existence of a "natural" national identity in that it points to specifically "German" characteristics, behaviors, and anxieties that are thought to pre-date the politically delineated, and thus *un*natu- ral, postwar boundaries. What brought the Wall down, accordingly, was not mere *Konsumterror*, a frenzy of commodity fetishism run amok, but rather the power of "Germanness" to provide a common identity that was able to neutralize and supersede differences in political ideology. "Germanness" was able, in Aziz Al-Azmeh's words, to "proffer a fetishism of the collective self as a socio-political imperative."[7]

This explanation seems all the more credible, given that we have witnessed what looks like convincing evidence of this "socio-political imperative" in the rampant outbreaks of xenophobic violence that erupted after the unification. These attacks were often carried out in the name of an essentialized German identity that was unwilling to tolerate the presence of anyone who could be defined as a foreigner, as expressed in the chant "Deutschland für die Deutschen, Ausländer 'raus!" – "Germany for the Germans, foreigners out!" Jeffrey Peck has noted both that the "fall of the Wall (November 1989) and subsequent German unification that subsumed the German Democratic Republic eleven months later (October 1990) occurred at breakneck speed," and that, within the year that followed, attacks on foreigners likewise rose "dramatically, notably in the eastern regions of the new Germany . . . Hoyerswerda, a small town in Saxony (in the former GDR) became the first city to announce that it would make itself *ausländerfrei* (free of foreigners)."[8] As is well known from numerous reports on the phenomenon, many of those responsible for the attacks have made a belligerent point of publicly challenging the Federal Republic's postwar taboo against displaying the iconography of National Socialism by wearing swastikas and engaging in other aggressively offensive behavior. Clearly, it does *look* as if the legacy of the Third Reich, far from having been finally laid to rest, has returned with a vengeance unanticipated by those who had initially rejoiced at the prospect of the citizens of the two German nations becoming "one people" again.

I want in the remainder of this paper to attempt, following Bloch's example, a different reading of what appears to be the return of a repressed Nazi unconscious in the former GDR. My focus thus far has been on the broader political questions raised by the collapse of the GDR. Certainly, we do need to ask what is to be salvaged of Germany's socialist and communist heritage, now that the project of a socialist Germany, i.e. the heritage of Liebknecht and Luxemburg, appears to be in ruins. We do need to ask how the heritage of the German Democratic Republic (and the German Democratic Republic *as* heritage) should be understood, now that it has been absorbed into a Federal Republic that apparently has no intention whatsoever of "reconciling" with its own socialist legacy, and in which the popular slogan "one currency, one people, one fatherland" could be chanted without apology at public gatherings. At the same time, however, I want to shift my attention from these more abstract questions and focus instead on the lived, experiential repercussions of the "gutting" of the German Democratic Republic as what Oskar Negt and Alexander Kluge would term a *Lebenszusamenhang*, or "context of living."[9] For it is here, I believe, that it might be possible to explain the apparent incongruity of these recent outbreaks of virulent xenophobia in formerly socialist communities, and to understand how, in Bloch's words, it could seem as if "from one day to the next the flag shops exchanged the soviet star for the swastika" (*Heritage of Our Times*, p. 145).

The period of the Weimar Republic, during which Germany moved in the course of less than two decades from fragile democracy through economic depression to belligerent dictatorship, is often celebrated as having been one of exuberant social transformation and artistic experimentation. It was during this period that German film came into its own, that the dada avant-garde flourished, and that Bertolt Brecht modernized political theater. However, many of the numerous studies that have focused on these spectacularly modern and modernist cultural phenomena have overlooked, and thus underestimated the importance of, an equally powerful conservative cultural and political reaction to German modernity specific to Weimar, the so-called "*Heimat*" movement.

As Anton Kaes has pointed out in his discussion of Edgar Reisz's

controversial 1984 television film of the same name, *Heimat* is a
particularly loaded term in German; in addition to meaning simply
"home" or "homeland," it also resonates

> with emotional connotations almost to the breaking point: *Heimat* means the
> site of one's lost childhood, of family, of identity. It also stands for the
> possibility of secure human relations, unalienated, precapitalist labor, and
> the romantic harmony between the country dweller and nature. *Heimat* refers
> to everything that is not distant and foreign.[10]

The *Heimat* movement first emerged in the 1890s, and can be said to
have functioned as a stabilizing counter-balance to the modernization,
urbanization, and destabilization that resulted from the changes in
German society that were relocating increasing numbers of rural
inhabitants to the rapidly growing cities. For many rural Germans, these
phenomena were experienced as threats to traditional and comfortable
provincial identities that had always been extraordinarily place-bound.
As Celia Applegate puts it, the concept of *Heimat* at first functioned as a
kind of security blanket, in that "*Heimat* in ... legal and political
contexts was essentially used as a term of obfuscation. It made fundamental changes seem less drastic... *Heimat* in the literary context
became a general term for the *Volk* in every German."[11] It reassured
provincial Germans that, however much the world around them seemed
to be changing, their familiar regional "contexts of living" were not in
danger.

This anxious but otherwise rather neutral use of the *Heimat* concept
changed considerably once this provincial anxiety had been exacerbated
by Germany's defeat in the Great War and by the accelerated pace of
both modernization *and* the political fractionalization that followed it.
Applegate has argued that it was precisely their increased sense of
"insecurity and confusion" after the war that led many Germans both in
rural areas and in the cities to reject the Weimar model of a modern
and thus rootless cosmopolitanism in favor of "the familiar certainties
of place and home" (65) offered by *Heimat* culture. These "certainties"
could be made all the more certain by increased recourse to an equally
place-bound model of an essentialized and pre-modern "Germanness"
that complimented, rather than contradicted, the various regional
identities, making them seem more compatible with each other because
more organically connected. Thus, the concept of *Heimat* as linked to a
provincial and specifically local identity was manipulated by National
Socialism in such a way that it could come to include the entire nation;
both village and nation now "offered a [reassuring] vision of the deeply
rooted life" (71). National Socialism could take advantage of what was
now, as it were, a doubled sense of an inherited German identity linked
specifically to place to justify the invasion of Eastern Europe in the

name of the "Volksdeutsche" or ethnic Germans who, so the argument went, needed to be able to practice their culturally German regional identities within the context of the larger German nation. The call "Heim ins Reich" was thus not intended to induce ethnic Germans who had been living for generations in Poland or the Soviet Union to come "home" to Germany proper, but to restore any soil upon which Germans had lived in communities to its "proper" place *as* Germany.[12] *Heimat* thus understood and lived, allowed Germans to figure utopia not as "no place on earth," but rather as "any place on earth" where Germans had established communities. Rather than superseding and neutralizing local identities, the concept of "Germanness" functioned as a kind of "meta-*Heimat*" in that, paradoxically, it made it possible to live anywhere, and still be home in Germany.

Ernst Bloch insisted on "refunctioning" *Heimat* in his work both during and after the war, taking the term back from both its Nazi appropriators and from the regional Germans who had first recognized in it a conceptual space within which to fix identity in an imagined past that felt more familiar and "homey" than the threatening present. Bloch used the term, in contrast, *not* to connote a nostalgic reconciliation with a past that, in the Germans' case especially, was mostly imagined; for Bloch, *Heimat* refers instead to an *anticipated* state of reconciliation with conditions of possibility that do not as yet exist, and indeed *will not* exist until present conditions have been radically reconceptualized so that they can be transformed into something as yet impossible to define. Anton Kaes has thus described Bloch's revolutionary *Heimat* as "the utopian antithesis to alienation per se;"[13] in contrast, *Heimat* as appropriated by National Socialism was fundamentally dependent on a condition of permanent anxiety and alienation which accounts for its peculiarly exaggerated component of "defensive and ... paranoid nationalism."[14]

What does this have to do with xenophobic violence in little towns in the former GDR? Wouldn't this model for belonging and for defining one's identity in relation to idealized and essentialized local or national places be incompatible with the history of those young people raised in the GDR after the war, a history within which the "familiar certainties of place and home" would presumably be socialist, internationalist, and decidedly anti-Nazi? It is my contention that the extraordinarily rapid absorption of the former GDR into the Federal Republic purposefully delegitimated everything about the culture within which these people had grown up, including these "familiar certainties." This gutting of their contexts of living, of everything that, to return to Kaes's definition of *Heimat*, "stood for the possibility of secure human relations," left them without a coherent identity, and with little choice in the way of options for a replacement outside that offered by the Federal Republic, an identity based in absolute "Germanness." In other words, the young former East Germans who found themselves facing "insecurity and confusion" at least as devastating as that experienced by their grand-fathers and grandmothers during the Weimar Republic were presented by the Federal Republic with precisely the same option for stabilizing identity that had been offered to them by National Socialism – an essentialized, transhistorical "Germanness" linked to place. Hence the desire to declare an insignificant town in the former GDR "free of foreigners." "Deutschland für die Deutschen, Ausländer 'raus!" reflects the same appeal to a "blood *and* soil" based fiction of inherited identity that resulted in the previous generation's anti-Semitism. This is thus not a vampire-like return of a "natural" German tendency toward fascism, but rather a politically sanctioned manipulation of the same fiction of fixed identity that was a necessary prerequisite to the appeal of fascism.

The morning after the Wall came down in Berlin, I was teaching an introductory course in German literature to undergraduates in Milwau-kee, Wisconsin, which prides itself on being America's "German city." Ironically, the assigned reading for the week was the text of a beautiful song by the East German dissident songwriter Wolf Biermann called "The Prussian Icarus." It is about, among other things, the agony of finding an honorable context in which to be German when the terms of the argument seem to have been frozen in concrete and barbed wire. My students, of course, suggested we cancel class to celebrate the fact that the East was now "free;" one of them wondered aloud "why the Berlin Wall had been up so long anyway." In my attempt to answer this question, I referred to the remark once made by Heiner Müller that the Berlin Wall had been socialism's revenge for the murders of Karl Liebknecht and Rosa Luxemburg. This information met with a pro-foundly indifferent silence – no one recognized the names. My students inadvertently proved Müller right; the Wall had been a kind of spectacu-lar international memorial to Weimar socialism's failed attempt to free the Germans, in the wake of the catastrophic war, from their particularly destructive fantasy of "Germanness." It made bitterly ironic sense that this memorial should have been destroyed; after all, one of the most disturbing manifestations of post-unification "Germanness" has been the desecration of Jewish cemeteries . . .

For Ernst Bloch, the past should never really be past. It should be instead "a beacon within the present, it illuminates the horizon of that possibility for happiness which has not yet fully come into view." What I hope to have suggested here is that Bloch's work, especially that pertaining to questions of memory and national identity, needs to be reread and re-evaluated precisely now, not only in light of its blind spots and his glaring political mistakes, but also its acknowledgement of the profound necessity of salvaging the utopian content of the past, however compromised and contradictory that past may be. This is especially true in the case of Germany in this vertiginous and dangerous moment of its self-redefinition. I would also argue that greater and more careful attentiveness to the past as a "beacon within the present" is crucially important just now to academic Marxism, which to a disturbing extent has seemed inclined in recent years to practice a kind of theoretical bulimia, a "binge and purge" style consumption and then wholesale rejection of its own compromised and often contradictory heritages. I am not suggesting by any means that we swallow Bloch whole, but only that such a re-evaluation might provide strategies for counter-balancing the theoretical and practical manifestations of patterns of forgetting in what Eric Santner has characterized as a "world that threatens to become absorbed, without remainder, into a global system of technolog-ically reproduced immediacy." This tendency, he argues, can only be resisted by wilfully cultivating the capacity to remember, a capacity for "preserv[ing] negative spaces, fissures, traces; to preserve, as it were, the wailing walls of the world and keep them from becoming so many tourist attractions."[15] A re-evaluation of the various pasts I have referred to here that manages to be critical without being dismissive might assist us in coming to terms with the clearly re-emerging power of national identity as a "cultural synthesis" throughout the world, a process that will be necessary if Marxism is to provide a meaningful alternative to that identity.

Notes

1. Cited in Charles Maier, *The Unmasterable Past: History, Holocaust, and German National Identity* (Cambridge, Mass., and London: Harvard University Press, 1988), p. 45. Maier's book is an excellent contextualization and analysis of the *Historikerstreit* and of the recent debates around German national identity. See also Jürgen Habermas, ed., *Observations on "The Spiritual Situation of the Age"*, trans. Andrew Buchwalter (Cambridge, Mass.: MIT Press, 1987), and *New German Critique*, 44 (Spring/Summer 1988), "Special Issue on the *Historikerstreit*."

2. Monika Maron, "Writers and the People," *New German Critique*, 52, (Winter 1991), p. 36

3. Anson Rabinbach, "Unclaimed Heritage: Ernst Bloch's *Heritage of Our Times* and the Theory of Fascism," *New German Critique*, 11 (Spring 1977), p. 5.

4. Ibid., p. 8.

5. Ibid., p. 19.

6. Stefan Heym, "Ash Wednesday in the GDR," *New German Critique*, 52 (Winter 1991), p. 31.

7. Aziz Al-Azmeh, *Islams and Modernities* (London and New York: Verso, 1993), p. 7.

8. Jeffrey M. Peck, "Rac(e)ing the Nation: Is There a German 'Home'?" *New Formations*, 17 (Summer 1992), p. 75.

9. This concept is discussed throughout their *Public Sphere and Experience*, originally published in 1972.

10. Anton Kaes, *From Hitler to Heimat: The Return of History as Film* (Cambridge, Mass., and London: Harvard University Press, 1989), p. 165.

11. Celia Applegate, "The Question of Heimat in the Weimar Republic," *New Formations*, 17 (Summer 1992), p. 66.

12. For a brief analysis of this logic, see my translator's introduction to H.G. Adler, "A

'*Mischling*' attempts to Fight for His Rights," in Angelika Bammer, ed., *Displacements: Cultural Identities in Question* (Bloomington: Indiana University Press, 1994), pp. 205–15.

13. Kaes, *From Hitler to Heimat*, p. 165.

14. Applegate, "The Question of Heimat," p. 71.

15. Eric L. Santner, *Stranded Objects: Mourning, Memory, and Film in Postwar Germany* (Ithaca and London: Cornell University Press, 1990), p. 145. Uncannily, Santner's book, a discussion of postwar German films that attempt to come to terms with German history, was published even as clever entrepreneurs in Berlin were selling fragments of the Berlin Wall as souvenirs.

Part II
Concrete Utopias:
The Big Picture

5

Educated Hope:
Ernst Bloch on Abstract and
Concrete Utopia
Ruth Levitas

In so far as Ernst Bloch's work has been incorporated into utopian studies, it has been seen as a justification and celebration of utopianism, and welcomed because of the ever-present need to defend utopia against those who regard it as trivial or dangerous. This essay argues that while this celebratory theme in Bloch's work is important, there is an equally important, though deeply problematic, distinction between abstract and concrete utopia. As with the distinction made by Friedrich Engels between utopian and scientific socialism, or that made by Karl Mannheim between ideology and utopia, its epistemological basis is dubious. Nevertheless, it remains an important issue. Indeed, a parallel problem arises in recent commentaries on William Morris, which similarly attempt to assert the virtues of dreaming and hence of utopianism while preserving a distinction between "disciplined" and "undisciplined" dreaming. Some distinction between abstract and concrete utopia, despite its difficulties, can consequently be seen to be fundamental to the relationship between utopia and Marxism – or, indeed, to the relationship between utopia and *any* political orientation involving a commitment to social transformation. Otherwise utopians can only continue to imagine alternative worlds; the point, however, is to create one.

In developing this argument, the essay first examines Bloch's overall project and the role of the distinction between abstract and concrete utopia within it. The distinction is then compared first with Mannheim's dichotomy between ideology and utopia, and secondly with the discussion of the relationship between Marxism and utopia elaborated by Edward Thompson in *William Morris: Romantic to Revolutionary*. The parallel between Bloch's *docta spes*, educated hope, which arises from the abstract/concrete distinction, is set alongside the idea of the "education of desire" which Thompson draws from Miguel Abensour.

We then return to Bloch, and the conflict between the epistemological
difficulty of differentiating abstract from concrete utopia and its political
necessity.

Bloch's central project in his magnum opus *The Principle of Hope* is the
rehabilitation of the concept of utopia. In attempting this, he draws
attention to the utopian element in a wide range of cultural forms. He
includes daydreams, fairy tales, myths, travelers' tales, the sea voyages of
medieval Irish monks, and the alchemists' attempts to synthesize gold,
besides the more conventional field of literary descriptions of ideal
societies. Utopia is not necessarily conceived of as a literary genre or
even a written work of any kind, although such definitions remain
current. For example, Darko Suvin has defined utopia as

> the verbal construction of a particular quasi-human community where socio-
> political institutions, norms and individual relationships are organized
> according to a more perfect principle than in the author's community, this
> construction being based on estrangement arising out of an alternative
> historical hypothesis.[1]

For Bloch, such a definition is far too narrow. Not only a broader field
of literature, but also architecture and music may be important vehicles
of utopia. What binds this diverse mass of material together is that all of
it can be seen as embodying "dreams of a better life." All of it ventures
beyond the present reality, and reaches forward to a transformed future.
It embodies both the act of wishing and what is wished for.

Wishing is a crucially important human activity, not just because the
range and variety of the content of wishes are an interesting aspect of
cultural anthropology. The importance of utopian wishes hinges on the
unfinishedness of the material world. The world is in a constant state of
process, of becoming. The future is "not yet" and is a realm of possibility.
Utopia reaches toward that future and anticipates it. And in so doing, it
helps to effect the future. Human activity plays a central role here in
choosing which possible future may become actual: "the hinge in human
history is its producer."[2] Utopia is the expression of hope, but that hope
is to be understood "not ... *only as emotion ... but more essentially as a
directing act of a cognitive kind*" (I: 12).

Bloch's discussion may be read as a celebration of the range and
tenacity of utopian wishing. Yet because the function of utopia is not
just to express desire, but to reach forward and to be the catalyst of a
better future, he is also critical of the content of these wishes. As Fredric
Jameson argues in *Marxism and Form*, we may locate within Bloch's work
a system of positive hermeneutics whose project is the restoration of lost
or hidden meanings, the recovery of the genuine element of aspiration
and anticipation which is at the heart of these various utopian
expressions; but there is also a philosophical system which is more

critical, and which is concerned not with recovery but with distinguishing between truth and falsehood (125). The way in which Bloch is being
incorporated into contemporary utopian studies emphasizes the celebratory and prophetic aspects of his work, rather than its more critical
elements. But the question of the evaluation of utopian wishes is also
essential, because Bloch did not seek merely to rehabilitate the concept
of utopia, but to rehabilitate utopia *within Marxism* as a neglected
Marxist category. Thus although Bloch remains adamant that all forms
of utopian venturing beyond are better than anti-utopian or pragmatic
attitudes which close off the future, not all utopian imagining is as good
as any other.

Fundamental to this more critical project is the distinction which Bloch
makes between abstract and concrete utopia. Abstract utopia is fantastic
and compensatory. It is wishfull thinking, but the wish is not accompanied by a will to change anything. In the daydream, it often involves
not so much a transformed future as a future where the world remains as
it is except for the dreamer's changed place in it – perhaps by a large win
in the lottery. Thus Bloch says, "Most people in the street look as if they
are thinking about something else entirely. The something else is predominantly money, but also what it could be changed into" (I: 33). Or, if
a transformed future is imagined, it may be one which could never be
effected. For although the future is open, in that there is a range of real
possibilities, it is not unconstrained. Concrete utopia, on the other hand,
is anticipatory rather than compensatory. It reaches forward to a real
possible future, and involves not merely wishfull but willfull thinking:
"There is never anything soft about conscious-known hope, but a will
within it insists: it should be so, it must become so" (I: 147). Concrete
utopia embodies what Bloch claims as the essential utopian function,
that of simultaneously anticipating and effecting the future. And not all
dreams of a better life fulfill this function. While abstract utopia may
express desire, only concrete utopia carries hope.

Thus despite Bloch's general project of recovery and rehabilitation,
he makes some harsh comments about abstract utopia. He regards the
customary sense of derogation associated with the term as appropriate,
although it should not be allowed to outweigh the positive connotations
of concrete utopia: "the category of the Utopian, beside the usual,
justifiably pejorative sense, possesses the other, in no way necessarily
abstract or unworldly sense, much more centrally turned towards the
world: of overtaking the natural course of events" (I: 12). The problem
of abstract utopia is described by Bloch as one of immaturity, and a
consequent tendency to become lost in fantasy and memory rather than
being oriented to real possibility:

> the thus determined imagination of the utopian function is distinguished
> from mere fantasizing precisely by the fact that only the former has in its

favour a Not-Yet-Being of an expectable kind, i.e., does not play around and get lost in an Empty-Possible, but psychologically anticipates a Real-Possible. [I: 144]

At one point, Bloch goes so far as to say that utopian function may not be present at all in "mere wishful thinking," or only as a glimmer which "flickers up" (I: 144). Consequently,

> Pure wishful thinking has discredited utopias for centuries, both in pragmatic political terms and in all other expressions of what is desirable; just as if every utopia were an abstract one. And undoubtedly the utopian function is only immaturely present in abstract utopianizing, i.e., still predominantly without solid subject behind it and without relation to the Real-Possible. Consequently, it is easily led astray, without contact with the real forward tendency into what is better. [I: 145]

Bloch's use of the term immaturity to describe abstract utopia is reminiscent of the discussions by Marx and Engels on utopian socialism. But so too is the defense that is implicit in the term and in the project of recovery. Despite the fact that, in the hands of Marx and Engels, the term "utopian" is derogatory, and despite their sharp criticisms of utopian socialism, they also praised it for its criticisms of bourgeois society. For example, in *The Manifesto of the Communist Party* we read:

> Such fantastic pictures of future society, painted at a time when the proletariat is still in a very underdeveloped state and has but a fantastic conception of its own position, correspond with the first instinctive yearnings of that class for a general reconstruction of society. But these Socialist and Communist publications contain also a critical element. They attack every principle of existing society. Hence they are full of the most valuable materials for the enlightenment of the working class.[3]

The same point is reiterated by Engels in *Anti-Dühring*. Although he observes that the social systems proposed by the early socialists were utopian, and that "the more completely they worked out in detail, the more they could not avoid drifting off into pure fantasies," he maintains that they contain a core which should be taken seriously.[4]

Moreover, Engels is much ruder about those who would throw the baby out with the bath water. Not only does he "delight in the stupendously grand thoughts and germs of thoughts that everywhere break out through their fantastic covering, and to which these philistines are blind" (246). In response to Dühring's dismissal of Fourier, Owen and Saint-Simon as social alchemists, Engels replies that alchemy was necessary in its epoch, and describes Dühring as an impertinent dwarf (186, 253, 279). (One can only speculate as to whether Bloch's inclusion of alchemy as a manifestation of utopianism was in any way related to

Engels's remarks!) The suggestion that it is a greater blindness to reject the thoughts than to be deluded by their fantastic coverings is echoed in Bloch's response to some of Heidegger's negative comments on wishfull thinking, which, says Bloch, are "like a eunuch accusing the infant Hercules of impotence" (I: 145). Thus,

> at least as suspicious as the immaturity (fanaticism) of the undeveloped utopian function is the widespread and ripe old platitude of the way-of-the-world philistine, of the blinkered empiricist whose world is far from being a stage, in short, the confederacy in which the fat bourgeois and the shallow practicist have always not only rejected outright the anticipatory, but despised it ... We do not need to emphasize that the genuine struggle against immaturity and abstraction, in so far as they adhered to the utopian function or potentially adhere to it, has nothing in common with bourgeois "realism." [I: 145]

It does however have something to do with "real realism." The problem concerns both the relationship between dreams and reality, and the definition of reality itself. Bloch's defense of dreaming in general is that it is potentially a way of venturing beyond the present, and may contain anticipation or concrete utopia. In vindication of this position, and in support of its Marxist credentials, Bloch quotes repeatedly from a letter from Marx to Arnold Ruge dated 1843:

> Our motto must therefore be; reform of consciousness not through dogmas, but through the analysis of mystical consciousness which is still unclear to itself. It will then become apparent that the world has long possessed the dream of a matter, of which it must only possess the consciousness in order to possess it in reality. It will become apparent that it is not a question of a great thought-dash between past and future, but of the *carrying-through* of the thoughts of the past. [I: 155–6]

Like many who have addressed the question of the relationship between Marxism and utopia, Bloch also refers to a passage in *What is to be Done?* where Lenin cites Pisarev:

> "There are rifts and rifts," wrote Pisarev concerning the rift between dreams and reality ... "The rift between dreams and reality causes no harm if only the person dreaming believes seriously in his dream, if he attentively observes life, compares his observations with his castles in the air and if, generally speaking, he works conscientiously for the achievement of his fantasies. If there is some connection between dreams and life then all is well." [I: 211]

Lenin adds, "of this kind of dreaming there is unfortunately too little in our movement" (I: 211). It is a passage, says Bloch, "which has come to be very much praised over the years, but not so eagerly taken to heart"

(I: 9). And "the point of contact between dreams and life, without which dreams only yield abstract utopia, life only triviality, is given in the utopian capacity which is set on its feet and connected to the Real-Possible" (I: 145–6).

However, it is fundamental to Bloch's argument that reality does not consist only of what is, but includes what is becoming or might become. The material world is essentially unfinished and in a state of process – a process whose direction and outcome are not predetermined. The future therefore constitutes a realm of possibility – real possibility, rather than merely formal possibility. And although the fact that the future is indeterminate means that not all real possibilities will in fact be realized, these possible futures must be seen as a part of reality. Concrete utopia, understood both as content and as function, is within the real, but relates to what Bloch describes as *Front*, or *Novum*, that part of reality which is coming into being on the horizon of the real. This location within but on the edge of the real means that utopia is transcendent, but "transcendent without transcendence" (I: 146).

The process of extracting concrete utopia from its abstract trappings results in what Bloch describes as *docta spes* or "educated hope." It involves

> knowledge and removal of the finished *utopistic element*, ... knowledge and removal of *abstract utopia*. But what then remains: the unfinished forward dream, the docta spes which can only be discredited by the bourgeoisie, – this seriously deserves the name utopia in carefully considered and carefully applied contrast to utopianism; in its brevity and new clarity, this expression then means the same as: *a methodical organ for the New, an objective aggregate form of what is coming up*. [I: 157]

Docta spes operates as a dialectic between reason and passion, and, as we shall see, this is one explanation of why Bloch sees utopia as a necessary concept within Marxism. Concrete utopia can be understood both as latency and as tendency. It is present historically, as an element in human culture which Bloch seeks to recover; and it refers forward to the emergent future. Concrete utopia is not simply a "correct" version of abstract utopia, but a praxis-oriented category characterized by "militant optimism":

> [U]topian function as the comprehended activity of the expectant emotion, of the hope-premonition, maintains the alliance with all that is still morning-like in the world. Utopian function thus understands what is exploding, because it is this itself in a very condensed way: its Ratio is the unweakened Ratio of a militant optimism. Therefore: the *act-content* of hope is, as a consciously illuminated, knowingly elucidated content, the *positive utopian function*; the *historical content* of hope, first represented in ideas, encyclopedically explored in real judgements, is *human culture referred to its concrete utopian*

horizon. The docta spes combine operates on this knowledge as expectant emotion in the Ratio, as Ratio in the expectant emotion. And predominant in this combine is no longer contemplation, which for centuries has only been related to What Has Become, but the participating, co-operative process-attitude, to which consequently, since Marx, the open becoming is no longer sealed methodically and the Novum no longer alien in material terms. [I: 146]

With the removal of abstract utopia, the utopian function "tears the concerns of human culture away from . . . an idle bed of contemplation" and "opens up, on truly attained summits, the ideologically unob-structed view of human hope" (I: 158). Jürgen Habermas says of Bloch's project of recovery and criticism that, "within the ideological shell Bloch discovers the Utopian core, within the yet false consciousness the true consciousness."[5]

Bloch's distinction between abstract and concrete utopia can be clarified by comparison with Mannheim's contrast between ideology and utopia, not least because one of the main points at which Bloch discusses the issue is headed "The Encounter of the Utopian Function with Ideology." There are similarities, similar problems, and important differences. Mannheim regarded both ideology and utopia as categories of ideas incongruous with reality. However, utopias are oriented to the future, and are those ideas which transform reality in their own image, whereas ideologies are oriented to the past and serve to legitimate the status quo. Consequently, not all forms of wishfull thinking are categor-ized as utopias. Mannheim does not disagree that "wishful thinking has always figured in human affairs." But despite the fact that "myths, fairy tales, other-worldly promises of religion, humanistic fantasies, travel romances, have been continually changing expressions of what was lacking in actual life,"[6] they are largely compensatory and therefore ideological. For Mannheim, those forms of wishfull thinking which do not serve to effect the future are not utopian at all. For Bloch, they are utopian, but largely comprise abstract utopia.

Both Bloch and Mannheim point out that their distinctions are analytical and their categories ideal types: concrete utopia contains abstract elements, ideology may contain utopian elements, and utopia may contain elements of ideology. Unlike Mannheim, who nevertheless consigns many forms of wishfull thinking to the scrap-heap of ideology without a second thought, Bloch carries this argument to its logical conclusion. The task is to recover the core of concrete utopia from the dross of the abstract elements in which it is embedded. In Bloch's case, therefore, the dichotomy is less crude, and does not imply that those who are not with us are against us. Whereas concrete utopia, like Mannheim's utopia, is anticipatory, transformative and linked to the future, abstract utopia (while compensatory) is not necessarily linked to the past in the sense of sustaining its social forms (although it does draw upon memory rather than imagination in the construction of its images). Mannheim's ideology is anti-utopian in function; Bloch's abstract utopia is not. It is superior to pessimism or bourgeois philistinism because it contains the intention toward a better life, and thus contains, if only vestigially, the utopian function.

A fundamental difference is in the relationship between utopia and reality. Mannheim sees reality as given, and, moreover, regards the question of what is real as unproblematic. Both ideology and utopia are consigned to a symbolic realm of ideas which is outside this reality and can be contrasted with it. For Bloch, reality is essentially unfinished and concrete utopia is important precisely because it is a possible future (or a range of possible futures) located within the real. It is not only anticipated subjectively in utopian thinking (as product of the "not yet conscious"), but has objective reality as the "not yet become" or as the real-possible future, whether or not in any particular case it becomes actual reality. Whereas Mannheim can only retrospectively define ideas as utopian, since they qualify only if they succeed in realizing themselves, Bloch's open future dispenses with the criterion of success in distinguishing between abstract and concrete utopia. Nevertheless, it is not clear that Bloch's criteria for making the distinction are any more adequate than Mannheim's. Both would seem to involve contentious subjective judgements, even if Bloch does not rely so heavily upon hindsight. This subjective element is reflected in a political difference between the two: whereas Mannheim fears the utopia as irrational and potentially revolutionary, Bloch welcomes the "red dream" and the revolution.

Although concrete utopia is ostensibly defined by Bloch in terms of a utopian function in relation to a range of real-possible futures, he is actually more specific than that. Among possible futures is "devastatingly, possible fascist Nothing" as well as "finally feasible and overdue, socialism" (I: 197), and the former is not utopian. When Bloch argues that "the world is full of propensity towards something, tendency towards something, latency of something" (I: 18), he is not indifferent as to what that something might be. And indeed Bloch identifies concrete utopia with Marxism, both as goal and as process. Concrete utopia is embodied in Marxism, where human will and social process meet, where we make history, if not under conditions of our own choosing. And Marxism rescues the concept of utopia, first by the recognition, in the concept of tendency, of the importance of what is becoming, and secondly, by revealing the process by which utopia has become possible. The development of socialism from utopia to science creates the space in which Marxism can reclaim utopia:

Thus the only seemingly paradoxical concept of a concrete utopia would be appropriate here, that is of an anticipatory kind which by no means coincides with abstract utopian dreaminess, nor is directed by the immaturity of merely abstract utopian socialism. The very power and truth of Marxism consist in the fact that it has driven the cloud in our dreams further forward, but has not extinguished the pillar of fire in those dreams, rather strengthened it with concreteness. [I: 146]

Bloch's discussion of Marxism raises again the relation between reason and passion which is crystalized in the concept of *docta spes*. He argues that Marxism contains both a cold and a warm stream. The cold stream is that of analysis. This establishes Marxism as a "science of conditions," which also gives rise to a process of unmasking and disenchantment. The warm stream is the "liberating intention" of Marxism, "towards whose goal all these disenchantments are undertaken" (I: 209). That goal, and the content of concrete utopia, are identified by Bloch as "the utopian Totum . . . that homeland of identity in which neither man behaves towards the world, nor the world behaves towards man, as if towards a stranger" (I: 209). The substance of concrete utopia, as expressed in *The Principle of Hope*, is the transcendence of alienation, although in *Natural Law and Human Dignity* Bloch is more forthcoming about the institutional foundations of this. The warm stream thus has a double aspect: it carries both the motivating passion for liberation, and the object and goal of that passion. The cold stream directs us toward the path. Bloch's point, however, is the interdependence of cold and warm streams: "only coldness and warmth of concrete anticipation together therefore ensure that neither the path in itself nor the goal in itself are held apart from one another undialectically and so become reified and isolated" (I: 209).

Educated hope, *docta spes*, is born out of and articulates this relationship between end and means, passion and reason, aspiration and possibility. It represents the transformation of wishfull thinking into wish-full and effective acting, the move from the dream to the dream come true. The distinction between abstract and concrete utopia is a necessary one if Bloch is to rehabilitate utopia as a transformative category and a category within Marxism, rather than as a repository of desire. Yet the distinction does not rely, in the end, upon function, but upon content, for the content makes the function possible. And Bloch does not offer us criteria for making such a distinction other than his explicitly teleological and evaluative specification of the utopian goal and its content.

Whereas Bloch uses the concept of educated hope to articulate the relationship between the cold and warm streams of Marxism and the function of concrete utopia, recent commentators on William Morris have used the term "the education of desire" to describe the utopian function. What started as a debate about the significance of Morris's utopian novel, *News from Nowhere*, became a question of the general relationship between Marxism and utopia. An examination of this debate offers interesting parallels with Bloch's argument, and raises the question of whether the problematic distinction between abstract and concrete utopia is fundamental to the relationship between Marxism and utopia.

The attitude of Marxists to utopian literature has generally been to regard it as at best an irrelevance, at worst a pernicious distraction from the class struggle and misdirection of political energies. Since *News from Nowhere* has always been the best known of Morris's socialist writings, responses to this have tended to color general interpretations of Morris's work. The general antipathy of Marxists to utopian speculation meant that he was largely ignored, despite repeated attempts to argue for his importance. Thus in 1934 Robin Page Arnot's *William Morris: A Vindication* (later updated as *William Morris: The Man and the Myth*) identified two myths about Morris, the "bourgeois myth" in which his socialism was ignored or denied, and the "Menshevik myth" in which he was portrayed as a gentle, eccentric, very English and specifically anti-Marxist socialist. (Bloch, to his shame, clearly subscribed to a view not dissimilar to the Menshevik myth, describing Morris as a "machine-wrecker" [II: 614]). In 1952, A.L. Morton argued from a Marxist standpoint in *The English Utopia* that *News from Nowhere* was the culmination of the English utopian tradition. In 1955, Edward Thompson published *William Morris: Romantic to Revolutionary*, in which he addressed Morris's transition from the Romantic tradition of Thomas Carlyle and John Ruskin to revolutionary socialism. Thompson's argument was that in making this shift, Morris created a synthesis between Romanticism and Marxism which transformed and enriched both. He described *News from Nowhere* as "the first Utopia which is not Utopian" (quoting Morton), and called it a "Scientific Utopia."[7] In 1958, Raymond Williams similarly argued in *Culture and Society* the importance of Morris's integration of Romanticism and Marxism, and thus the transformation of that earlier tradition: "The economic reasoning, and the political promise, came to him from Marxism; the general rebellion was in older terms."[8] The broader implications of the argument about Morris did not become apparent, however, until the re-issue of Thompson's book in 1977 with a postscript discussing the debate that had followed the publication of the first edition. This postscript remains one of the most important discussions, apart from Bloch's, of the general relationship between Marxism and utopia.

Thompson develops his argument in relation to three commentators: Paul Meier, John Goode, and Miguel Abensour. Meier's work, a long study of Morris entitled *Le Pensée utopique de William Morris*, translated into English under the more revealing title of *William Morris: The Marxist Dreamer*, is seen by Thompson as perpetuating a third myth about Morris, a Marxist myth in which Morris is similarly assimilated to

Marxism. Since Meier's project involves comparing *News from Nowhere* and Morris's other socialist writings with the views of capitalism, socialism, communism, and the transitions between them that can be extracted from the writings of Marx and Engels, Thompson's objection has some foundation, although, as I have argued in *The Concept of Utopia* (119), Meier's position can be argued to be less extreme than Thompson suggests. Morris's utopianism, for Meier, is vindicated because it corresponds (in his view) to Marxist orthodoxy. Besides his general objection to the interpretation of Morris that is involved here, Thompson turns to Goode and Abensour to argue that Meier's treatment misunderstands the function of dreaming and the function of utopia.

Goode argues that the function of utopian speculation in Morris's work, and specifically in his utopian fiction, is neither escape and compensation, nor the description of a plan for the future. It is not didactic, but exploratory and educative, emphasizing both the necessity of social transformation and the centrality of human imagination and will in effecting that transformation:

> Morris . . . invents new worlds or reinvokes dream versions of old worlds, not in order to escape the exigencies of the depressing actuality but in order to insist on a whole structure of values and perspectives which must emerge in the conscious mind in order to assert the inner truth of that actuality, and give man the knowledge of his own participation in the historical process that dissolves that actuality.[9]

The vision set out in the dream is thus not a literal goal, as Meier's approach suggests, but an exploration of the values on which a socialist society should be based.

A similar case is put by Abensour, who, like Thompson, rejects Meier's attempt to reduce Morris's thought to an illustration of Marxist truth as an exercise in theoretical repression. *News from Nowhere* should not be read literally, since its purpose is "to embody in the forms of fantasy alternative values sketched in an alternative way of life."[10] Utopia's function is estrangement, the disruption of the taken-for-granted nature of present reality. Thus,

> in such an adventure two things happen: our habitual values (the "common sense" of bourgeois society) are thrown into disarray. And we enter Utopia's proper and new-found space: *the education of desire.* This is not the same as "a moral education" towards a given end: it is rather, to open a way to aspiration, to "teach desire to desire, to desire better, to desire more, and above all to desire in a different way".[11]

This passage contains ambiguities which relate directly to our original problem, the dependence of the distinction between abstract and concrete utopia upon specification of the utopian content in Bloch's notion of educated hope. First, though, we need to see how Thompson develops from this debate about Morris the general problem of the relationship between Marxism and utopia.

Thompson reiterates that the essence of his original argument was that Morris transformed the Romantic tradition by integrating Marxist ideas into it "in such a way as to constitute a rupture in the older tradition," thereby creating a synthesis between the two which enriched both. That is, he did not simply "correct" the Romantic critique by the addition of Marxism, but recovered an element missing from Marxism. Thus when orthodox Marxism ignored or rejected Morris, it "turned its back upon a juncture which it neglected to its own peril and subsequent disgrace" (779). For Abensour, too, the problem became not whether Marxists should criticize Morris, but whether questions were raised about the adequacy of Marxism. Thus Thompson suggested that Morris's work raised the general question of the relationship between Marxism and utopia:

> what may be involved ... is the whole problem of the subordination of the imaginative utopian faculties within the later Marxist tradition: its lack of a moral self-consciousness or even a vocabulary of desire, its inability to project any images of the future, or even its tendency to fall back in lieu of these upon the Utilitarian's earthly paradise – the maximization of economic growth ... to vindicate Morris's utopianism may be at the same time to vindicate utopianism itself, and set it free to walk the world once more without the shame and without accusations of bad faith. [792]

Thompson suggests, however, that the relationship between Marxism and utopia is intrinsically problematic, since they relate to what he calls different "operative principles." Utopia concerns desire, Marxism concerns knowledge. Since "one may not assimilate desire to knowledge," the goal is the dialectical relationship between Marxism and utopia (807). In many ways, this parallels the relationship which Bloch claims for the cold and warm streams in Marxism – although there the relationship is perceived as within Marxism, rather than between Marxism and an external element.

However, Thompson goes on to make the point, as Bloch does, that the general vindication of utopianism in terms of the expression, exploration, and education of desire "does not ... mean that *any* ... utopian work is as good as any other":

> The "education of desire" is not beyond the criticism of sense and of feeling, although the procedures of criticism must be closer to those of creative literature than those of political theory. There are disciplined and undisciplined ways of "dreaming," but the discipline is of the imagination and not of science. [793]

This suggests that Thompson also wants to make a distinction between good and bad, or at least better and worse, utopia; but he does not make clear the basis of such evaluation. The lack of clarity of his statement can be set alongside Abensour's argument that the function of utopia is the education of desire. What is desired will be not only more and different but better; but the distinction between the education of desire and a moral education is made on the basis that a desired end is not specified. Goode is a little clearer, since his final judgement of Morris is a critical one. Goode argues that utopia involves "the collectivization of dream," its communication and thus its transition from the private to the public domain. He suggests that it is a weakness in *News from Nowhere* that, despite the discussion of the revolution, the transition remains insufficiently explained. The connection between the end and the means, in terms of political activity in Morris's own times, is not established: "the collectivity of the dream is not brought into relationship with the possible collectivity of the present."[12] Whether Goode's criticism is correct is debatable. What is important here is the assertion that utopia should make this connection. Its role is not just the exploration and education of desire, but the transformation of society. In Bloch's terms, it should articulate both the warm and cold streams, both ends and means.

Because the "education of desire" eschews the prescription of a desired end, it appears to be more open, more explanatory than Bloch's "educated hope." Yet this is probably only because Bloch's specification of the content of "good" utopia is clearer and more explicit than Abensour's or Thompson's. The question of "disciplined dreaming" is comprehensible only insofar as it does refer to the desirability and possibility of the utopian vision. And the education of desire, the disruption of the taken-for-granted present is implicitly directed to a further end, that of transformation. Thus Williams argues that "the element of transformation, rather than the more general element of otherness" is crucial to the utopian mode.[13]

Yet these debates about the significance of Morris and of *News from Nowhere* in particular are, while dealing with similar issues, rather less clear about the nature of the problem than Bloch was. Because of the tradition of negativity toward utopianism that became characteristic of Marxism after Marx, the emphasis in both Thompson and Bloch is on defending utopia. And indeed it is true that *The Principle of Hope* is an elaborated defense of utopia, since utopia represents the reach forward to something better, something missing. Contemporary use, or perhaps appropriation, of Bloch emphasizes his celebration both of the ubiquity of utopia and of its positive value in the world. But much of this appropriation misses an essential feature of Bloch's work, which arises from its Marxist, or more generally its politically committed, nature. Educated hope aims not only at an estrangement effect, but at social transformation. It is less open than the education of desire precisely because the distinction between "good" and "bad" utopia is pushed further.

It is pushed further. But it is at the same time pushed too far and not far enough. Too far, in the sense that epistemologically Bloch's distinction between abstract and concrete utopia is no more tenable than Mannheim's separation of ideology and utopia. Not far enough, in that the grounds of such a distinction are insufficiently spelled out, especially given its centrality to Bloch's project, and ultimately rest upon a teleological closure. To have pursued it further would have revealed the intrinsically political nature of the dichotomy and undermined the pretensions of Marxism to absolute verity and scientificity.

Yet for Bloch's critical project, the separation of abstract and concrete utopia, the identification of educated hope is essential. Without it, the argument that utopia is anticipatory thinking falls flat on its face. At best, it becomes indistinguishable from the much repeated idealist theme common to early commentaries on utopia that utopian images have a value only as attainable goals, the pursuit of which constitutes a spur to human progress. And the centrality of educated hope arises from something quite opposed to this: it arises out of political, rather than epistemological necessity – out of the commitment to the realization of utopia through, as well as its rehabilitation within, Marxism.

Bloch does not solve the problem of how such a distinction is to be made, but he correctly identifies it as a key distinction in the relationship between Marxism and utopia. And the problem remains intrinsic to that relationship. For if utopia is the repository of desire, Marxism even (or perhaps especially) when most informed by the passion of the warm stream – and thus at its most utopian – is about the hope for a transformed future with a specifically socialist content. Any Marxist rehabilitation of utopia which seeks to do more than explain the variation in utopian imagery as an expression of what is missing is going to stumble on some version of the distinction between abstract and concrete utopia. The distinction between compensatory and transformative visions of the good life is bound to be central to a perspective whose central *raison d'être* is change rather than interpretation. In consequence, the retrieval of utopia by Marxism does need a concept like that of educated hope. It is a necessary distinction, albeit one which cannot be made on grounds which are objective in the sense of epistemologically unassailable. For both educated hope and the education of desire are intrinsically evaluative concepts which cannot be made other than through the specification of the content of the good society, and through judgements about the possibility and desirability of different aspirations toward the good life. By this I do not mean to imply that a rapprochement between Marxism and utopia is mistaken; rather that the process of education implied in both the education of hope and the education of desire must be recognized as one which involves explicit value-based choices, not one in which the end is, as Bloch argues, somehow objectively given as the end of a teleological unfolding of what we have all "really" wanted since time immemorial. The problem with which Bloch wrestles in the concept of *docta spes* remains a central problem for utopian studies – and may be more important to an understanding of Bloch and our own predicament than his unparalleled vindication of utopia.

Notes

1. In Tom Moylan, *Demand the Impossible* (London: Methuen, 1986), p. 33.

2. Ernst Bloch, *The Principle of Hope*, trans. Neville Plaice, Stephen Plaice, and Paul Knight (Oxford: Basil Blackwell, 1986), 3 vols., vol. I, p. 249. Subsequent in-text refereneces to this work cite volume and page number.

3. Karl Marx and Friedrich Engels, *Collected Works* (London: Lawrence & Wishart, 1975–), vol. 25, p. 246.

4. Ibid.

5. James Bentley, *Between Marx and Christ* (London: Verso, 1982), p. 87.

6. Karl Mannheim, *Ideology and Utopia* (London: Routledge & Kegan Paul, 1979), p. 184.

7. E.P. Thompson, *William Morris: Romantic to Revolutionary* (London: Merlin, 1977), pp. 695, 697.

8. Raymond Williams, *Culture and Society* (London: Penguin, 1958), p. 258.

9. John Goode, "William Morris and the Dream of Revolution," *Literature and Politics in the Nineteenth Century*, ed. J. Lucas (London: Methuen, 1971), pp. 269–70.

10. Thompson, *William Morris*, p. 790.

11. Ibid., pp.790–91.

12. Goode, "William Morris and the Dream of Revolution," pp. 275, 278.

13. Raymond Williams, "Utopia and Science Fiction," *Problems in Materialism and Culture* (London: Verso, 1980), p. 197.

6

Ernst Bloch, Utopia, and Ideology Critique

Douglas Kellner

The utopian Marxist philosopher Ernst Bloch developed a method of cultural criticism which expands conventional Marxian approaches to culture and ideology and provides one of the richest treasure houses of ideology critique to be found in the Marxian tradition. In this article, I want to suggest how Bloch provides a method for discerning and criticizing ideological content in theories, philosophies, and cultural artifacts whose ideological nature and effects are often overlooked. Bloch's practice of ideological criticism discerns emancipatory utopian dimensions even in ideological products, ferreting out those aspects that might be useful for radical theory and practice. Bloch therefore provides exciting methods of cultural criticism, a new approach to cultural history, and novel perspectives on culture and ideology. He also contributes uniquely distinctive perspectives on Marxism, socialism, and revolutionary theory, though these will not be my focus in this study.[1]

Reading *The Principle of Hope*

Now that Bloch's magnificent magnum opus *The Principle of Hope* has been translated, his mature philosophy is accessible to English-speaking readers.[2] Problems in appropriating Bloch's work and using it for cultural and political analysis and critique remain significant, however, as Bloch's text is extremely difficult, elusive, and very long (over 1,400 pages in the English translation). Consequently, if Bloch is to have any real impact on political and cultural analysis in the English-speaking world, efforts must be made to explain and interpret what he is up to, and convincing arguments must be provided to persuade people that reading Bloch is worth the time and effort.

The Principle of Hope consists of three volumes, divided into five parts, and fifty-five chapters. The three volumes roughly correspond to Hegel's division of his system into interrogations of subjective, objective, and absolute spirit. The first volume queries "Little Daydreams" (Part 1), "Anticipatory Consciousness" (Part 2), and "Wishful Images in the Mirror" (Part 3). The last two studies analyze the utopian dimensions of fashion, advertising, display, fairy tales, travel, film, theater, jokes, and other cultural phenomena. The second volume (Part 4) depicts "Outlines of a Better World," focusing on social and political utopias, including technological, architectural, and geographical utopias, as well as quests for world peace and a life of leisure. Volume III (Part 5) discusses "Wishful Images of the Fulfilled Moment," including morality, music, images of death, religion, morning-land of nature, and the highest good.

Just as Hegel's philosophy articulated the odyssey of spirit through history and culture, so too does Bloch's philosophy chart the vicissitudes of hope. For Bloch, hope permeates everyday consciousness and its articulation in cultural forms, ranging from the fairy tale to the great philosophical and political utopias. For Bloch, individuals are unfinished, they are animated by "dreams of a better life," and by utopian longings for fulfillment. The "something better" for which people yearn is precisely the subject matter of *The Principle of Hope*, which provides a systematic examination of the ways that daydreams, fairy tales and myths, popular culture, literature, theater, and all forms of art, political and social utopias, philosophy, and religion – often dismissed *tout court* as ideology by some Marxist ideological critique – contain emancipatory moments which project visions of a better life that put in question the organization and structure of life under capitalism (or state socialism).

Bloch urges us to grasp the three dimensions of human temporality: he offers us a dialectical analysis of the *past* which illuminates the *present* and can direct us to a better *future*. The past – what has been – contains both the sufferings, tragedies, and failures of humanity – what to avoid and to redeem – and its unrealized hopes and potentials – which could have been and can yet be. For Bloch, history is a repository of possibilities that are living options for future action; therefore, what could have been can still be. The present moment is thus constituted in part by *latency* and *tendency*: the unrealized potentialities that are latent in the present, and the signs and foreshadowings that indicate the tendency of the direction and movement of the present into the future. This three-dimensional temporality must be grasped and activated by an *anticipatory consciousness* that at once perceives the unrealized emancipatory potential in the past, the latencies and tendencies of the present, and the realizable hopes of the future. Above all, Bloch develops a philosophy of hope and the future, a dreaming forward, a projection of a vision of a future kingdom of freedom. It is his conviction that only when we project our future in the light of what is, what has been, and what could be can we engage in the creative practice that will produce a world in which we are at home and realize humanity's deepest dreams.

In his magnum opus, Bloch carries through both a thorough examination of the ways that hope and visions of a better world exist in everything from daydreams to the great religions, and a cultural studies which trace throughout history anticipatory visions of what would later be systematized, packaged, and distributed as socialism by Karl Marx and his followers. Consequently, Bloch provides a critical hermeneutic of the ways that cultural history and socio-economic developments point to socialism as the realization of humanity's deepest dreams and hopes, and that encourages us to look for the progressive and emancipatory (rather than the merely ideological and mystificatory) content of cultural artifacts.

Bloch's Concept of Ideology Critique

Bloch is most useful today in providing a model of cultural theory and ideology critique that is quite different from, and arguably better than, dominant models which present ideology critique as the demolition of bourgeois culture and ideology, thus, in effect, conflating bourgeois culture and ideology. This model – found in Lenin and most Marxist-Leninists like Althusser, but also to some extent in the Frankfurt School – interprets dominant ideology primarily as the instruments of mystification, error, and domination which are contrasted to science or Marxist theory, or "critical theory." The function of ideology critique on this model is simply to demonstrate the errors, mystifications, and ruling-class interest within ideological artifacts which are then smashed and discarded by the heavy hammer of the ideology critic.

Such a model is, of course, rooted in Marx's own texts, in which ideology was the ideas of the ruling class, ideas which legitimated bourgeois rule, ideas which mystified social conditions and thereby covered over oppression and inequality, and ideas which thus produced false consciousness and furthered bourgeois class domination.[3] Within the Marxian tradition, there is also a more positive concept of ideology, developed by Lenin, which sees socialist ideology as a positive force for developing revolutionary consciousness and promoting socialist development. Bloch, however, is more sophisticated than those who simply denounce all ideology as false consciousness, or who stress the positive features of socialist ideology. Rather, Bloch sees emancipatory-utopian elements in all living ideologies, and deceptive and illusory qualities as well.

For Bloch, ideology is "Janus-faced": it contains errors, mystifications, and techniques of manipulation and domination, but it also contains a utopian residue or surplus that can be used for social critique and to advance progressive politics. In addition to reconstructing and refocusing the theory and practice of ideology critique, Bloch also enables us to see ideology in many phenomena usually neglected by Marxist and other ideology critiques: daydreams, popular literature, architecture, department-store displays, sports, or clothing. In this view, ideology pervades the organization and details of everyday life. Thus, ideology critique should be a critique of everyday life, as well as critique of political texts and positions, or the manifestly evident political ideologies of Hollywood films, network television, or other forms of mass-mediated culture.[4]

Previous Marxist theories of ideology, by contrast, tended to equate ideology with texts, with political discourses, and with attempts to mystify class relations and to advance class domination. Ideology critique, on this model, would simply expose and denounce the textual mechanisms of mystification and would attempt to replace ideology with truth. Bloch would dismiss this merely denunciatory approach to ideology critique as "half-enlightenment," which he compares to genuine enlightenment. Half-enlightenment "has nothing but an attitude," i.e. rationalistic dismissal of all mystification, superstition, legend, and so on that does not measure up to its scientific criteria.[5] Genuine enlightenment, on the other hand, criticizes any distortions in an ideological product, but then goes on to take it more seriously, to read it closely for any critical or emancipatory potential. Half-enlightenment deludes itself, first, by thinking that truth and enlightenment can be obtained solely by eliminating error rather than offering something positive and attractive. Indeed, Bloch believes that part of why the left was defeated by the right in Weimar Germany is because the left tended to focus simply on criticism, on negative denunciations of capitalism and the bourgeoisie, whereas fascism provided a positive vision and attractive alternatives to masses desperately searching for something better.

Against merely negative ideology critique, Bloch urges us to pay close attention to the potential progressive content within artifacts or phenomena frequently denounced and dismissed as mere ideology. For Bloch, ideology contained an "anticipatory" dimension, in which its discourses, images, and figures produced utopian images of a better world. Utopian elements, however, coexist with "merely embellishing ones" (148). In some cases, this amounts to a "merely dubious polishing of what exists" (149). Such apologetic functions "reconcile the subject with what exists" (ibid.). Such purposes appear above all "in periods of class society which are no longer revolutionary" (ibid.). Even in this situation, however, ideologies may contain embellishing elements that anticipate a better world, that express in abstract and idealist fashion the potentialities for a better future. If such ideologies deceive individuals into believing that the present society has already realized such ideals, they serve mystificatory functions, but Bloch's method of cultural criticism also wants us to interrogate these ideologies for their utopian

content, for their anticipations of a better world, which can help us to
see what is lacking in this world and what should be fought for to
produce a better (that is, freer and happier) future.

Bloch therefore restores to radical theory a cultural heritage that is
often neglected or dismissed as merely ideology. Critique of ideology,
Bloch argues, is not merely unmasking (*Entlarvung*) but is also uncovering and discovery: revelations of unrealized dreams, lost possibilities,
abortive hopes that can be resurrected, enlivened, and realized in our
current situation. Bloch's cultural criticism thus accentuates positive
utopian-emancipatory possibilities, the testimony to hope for a better
world. As Jürgen Habermas dramatically puts it:

> What Bloch wants to preserve for socialism, which subsists on scorning
> tradition, is the tradition of the scorned. In contrast to the unhistorical
> procedure of Feuerbach's criticism of ideology, which deprived Hegel's
> "sublation" (*Aufhebung*) of half of its meaning (forgetting *elevare* and being
> satisfied with *tollere*), Bloch presses the ideologies to yield their ideas to him;
> he wants to save that which is true in false consciousness: "All great culture
> that existed hitherto has been the foreshadowing of an achievement,
> inasmuch as images and thoughts can be projected from the age's summit
> into the far horizon of the future."

Bloch believed that even ideological artifacts contain expressions of
desire and articulations of needs that radical theory and politics should
heed to provide programs and discourses which appeal to deep-seated
desires for a better life. Ideologies also provide clues to possibilities for
future development and contain a "surplus" or "excess" that is not
exhausted in mystification or legitimation. And ideologies may contain
normative ideals whereby the existing society can be criticized, as well
as models of an alternative society. For example, the notion of the *citoyen*
(citizen) in bourgeois ideology with its individual rights, civil liberties,
and actively engaged autonomy expressed something more than mere
legitimation and apologetics for bourgeois institutions and practices.
Bloch takes seriously Marx's position that the task of socialism is to fully
realize certain bourgeois ideals. Throughout his life, Bloch argued that
Marxism, as it was constituted in its Social Democratic and other leading
versions, was vitiated by a one-sided, inadequate, and merely negative
approach to ideology.

For Bloch, the problem of ideology "is broached from the *side of the
problem of cultural inheritance*, of the problem as to how works of the
superstructure progressively reproduce themselves in cultural consciousness even after disappearance of their social bases" (154). Such notions
contain a *cultural surplus* that lives on and provides a *utopian function*
whereby the ideal can still be translated into a reality and thus be fully
realized for the first time. Although for Bloch the primary site of

ideology is the cultural superstructure – philosophy, religion, art, and so on – the superstructure contains a cultural surplus and thus cannot be reduced to mere ideology. For Bloch, the cultural surplus preserves unsatisfied desires and human wishes for a better world; because these wishes are usually not fulfilled they contain contents which remain relevant to a future society which may be able to satisfy these wishes and needs. In other words, ideology contains hints as to what human beings desire and need which can be used to criticize failures to satisfy these needs and to realize these desires in the current society.

Ideology critique thus requires not only demolition but also herme- neutics, for ideology, in Bloch's view, contains pre-conscious elements or what Bloch calls the "Not-Yet-Conscious." Properly understood, the Not-Yet-Conscious may point to real possibilities for social development and real potentials for human liberation. Bloch tends to present the theory of utopian surplus along historical-materialist lines in terms of the rise and fall of social classes. Utopian surplus generally appears when a class is rising: the ascending class criticizes the previous order and projects a wealth of proposals for social change, as when the bourgeoisie attacked the feudal order for its lack of individual freedom, rights, democracy, and class mobility. Bourgeois critiques of feudalism proliferated, as did revolutionary proposals for a new society. Some of these ideas were incorporated into bourgeois constitutions and declar- ations of rights, and some were even institutionalized in the bourgeois order.[6]

Thus culture ranges for Bloch from an ideal type of pure ideology to purely non-ideological emancipatory culture. Purely ideological artifacts embellish or legitimate an oppressive existing reality, as when Bloch speaks of ideology as that which excludes all progressive elements (9). Most cultural artifacts, however, contain a mixture of ideology and utopian elements. Since ideologies are rhetorical constructs that attempt to persuade and to convince, they must have a relatively rational and attractive core and thus often contain emancipatory promises or moments. Drawing on Bloch, Fredric Jameson has suggested that mass cultural texts often have utopian moments and proposes that radical cultural criticism should analyze both the social hopes and fantasies in cultural artifacts, as well as the ideological ways in which fantasies are presented, conflicts are resolved, and potentially disruptive hopes and anxieties are managed.[7]

In his reading of *Jaws*, for instance, the shark stands in for a variety of fears (uncontrolled organic nature threatening the artificial society, big business corrupting and endangering community, disruptive sexuality threatening the disintegration of the family and traditional values, and so on) which the film tries to contain through the reassuring defeat of evil by representatives of the current class structure. Yet the film also contains utopian images of family, male bonding, and adventure, as well

as socially critical visions of capitalism which articulate fears that
unrestrained big business would inexorably destroy the environment
and community. In Jameson's view, mass culture thus articulates social
conflicts, contemporary fears and utopian hopes, and attempts at
ideological containment and reassurance. In his view,

> works of mass culture cannot be ideological without at one and the same
> time being implicitly or explicitly Utopian as well: they cannot manipulate
> unless they offer some genuine shred of content as a fantasy bribe to the
> public about to be so manipulated. Even the "false consciousness" of so
> monstrous a phenomenon as Nazism was nourished by collective fantasies of
> a Utopian type, in "socialist" as well as in nationalist guises. Our proposition
> about the drawing power of the works of mass culture has implied that such
> works cannot manage anxieties about the social order unless they have first
> revived them and given them some rudimentary expression; we will now
> suggest that anxiety and hope are two faces of the same collective conscious-
> ness, so that the works of mass culture, even if their function lies in the
> legitimation of the existing order – or some worse one – cannot do their job
> without deflecting in the latter's service the deepest and most fundamental
> hopes and fantasies of the collectivity, to which they can therefore, no matter
> in how distorted a fashion, be found to have given voice.[8]

A film like *Jaws*, for instance, might use utopian images to provide a
critique of the loss of community, and its destruction by commercial
interests. Popular texts may thus enact social criticism in their ideological scenarios and one of the tasks of radical cultural criticism is to
specify utopian, critical, subversive, or oppositional meanings, even
within the texts of so-called mass culture. For these artifacts may contain
implicit and even explicit critiques of capitalism, sexism, or racism, or
visions of freedom and happiness which can provide critical perspectives
on the unhappiness and unfreedom in the existing society. *The Deer
Hunter*, for instance, though an arguably reactionary text, contains
utopian images of community, working class and ethnic solidarity, and
personal friendship which provide critical perspectives on the atomism,
alienation, and loss of community in everyday life under contemporary
capitalism. The utopian images of getting high and horsing around in
the drug hootch in *Platoon* present visions of racial harmony and
individual and social happiness which provide a critical perspective on
the harrowing war scenes and which code war as a disgusting and
destructive human activity. The images of racial solidarity and transcendence in the dance numbers of *Zoot Suit* provide a utopian and critical
contrast to the oppression of people of color found in the scenes of
everyday and prison life in the film. And the transformation of life in
the musical numbers of *Pennies from Heaven* provide critical perspectives
on the degradation of everyday life due to the constraints of an unjust
and irrational economic system which informs the realist sections of the

film. Ideologies thus pander to human desires, fantasies, anxieties, and hopes and cultural artifacts must address these, if they are to be successful. Ideology and utopia are thus interconnected and culture is saturated with utopian content. On the other hand, ideologies exploit and distort this utopian content and should be criticized to expose their merely embellishing, legitimating, and mystifying elements.

Everyday Life, Human Beings, and Psychology

Certain versions of Marxist ideology critique and half-enlightenment err, Bloch believes, by failing to see the importance of culture in everyday life. A rationalistic ideology critique believes that simply by exposing error and pointing to the truth it can motivate people to action. Such a belief, on Bloch's account, errs both in its overestimation of rationalistic enlightenment and in its underestimation of subrational desires, fantasies, beliefs, and so on. Properly understanding human motivation and psychology, Bloch believes, requires taking fantasy, imagination, wishes, and desires more seriously.

Bloch's thought is rooted in a humanist anthropology which grounds his critique of oppression and emancipatory perspectives. Bloch always begins with the wishing, hopeful, needy, and hungry human being and analyzes what prohibits realization of human desire and fulfillment of human needs. Thus, humanism for Bloch is revolutionary and provides standards for critique and impetus for political action and social change.

Unlike most Marxists, Bloch thus takes human needs, desires, and psychology very seriously. Here Bloch's thinking runs parallel to that of Wilhelm Reich and the Freudo-Marxists, though in significant ways it also differs from this tendency.[9] For Reich and others urged the communists to pay more attention to sexual needs and desires and to unconscious wishes and fears. But they tended to overestimate the role of sexuality in constituting human psychology and motivation, and downplayed such things as hunger, needs for security, home, community, and many other things which Bloch believes the fascists addressed with more success than the left.[10]

In *The Principle of Hope*, Bloch carries out an extremely interesting appreciation and critique of Freud, and develops his own psychological theories of imagination, needs, and hope against Freud. In fact, I would think that Bloch could productively be used to develop a Marxian anthropology and social psychology today and that his own anthropological and psychological perspectives are deeper and more illuminating than Freudo-Marxist approaches associated with the Frankfurt School or contemporary French theory like that of Deleuze and Guattari, or Lyotard. Briefly examining Bloch's critique of Freud will enable us to perceive how he is able to point to ideological tendencies in thinkers and theories often not perceived by standard Marxist ideology critique, as well as articulating Bloch's own distinctive anthropological and psychological perspectives. This discussion will also show how Bloch is, if anything, more critical and devastating in his attack on ideologies like psychoanalysis than many Marxist critics.

Given Bloch's emphasis on the importance of the subjective dimension in the constitution of human experience and for radical theory and politics, it is necessary that he distinguish his theory of subjectivity from psychoanalytic theories. He does this, first, by rooting psychological tendencies in the body and in human needs, and primarily hunger, rather than in instincts and the unconscious, as does Freud (45 ff.). He also conceptualizes "man as a quite extensive complex of drives" (47 ff.) and constantly emphasizes cravings, wishing, desiring, and hoping for a better life opposed to Freudian emphases on castration, repression, and the conservative political economy of the instincts which are characterized more by repetition, excitation-release, and ultimately entropy (the death instinct) than the development of new drives, impulses, and tendencies and possibilities for change and transformation such as one finds at the center of Bloch's theory (whereas Freud tends to present a fixed view of human nature).

At the end of the first stage of his critique of Freud, Bloch concludes: "In short, we realize that man is an equally changeable and extensive complex of drives, a heap of *changing,* and mostly badly ordered wishes. And a permanent motivating force, a single basic drive, in so far as it does not become independent and thus hang in the air, is hardly conceivable." Rather, there are several basic drives which emerge as primary at different times in social and individual life depending on the conditions prevailing at the time (50).

In a discussion of "Various Interpretations of the Basic Human Drive," Bloch critiques Freud's notion of the privacy of the sexual drive, as well as his notions of the ego drive and repression, repression and the unconscious, and sublimation (51 ff.). The key point is that

> [t]he unconscious of psychoanalysis is therefore, as we can see, *never a Not-Yet-Conscious,* an element of progressions; it consists rather of regressions. Accordingly, even the process of making this unconscious conscious only clarifies What Has Been; i.e. *there is nothing new in the Freudian unconscious.* This became even clearer when C.G. Jung, the psychoanalytic fascist, reduced the libido and its unconscious contents entirely to the primeval. According to him, exclusively phylogenetic primeval memories or primeval fantasies exist in the unconscious, falsely designated "archetypes"; and all wishful images also go back into this night, only suggest prehistory. Jung even considers the night to be so colorful that consciousness pales beside it; as a spurner of the light, he devalues consciousness. In contrast, Freud does of course unhold illuminating consciousness, but one which is itself surrounded by the ring of the id, by the fixed unconsciousness of a fixed libido. Even

highly productive artistic creations do not lead out of this Fixum; they are simply *sublimations* of the self-enclosed libido. [56]

In his analysis, Bloch positively valorizes Freud's enlightenment rationalism over Jung's irrationalism, and while he carries through a rehabilitation of what is sometimes dismissed as "the irrational," he also carries out a devastating critique of obscurantist, reactionary, irrationalist tendencies, especially those connected with fascism. Indeed, continuing to examine his critique of Jung, and his critique of Freud's disciple Adler who claimed that the will to power was the primary human drive, should help differentiate Bloch's theory of the subjective from more reactionary variants with which he might be wrongly identified. This exercise will also illustrate the sharp and powerful critique of ideology Bloch carries through, how he discerns ideological tendencies in phenomena often overlooked and is able to connect ideological theories to socio-historical tendencies.

Bloch discerns, for example, how Adler's will to power is related to competitive capitalist drives to move from the bottom to the top and how his theories of inferiority complex and neurosis reproduce the feelings of those strata of capitalist societies who have failed economically and who thus blame themselves for their failures (57 ff.). Bloch concludes:

> Because Adler therefore drives sex out of the libido and inserts individual power, his definition of drives takes the ever steeper capitalist path from Schopenhauer to Nietzsche and reflects this path ideologically and psychoanalytically. Freud's concept of libido borders on the "will to life" in Schopenhauer's philosophy; Schopenhauer in fact described the sexual organs as "the focal points of the will." Adler's "Will to Power" conversely coincides verbally, and partly also in terms of content with Nietzsche's definition of the basic drive from his last period; in this respect, Nietzsche has triumphed over Schopenhauer here, that is to say, the imperialist elbow has triumphed over the gentlemanly pleasure–displeasure body in psychoanalysis. The competitive struggle which hardly leaves any time for sexual worries stressed industriousness rather than randiness; the hectic day of the businessman thus eclipses the hectic night of the rake and his libido. [58]

Bloch then points out that the hecticness of life and the structural anxiety that permeates life in capitalist society, which submits the underlying population to the vagaries and uncertainties of the market, produce tendencies toward escape and regression, especially among the middle and lower *petit bourgeois* strata. Thus Adler's celebration of a will to power, which implicitly summons one to muster one's energies for production and competition, loses appeal as it becomes increasingly difficult to succeed in the marketplace. "Above all the path to the so-called heights lost some of its interest and prospects, in exact proportion

to the decline of free enterprise, as a result of monopoly capitalism"
(59).

The class strata which had previously responded to follow the calls by
Nietzsche, Adler, and others to scale the heights of competition and
worldly success began to look backward toward "the so-called depths, in
which the eyes roll instead of aiming at a goal" (59). Consequently, the
appeal grew of C.J. Jung, "the fascistically frothing psychoanalyst" who
"consequently posited the frenzy-drive in place of the power drive" (59).
I cite the following passage in its entirety to provide a sense of Bloch's
power as a critic of ideology:

> Just as sexuality is only part of this Dionysian general libido, so also is the will
> to power, in fact the latter is completely transformed into battle-frenzy, into
> a stupor which in no way strives toward individual goals. In Jung, libido thus
> becomes an archaically undivided primeval unity of all drives, or 'Eros' per
> se: consequently it extends from eating to the Last Supper, from coitus to
> unio mysterica, from the frothing-mouth of the shaman, even the berserker,
> to the rapture of Fra Angelico. Even here, therefore, Nietzsche triumphs
> over Schopenhauer, but he triumphs as the affirmation of a mescaline
> Dionysus over the negation of the will to life. As a result, the unconscious
> aspect of this mystified libido is also not contested and there is no attempt to
> resolve it into current consciousness as in Freud. Rather the neurosis,
> particularly that of modern, all too civilized and conscious man, derives
> according to Jung precisely from the fact that men have emerged too far out
> of what is unconsciously growing, outside the world of "elemental feel-
> thinking." Here Jung borders not only on the fascist version of Dionysus, but
> also partly on the vitalistic philosophy of Bergson. [59–60]

Those who might be inclined to dismiss Bloch as an irrationalist should
first read his critique of German irrationalist thought and fascist
ideologies. After critiquing Adler and Jung, Bloch goes after Bergson,
the "sentimental penis-poet" D.H. Lawrence, the "complete Tarzan
philosopher" Ludwig Klages, the celebrator of Neanderthal man Gott-
fried Benn, and the *petit bourgeois* mystifier Martin Heidegger (60 ff.).[11]
While Bergson's vitalism contained some progressive moments, by
contrast D.H. Lawrence,

> and Jung along with him, sings the wildernesses of the elemental age of love,
> which to his misfortune man has emerged from; he seeks the nocturnal
> moon in the flesh, the unconscious sun in the blood. And Klages blows in a
> more abstract way on the same bull-horn; he does not only hark back like
> the early Romantics to the Middle Ages, but to the diluvium, to precisely
> where Jung's impersonal, pandemonic libido lives. [59–60]

Bloch continues his provocative critique of German irrationalism (61
ff.), which rivals that of his friend Lukács,[12] and then presents his own

theories of subjectivity, hope, the preconscious, the Not-Yet-Conscious, and so on (65 ff.). This anthropological analysis of the elements in subjective experience which strive for a better life far surpasses the theory of the subjective dimension of Lukács, or almost any other Marxist. Indeed, *The Principle of Hope* provides a treasure house of insights into many topics neglected in standard Marxism, as well as providing an extremely useful concept of culture and ideology critique. In the next section, I thus want to examine some of the richest sections of *The Principle of Hope*, which I believe are most productive for cultural criticism today.

Bloch's Cultural Criticism and the Panorama of Culture

I have stressed how Bloch's theory of cultural criticism is rooted in his anthropological and philosophical perspectives, which are delineated in the first two parts of *The Principle of Hope*.[13] Part 3 contains explorations of "Wishful Images in the Mirror," in which Bloch decodes traces of hope permeating everyday life and culture. No philosopher since Hegel has explored in such detail and with such penetration the cultural tradition, which for Bloch contains untapped emancipatory potential. Yet Bloch concentrates not only on the great works of the cultural heritage, but on familiar and ordinary aspects of everyday experience within which he finds utopian potential. Fashion, grooming, new clothes, and how we make ourselves appear to others – all these activities exhibit the utopian potential of transforming us into something better. Perceiving the utopian potential of advertising, Bloch recognizes that it invests magical properties into commodities, which will produce allegedly magical results for the customer. "Shop-windows and advertising are in their capitalist form exclusively lime-twigs for the attracted dream birds" (344). To be sure, the promises of advertising and consumer culture are often false promises and often produce false needs, but their power and ubiquity show the depth of the needs that capitalism exploits and the wishes for another life that permeate capitalist societies. Moreover, many people wear masks, often derived from magazines or mass cultural images, to transform themselves, to attempt to invent a more satisfying life. Thus, youths join subcultures, even fascist ones like the Ku Klux Klan. Criminals and crime provide powerful attractions to oppressed youth, promising transcendence of their everyday misery.[14] Similar motivations lead individuals to join the Klan and other racist groups, to try to get a new and more satisfying identity through immersion in violent subcultures. Magazines, best-selling novels, and film and television also offer advice and models for self-transformation and how to achieve romance, success, and wealth.

Fairy tales celebrate the courage and cunning whereby ordinary individuals achieve their dreams. The realization of wishes is the very substance of fairy tales, and images of artifacts like Aladdin's lamp provide powerful fantasies of wish-fulfillment. Travel to exotic faraway places enables individuals to dream of better lives, while the circus provides access to a "wishful world of eccentricity and precise dexterity" (364). Adventure stories are vehicles of escape to a world of excitement and often show ordinary individuals defeating evil villains and oppressors. These are "immature, but honest substitute(s) for revolution" (368) and expressions of deep-seated desires for more power and satisfaction in their daily lives among ordinary people.

These forms of popular culture thus demonstrate desire for change and transformation and contain utopian energies which can make individuals yearn for a better world and attempt to transform themselves and their world. This culture is not, however, completely innocent or positive in its effects. Travel stories and images are exploited by travel agencies, promoting colonialism and the decline of everything, "with the exception of the West" (376). Much culture simply expresses and furthers the decadence of capitalist societies. In an attack on American popular music and dance that outdoes Adorno, Bloch writes:

> Where everything is disintegrating though, the body also contorts itself effortlessly along with it. Nothing coarser, nastier, more stupid has ever been seen than the jazz-dances since 1930. Jitterbug, Boogie-Woogie, this is imbecility gone wild, with a corresponding howling which provides the so to speak music accompaniment. American movement of this kind is rocking the Western countries, not as dance, but as vomiting. Man is to be soiled and his brain emptied; he has even less idea amongst his exploiters where he stands, for whom he is grafting, what he is being sent off to die for. [394]

Against this "American filth," however, Bloch claims that "a kind of movement of purification emerged" in the "new schools of dance developing from Isidora Duncan" which attempted "to demonstrate a more beautiful human image in the flesh" (394). Bloch also celebrates the Russian folk dance which expresses a "joy beyond the day of drudgery. The calmness and boisterousness both say: Here I am human, here I am entitled to be" (395). Expressionist dance, however, is more ambivalent, rebelling against "the spirit of gravity," but also flowing into "the local bloodlake of fascism; for which this kind of roaring of wings was already foreseeable in its imperialist premises" (398).

These examples show that Bloch carries out a differentiated critique of cultural forms, tending to attack those which he sees involved with fascist culture, or a decadent capitalism, and praising those which rebel against capitalism or celebrate a healthy socialism. He contrasts, for example, the "incomparable falsification" of Hollywood film, contrasted with the "realistic film in its anti-capitalist, no longer capitalist peak performances" (408). While Bloch is sharply critical of Hollywood film (see especially p. 410), he believes that film per se contains much utopian potential in its ability to project images of a better life, to explore and redeem concrete reality, and to transmit utopian dreams and energies.

In sum, Bloch finds utopian traces throughout the field of culture, demonstrating that: "Mankind and the world carry enough good future; no plan is itself good without this fundamental belief within it" (447). While it is beneficial to affirm Bloch's methodological imperative of searching for utopian and emancipatory potential within all forms of culture, while also attending to embellishing and mystifying ideological elements, one might quarrel with his specific evaluations and judgements. As my presentation makes clear, he tends to attack culture that affirms capitalism, fascism, and philosophical idealism, and to praise culture which promotes socialism.

The limitations of his evaluations, I believe, derive from his overly dogmatic Marxism and his exile experiences which provide consistently negative depictions of the United States.[15] The Principle of Hope was written while Bloch was a relatively emphatic Marxist, and his political hermeneutic deeply influenced his readings. His discussion of theater, for instance, celebrates Brecht (413 ff.) and progressive German and Soviet theater, and exalts theater which promotes "defiance and hope" rather than the catharsis of pity and fear of Greek theater (429 ff.). He also constantly attacks the enemies of utopia, such as the French artist Grandville and Aristophanes (434; 435 ff.) and above all American culture.

Utilizing Bloch for cultural criticism thus requires distancing oneself from some of his specific judgements and analyses while making use of his double-coded concept of ideology and his method of cultural criticism. Cultural studies for Bloch rejects distinctions between high and low culture, seeing utopian potential in cultural artifacts ranging from advertising and display to Beethoven and opera. Bloch's politicization of cultural critique forces one to make political evaluations of cultural artifacts, though one may make different judgements, and utilize different political perspectives, from Bloch's. Indeed, cultural studies for Bloch was intimately bound up with his social and political theory, so that cultural criticism for him was an important part of political practice.[16]

Socialism, Revolution, and the Red Arrow

Part 4 of The Principle of Hope interrogates the "Outlines of a Better World" in a variety of utopias. Bloch finds utopian dreams not only in the social and political utopias of the great utopian theorists, but also in a variety of technological, architectural, and geographical utopias, as well as in painting, opera, literature, and other forms of art. Part 5 describes "Wishful Images of the Fulfilled Moment," in which morality, music, religion, and philosophies project images and visions of supreme fulfillment, culminating in the figure of an individual who "has grasped himself and established what is his, without exploitation and alienation." In this situation, "in real democracy, there arises in the world something which shines into the childhood of all and in which no one has yet been: homeland" (1,376).

Culture for Bloch contains traces of what he calls red arrows which migrate through history looking for realization in socialism. Bloch finds a red path weaving through history, revolting against alienation, exploitation, and oppression, struggling for a better world. The social and political utopias present imperfect yearnings for what was more fully developed in Marxism and socialism. Thus Bloch develops an explicitly political hermeneutic that interprets certain cultural artifacts and residues from the past as pointing toward socialism.

Certain aspects of the bourgeois revolutions, for instance, were never realized and contain a surplus of critical and emancipatory potential that can be used to criticize bourgeois society on the grounds that it was not realizing its own potentials. One of Bloch's more productive ideas is that the ideological surplus or cultural surplus is not just an expression of the socio-economic base or the dominant mode of production but is *ungleichzeitig*, describing what is non-contemporaneous or non-synchronic with the present.[17] This concept points to the fact that residues and traditions from the past continue to be effective in the present, even though it might appear that they are completely archaic and historically surpassed (i.e. fascist primitivism, or the strange phenomenon of Reaganism in a technological United States).

But *Ungleichzeitigkeit* also points to elements from the past which anticipate future developments, which appear before their time, which point ahead to the future (i.e. earlier anticipations of socialism) and which have yet to be realized. However, the utopian surplus contains the potential to project long-term goals for an individual or society and for political practice that provides alternatives to the status quo which is far-seeing and future-oriented. For Bloch, ideology and utopia are therefore not simply opposites, because utopian elements appear in ideology and utopias are often permeated with ideological content and mystification. Cultural surplus for Bloch has the potentiality of utopian surplus which anticipates, previews, and points to a better organization of society and everyday life, and it is the task of the cultural critic to discern and unfold this progressive potential and to relate it to the struggles and possibilities of the present. Bloch's cultural hermeneutic is thus deeply political, and cultural studies for him is thus intimately bound up with political practice.

Notes

1. For my reflections on Bloch's Marxism, see my articles (with Harry O'Hara) "Utopia and Marxism in Ernst Bloch," *New German Critique*, 9 (Fall 1976), pp. 11–34, and "Introduction to Ernst Bloch, 'The Dialectical Method,'" *Man and World*, 16 (1983), 281–4.

2. Ernst Bloch, *The Principle of Hope* (Cambridge, Mass.: MIT Press, 1986), 3 vols. This study will focus mainly on the use for cultural studies and ideology critique of Bloch's magnum opus, though I also draw on some of his other writings and my own previous research into Bloch's thought.

3. There are, of course, numerous books on Marx's concept of ideology, and an equal volume of heated debates over its relative merits and limitations and which aspects of the critique should be emphasized. For my own position within these debates, which I will not rehearse here, see Douglas Kellner, "Ideology, Marxism, and Advanced Capitalism," *Socialist Review*, 42 (Nov.–Dec. 1978), pp. 37–65.

4. Bloch's starting point is always the everyday life and existential situation of the individual, and thus his approach is similar to that of Henri Lefebvre and the French situationists who also undertook a critique of everyday life and were concerned with the existence of concrete individuals.

5. See Wayne Hudson, "Ernst Bloch: 'Ideology' and Postmodern Social Philosophy," *Canadian Journal of Political and Social Theory* 7: no. 1–2 (Winter 1983), pp. 136. I draw on Hudson's presentation of Bloch's concept of ideology here, but do not accept his critiques of Bloch, or his curious sketch of a "postmodern social philosophy," which anticipates in an eccentric fashion the current craze for postmodern theories. He presents Bloch as a prototype of modern theory.

6. Bloch's *Natural Law and Human Dignity* (Cambridge, Mass.: MIT Press, 1986) expands on this notion.

7. Fredric Jameson, "Reification and Utopia in Mass Culture," *Social Text*, 1 (Winter 1979), pp. 130–48.

8. Ibid., p. 144.

9. See Wilhelm Reich, *Sex-Pol* (New York: Vintage, 1972), and, on French Freudo-Marxism, Mark Poster, *Existential Marxism in Postwar France* (Princeton, NJ: Princeton University Press, 1975).

10. See Ernst Bloch, *Heritage of Our Times* (Berkeley: University of California Press, 1990).

11. Bloch was an early and consistent critic of Heidegger, perceiving the link between his philosophy and fascism that was later discovered by historiographic and ideological critiques.

12. Compare, for example, Georg Lukács, *The Destruction of Reason* (London: Merlin, 1980).

13. For further discussion of Bloch's philosophy, see Wayne Hudson, *The Marxist Philosophy of Ernst Bloch* (New York: St. Martin's Press, 1982).

14. This is a motif of many films dealing with the dilemmas of black youth in the US, including *Straight Out of Brooklyn, New Jack City, Boys N'the Hood, Juice*, and the earlier cycle of blaxploitation films that celebrated drug dealers and gangs. The other utopia offered for young black audiences is that of success in the music industry, as evidenced in the films of Prince and the ubiquitous rock videos of Michael Jackson, various rap groups, and others.

15. An exile from fascist Germany, Bloch lived in the US from 1938 until 1949. Yet he learned little English, and mainly immersed himself in writing his major works and in German exile politics while being supported by his wife, who worked as an architect (as I learned in personal interviews with the Blochs in 1974). Like the Frankfurt School exiles, he thus had a predominantly negative view of American culture.

16. For my own concept of a multi-perspectival cultural studies, see my articles, "Film, Politics, and Ideology: Reflections on Hollywood Film in the Age of Reagan," *The Velvet Light Trap*, 27 (Spring 1991), pp. 9–24, and "Toward a Multi-perspectival Cultural Studies," *Centennial Review*, 20: 446.

17. See Ernst Bloch, "Nonsynchronism and Dialectics," *New German Critique*, 11 (Spring 1977), pp. 22–38. The text is also now available in translation in *Heritage of Our Times*.

7

Bloch against Bloch:
The Theological Reception of *Das Prinzip Hoffnung* and the Liberation of the Utopian Function

Tom Moylan

I

If you look into the dark long enough, there is always
something there.

W.B. Yeats[1]

In the 1930s, Walter Benjamin recommended that historical materialism
could become the victor in the battle against fascism if it enlisted the
services of theology.[2] That critical encounter never occurred, but the
Marxist-Christian dialogues of the 1960s launched an interchange that
resembled what Benjamin had recommended.[3] This time, however, the
pressing issue was not fascism but a constellation of problems which
included the conflicts of the Cold War, the effects of de-colonialization
and neo-colonialization, and the impact of the bureaucratic-consumer
societies of late capitalism. Furthermore, the initiative was taken by
theologians rather than by Marxists, and yet an important influence on
this theoretical rejuvenation was the unorthodox Marxism of Benjamin's
friend, Ernst Bloch. In this provocative conversation, what had become
the closed discursive space of Western theology was broken open by the
external, secular discourse of critical Marxism. In turn, the rigidity of
the residual orthodox Marxism that runs through Bloch's own polyvocal
text was also challenged.[4] As a result, the reception of Bloch by liberal
and left theologians in the late twentieth century broke through the
philosophical and ideological limitations of his work and refunctioned
it for a post-Western appropriation of the utopian function in what
Gustavo Gutiérrez calls the "entirely worldly world" (66).[5]

II

The world has long possessed the dream of a matter, of which it must only possess the consciousness in order to possess it in reality.

Karl Marx[6]

Having worked on it for decades, Bloch completed *Das Prinzip Hoffnung* in 1959, just a few years before leaving the German Democratic Republic and settling into a professorship at Tübingen in the Federal Republic. The reception of Bloch's "esoteric Marxism,"[7] with its extensive and sympathetic analysis of religion and utopia, began at Tübingen in conversations between Bloch and theologians such as the Lutheran Jürgen Moltmann and the Catholic Johannes Metz. From there it spread rapidly, and his philosophy of radical hope became what one theologian in 1968 described as the "cultural pivot in historical theology as well as a contemporary point of contact between Christian theology and the world culture."[8] Wolfgang Pannenberg, one of the theologians influenced by Bloch at that time, noted that Bloch "taught us about the overwhelming power of the still-open future and of the hope that reaches out to it."[9] And, in the *Journal of Religion* in 1969, Ronald Green clearly appreciated that Bloch was concerned "not with the negation of religious belief, but with the attainment of a positive position by means of the criticism of religion."[10] As Green saw it, Bloch's dialectical critique involved a "constructive and creative reappropriation of the kernel of religious experience itself" (128). Over the course of the past thirty years, then, Bloch's work has had a major impact on political theology in Europe, on secular theology in the United States, and, perhaps most importantly, on liberation theology in Latin America and elsewhere in the Third World.

At the heart of Bloch's theory is his concept of the utopian function. For Bloch, the category of the Not-Yet-Conscious is the "psychological representation" of the materially "Not-Yet-Become in an age and its world" (127). In the unfolding of the forward-looking wishes of humanity, the Not-Yet-Conscious becomes "*conscious* in its act, *known* in its content" (144) in order to be an effective force in society. In this process, hope, the "expectant emotion in the forward dream," emerges "in a *conscious-known way* as *utopian function*" (144). Consequently, the imaginative ideas and images generated by the utopian function "extend, in an anticipating way, existing material into the future possibilities of being different and better" (144). Always the historical materialist, however, Bloch stresses that this utopian capacity achieves concrete expression only when it is "set on its feet and connected to the Real-Possible" conditions in a particular historical situation (146). Thus, the utopian function is rooted in the world yet "is transcendent without transcendence" (146).

Bloch's exploration of the utopian function in the history of religious discourse superseded the mechanical materialism of Feuerbach and the positivist versions of Marxism that had relegated religion to the dustbin of history.[11] Bloch returned to Marx's own assessment of religion as not merely a disempowering opiate but also a powerful "sigh of the oppressed" which must be accepted as a valid component of the long-term human efforts toward emancipation.[12] The central theoretical move in this deconstruction of religious discourse is a philosophical and historical critique that removes the hypostatized figure of God from the social space of religious discourse and practice and refunctions that "hollow space" for the utopian impulse. In his study of the major world religions, Bloch traces the historical movement away from non-human astral gods of nature toward gods who are implicated in the human project and finally toward the elimination of God and occupation of the site of religious mystery by the human utopian function itself.[13]

In Judaism and Christianity, especially, Bloch finds historical individuals who founded their religions by reacting against traditional customs and natural religion. Moses first establishes a contract with a single God and "forces his god to go with him, makes him into the exodus-light of his people" (1,191). The God of Moses is less a creator God and more a *Deus Spes*, a God of hope who helps his people arrive at the promised land. By the time of Jesus, religious hope had been placed in the figure of a messiah who "appears as a scarcely concealable vote of no-confidence" in a God, Yahweh, who had become identified with the "opium-priests" (1,235) of an institutionalized religion that had lost its prophetic exodus mission.[14] Instead of representing such an institutional God, Jesus "pervades the transcendent as a human tribune" (1,191) and "utopianizes" the transcendent figure of God into the Kingdom of God. Consequently, Jesus places the responsibility of building the new heaven and the earth in the hands of the community of believers.

The heart of the Christian message, then, is *Eritis sicut Deus*: you shall be like god. Thus, the *Novum* of religion moves away from that which is above humanity to humanity itself: "the glory of God becomes that of the redeemed community and of its place" (1,274). Yet, in Bloch's version of the humanization of religion there is a synchronic as well as a diachronic factor. For all along the way, he recognizes the importance of religious discourse as a privileged place of awe and mystery, as the site of the Utterly Different. It is only that the Utterly Different is now articulated within the realm of a human anticipation which is itself constantly open to that which has not yet been imagined or achieved.

Underlying this liberation of religious space is a "properly understood

atheism" (1,198): not the nihilistic atheism of the mechanical material-
ists that eliminates both God and religious space but rather a creative
atheism that negates the idolatrous god figure yet retains and transforms
the space of religion so that "the kingdom, even in secularized form,
and all the more so in its utopian-total form, *remains as a messianic Front-
space even without any theism*" (1,200). This liberating atheism is therefore
the precondition for religious utopia, for "without atheism messianism
has no place" (1,200). Consequently Bloch concludes that "religious
imagination certainly cannot be dismissed in toto by the achieved
demystification of the world-picture" (1,202), for "in the midst of the
. . . nonsense about the mythical there lives and rises the undischarged
question, which has been a burning question only in religion, about the
unestablished – meaning of life" (1,202).

Bloch argues that with historical materialism, the mythology of the
divine and theology as "real science" is finished, and yet, contrary to
Feuerbach and the positivist Marxists, the "hope-content" which mythology and theology sought to express is not finished – nor will it ever be.
Bloch, however, does not claim full credit for historical materialism or
his own project. Rather, he sees this atheist strategy as a fundamental
aspect of the Jewish and Christian traditions. He interprets Moses'
replacement of the astral gods with a god under contract for the exodus
as an implicitly atheist gesture, and he argues that "long before God as
an existent object of being had been overthrown by the Enlightenment,
Christianity put *man* and his claim, or precisely the *son of man* and his
representative mystery, into the Lord of Heaven of former days"
(1,284).[15] In this religious elimination of what is basically idolatry, the
critical atheist is not an anti-christ but actually a prophetic voice first
spoken by Moses and continuing into the present. Paradoxically, then,
the utopian element in this religious tradition is "irreligious" because it
is insistently "meta-religious" in that it "keeps the world open at the
front and frontwards" (1,293).

The result of this atheist religious tradition and Bloch's own secular
analysis which continues in its spirit is the preservation and transformation of the "*hollow space* which the dispatching of the God-hypostasis
leaves behind" (1,294). What persists in that meta-religious zone is "the
Novum into which human ranks of purpose continue to run in mediated
form" (1,296). In this space of mystery and undischarged questions,
humanity has projected not only its nostalgic myths of perfection but
also its expressions of tendencies toward a fulfillment not yet achieved.
In this way, Bloch distinguishes between religious hypostasis and the
field wherein religious hypostasis occurs, for that field is the most
profound site of the utopian function. As Bloch puts it: "If there is no
utopia of the kingdom without atheism, then there is implicitly also
none without the utopian-real hollow space itself which atheism has
both left behind and revealed" (1,297), for

here and nowhere else the entire history of religion has journeyed; but the kingdom needs space. So much space that all expressions and extensions so far are not enough for it, and again so little space, such intensively penetrated space, that only the narrow path of Christian mysticism indicates it ... For this and for this end the religious hollow space is and remains non-chimera, although all the gods in it were chimeras. [1,298]

III

> This kind of correlation does not reduce Marxism to Christianity, nor does it reduce Christianity to Marxism. The specific element in Marxism is praxis that leads to transcendence within real life. The specifically Christian element is hope in the potentialities of praxis, going beyond what can be calculated to be humanly achievable. The connecting link between them is real material life as the ultimate basis for all human life.
>
> Franz J. Hinkelammert[16]

Bloch's transformation of religious space into a privileged site of the utopian function profoundly influenced liberal and left theology in the 1960s. His critique enabled theologians to break out of inherited religious discourses and to pursue an agenda of hope without becoming trapped in the compensations promised by a supernatural deity or a technocratic society. In his introduction to a 1986 English-language edition of Bloch's essays, the US theologian Harvey Cox summarizes Bloch's dialogue in the 1950s with Paul Tillich and then explains Bloch's impact on the younger group of theologians of the 1960s. According to Cox, Bloch and Tillich agreed that the supernatural, personal God created through centuries of institutional Christianity no longer existed in any meaningful way and that humanity was no longer subject to that overwhelming and distant deity. They disagreed, however, on where the reality previously signified by that transcendental signifier was now to be located. Tillich looked to "the depths" of existence for God as the source of being; while Bloch looked to the "forward edge" where humanity moves into the future.[17]

The younger theologians influenced by Bloch included three basic groups: (1) the "death-of-God thinkers" such as Thomas Altizer who saw Bloch as a "threat from the left" to their non-historical, "quasi-pantheistic mysticism"; (2) the "development" theologians such as Leslie Dewart who sought to retrieve some acceptable concept of a personal God but who became trapped in existential notions of "presence" rather than the possibilities of an emancipating future; and (3) the "secular theologians" such as Cox who welcomed Bloch's insights that the secular society is "bounded by a future toward which it hastens every day, a future it never attains but which continually prevents it from accepting itself as finished and final."[18] For secular theology, Bloch's principle of hope provides a way to be concerned with the everyday world "without sacrificing the transcendent," for Bloch helps to locate the space represented by the figure of God at the horizon of a future that challenges the secular society not to be content with the false promises of its apparently fulfilling present.

Bloch's contribution to the removal of the traditional God of Christianity and his insistence on the power of the future possibilities that humanity has yet to know and appreciate also had a major impact on two influential theologies developed at Tübingen in the 1960s. The "theology of hope" grew out of the work of the Lutheran theologian Jürgen Moltmann. His book, *The Theology of Hope*, published in German in 1965 and English in 1967, restored eschatology or the doctrine of the "last things" to a central place in Christian thought.[19] Although Moltmann was directly influenced by Bloch, a substantial difference between the two rests in their assessments of the role of human activity in the movement toward the eschaton. For Moltmann, the first cause of this forward movement is the non-historical Promise of salvation given by a God who resembles the Aristotelian prime mover. That is, the hoped-for salvation of humanity comes about not in the historical incarnation of hope represented in the activities of Jesus and a community of believers but rather in a transcendent future which makes the Promise available to a receptive humanity. Thus, although Bloch's influence on Moltmann furthers a theology that gives primary emphasis to the process of hope and the powerful pull of the future, the theology of hope itself remains locked in a set of non-historical categories.

A more dynamic Blochian influence is evident in the work of another Tübingen colleague, Johannes Metz, a Catholic theologian who developed what he called "political theology." Metz, too, situates eschatology at the core of his work, but he goes further than Moltmann and links eschatology and hope with human political struggle. Celebrating the political maturity of the Enlightenment, Metz asserts that the proper concern of politics in the modern age is the question of freedom. Influenced by the analysis of the public sphere by Jürgen Habermas, Metz first identifies a public sphere for religion which negates the privileging of religion as an activity reserved for an entirely "private" sphere that ignores the political world. He then distinguishes between the public sphere of politics and the public sphere of religion in order to remove religious institutions from the temptations of direct political rule (a rule which in the history of the Roman Catholic Church was all too regularly associated with privilege and wealth rather than with the needs of the poor and exploited). He consequently stresses that while modern religion as a *public* entity must involve itself in the questions of political agenda, it must remain aware that it works in a sphere separate from that of direct political rule. Given this distinction, Metz sees the appropriate involvement of religion in the political quest for human freedom as one of engagement through critique rather than control.[20]

The shortcoming of Metz's theology, as interpreted by the more radical theologians developing Third World theologies of liberation (such as Gustavo Gutiérrez), was that his analysis comes from a position of relative freedom in the First World. Consequently, Metz's understanding of religious engagement in politics does not take into account the more complex and acute situations in countries where exploitation and suffering are more pointed and the Church itself is often the only public institution capable of effective opposition. Thus, this critique of Metz's binary opposition of the public spheres of religion and the state explains how the privileges of the secular societies of the advanced industrial world prevent a non-mediated political theology from recognizing the difficulties of engagement required by people in areas of greater, or at least more overt, oppression. As Gutiérrez, also influenced by Bloch, puts it, "in places like Latin America, things are different. The process here does not have the characteristics it exhibits in Europe. Faith, the Gospel, the Church, have . . . a complex public dimension which has played (and still plays) an important role in support of the established order" (225).

Bloch's critique of religious discourse and his analysis of the utopian function had its deepest and most persistent influence in those religious circles which sought to confront situations of suffering and political struggle in Latin America and in other Third World locations such as South Africa, South Korea, and the Philippines.[21] Gutiérrez's *Theology of Liberation*, published in Spanish in 1971 and in English in 1973, is one of the key texts of Latin American liberation theology.[22] Bloch's influence can be seen throughout the book: for example, in Gutiérrez's argument for an "entirely worldly world" which refuses the traditional separation of reality into distinct supernatural and natural planes of existence and instead claims that "the world has gradually been acknowledged as existing in its own right" (66); or, in his related argument that rejects the notion of separate sacred and profane histories and recognizes only "one human destiny, irreversibly assumed by Christ, the Lord of history" (153). Gutiérrez, therefore, regards human history as the privileged site of *both* material and spiritual liberation, which are themselves interconnected in the movement of humanity toward the Kingdom of God. This interconnection is explained by Gutiérrez in his chapter on "Encountering God in History" as he discusses the dynamics of Christian conversion in the ongoing project of liberation: "To be converted is to commit oneself to the process of the liberation of the poor and oppressed, to commit oneself lucidly, realistically, and concretely. It means to commit oneself not only generously, but also with an analysis of the situation and a strategy of action. To be converted is to know and experience the fact that, contrary to the law of physics, we can stand straight, according to the Gospel, only when our center of gravity is outside ourselves" (205). Here Christian theology and pastoral service connect with Marxist analysis and action in the figure of Bloch's "upright gait" as it is inspired by that which is Utterly Different and beyond the limits of any given individual or people.[23]

Gutiérrez's debt to Bloch is most directly found in his chapter on "Eschatology and Politics." He says straight away that the "commitment to the creation of a just society and, ultimately, to a new man presupposes confidence in the future" (213). This future orientation calls for people to take control of their "own destiny" and to engage in a "revolutionary process" that leads to the "building up of a just society, qualitatively different from the one which exists today" (213–14). In this process, then, the premises of a revised eschatology enable the Church to become *directly* involved in history in a way that does not compromise its basic agenda of salvation. Gutiérrez directly refers to Bloch's principle of hope as an activity which "subverts the existing order" (216). Referring to the utopian function that mobilizes human action in history, he argues that Bloch's important concept "brings us into the area of the possibilities of potential being" in a way that "allows us to plan history in revolutionary terms" (216). Indeed, while he respects and uses the theologies of both Moltmann and Metz, Gutiérrez finds that Bloch's analyses are much more soundly connected to history and human struggle than either of the European theologies (217–25).

Gutiérrez proceeds by developing an interpretation of Jesus that dehypostatizes the founder of Christianity in much the same way that Bloch does. He breaks with the dominant Christian tradition that reduces the historical Jesus to the status of a theological icon "unrelated to the real forces at play" (226). Instead, with clear echoes of Bloch's critique of idolatry, he accepts Jesus as a complex, historical actor whose insights and agenda exceeded the goals of both the political zealots and the religious reformers of his own time even as he combined both tendencies in his call for humanity to enter the Kingdom of God. The subversive message of Jesus' story, then, is not only the end of the domination of God over man but also the end of the domination of man over man. Gutiérrez, like Bloch, cautions that this anticipated Kingdom exceeds any given hope-content known to humanity, for "the announcement of the Kingdom ... leads it to discover unsuspected dimensions and unexplored paths" (231–2).

In the closing section of the chapter, Gutiérrez links "faith, utopia and political action" in a dynamic relationship that constitutes the core structure of liberation theology. He first rescues the term "utopia" from its negative connotation of useless dreaming and identifies it as the necessary mediation of a progressive faith and politics. He then argues for its "quality of being subversive to and a driving force of history" by identifying three elements which characterize utopian longing as a material force: "its relationship to historical reality, its verification in praxis, and its rational nature" (232).[24] He explains the three elements by means of the radical pedagogy of Paulo Freire. First, he recalls Freire's characterization of utopia's negative denunciatory power that repudiates the existing order of things and its positive annunciatory power that calls forth a new and just society. Then, following Freire, he links both approaches to historical praxis, for "if utopia does not lead to action in the present, it is an evasion of reality" (234). Finally, drawing on Freire's understanding of the relationship between learning and political action, he situates the utopian function as a "mediation of the creative imagination" within the larger processes of a critical reason by which one can not only know the world but also change it (234). Thus, for Gutiérrez, the utopian function provides the connection between salvation and history that Moltmann's theology avoided, and it provides the connection between the religious and the political public spheres that Metz's theology lacks.

The Blochian version of utopia, therefore, is the keystone of Gutiérrez's theology of liberation. It is the element which allows this radical theology to link, but also to challenge the limits of, Christian and Marxist thought and action. For within the single process of liberation, the complexity of levels that include the economic, the political, the social, and the spiritual is negotiated by means of the utopian function with its multiple dimensions of anticipation – some of which speak to the immediate moment and some of which go beyond all known images of the possible future society. In the interrelationships of faith, utopia, and politics, then, a complex intersection of discourses ensures that no provisional positions will hold back the larger revolutionary process. Political discourse keeps both faith and utopia focused on current struggles and future developments. Arising out of those struggles, the religious attitude of faith inspires both political action and utopian anticipation to resist their tendencies to be frozen in historically bound ideologies. And, utopian discourse – energized by the specificities of politics and the mysteries of faith – keeps faith and politics from becoming limited to present power structures, whether religious or secular. Gutiérrez ends his chapter with an account of Christian hope as it has been transformed by Blochian theory:

> Christian hope ... keeps us from any confusion of the Kingdom with any one historical stage, from any idolatry toward unavoidably ambiguous human achievement, from any absolutizing of revolution. In this way, hope makes us radically free to commit ourselves to social praxis, motivated by a liberating utopia and with the means which the scientific analysis of reality provides for us. And our hope not only frees us for this commitment, it simultaneously demands and judges it. [238]

Thus, he breaks open the ideological limits and idolatries at work in the Christian tradition and radicalizes that deconstructed Christianity with the infusion of the utopian function so that he can support and transform the secular revolutionary project in his own region of the world.

A more overt example of the dehypostatizing power of the discursive intersection of a Christianity and a Marxism that reciprocally subvert each other's traditional tendencies toward teleological closure can be found in the work of another Latin American liberation theologian, Franz Hinkelammert. Although his 1977 book contains only one direct reference to Bloch, Hinkelammert's *The Ideological Weapons of Death: A Theological Critique of Capitalism* (1986) is written in the spirit of Bloch's method of dehypostatization and utopian anticipation and Gutiérrez's use of that method in liberation theology. However, Hinkelammert focuses more specifically on the immediate conditions of exploitation and suffering caused by capitalism and its allied national security states in Latin America in the 1970s. In a direct engagement with economic theory, Hinkelammert employs a combination of Marxist political economy and biblical exegesis to interrogate the theories of Milton Friedman and the Trilateral Commission as they have affected Central and South America. In addition, he challenges the conservative theologies that justify the institutional Church in its legitimation of those capitalist theories and the practices that result from them. Following from this indictment of the dominant secular and sacral ideologies of power, Hinkelammert works from liberation theology's epistemological privileging of the poor to develop a "theology of life" that recognizes the rights and needs of the poor and that opposes the official "theology of death" that only offers patient suffering in this world and a transformed existence in a non-historical afterlife.

The central concept of the theology of life comes from Hinkelammert's reinterpretation of the resurrection of the body of Jesus as the fundamental sign of the *material* salvation of humanity. Hinkelammert argues that the promise of the resurrection provides the necessary link between present human existence and the utopian anticipation of the "new body" and "new earth" that challenges sacral and secular power. He notes, however, that such challenges must be continually "self-correcting" (225). For even as utopian praxis clashes with the limits of reality, it has to negotiate within those limits since it cannot in actual practice go beyond them. This does not deny the powerful, pre-conceptual activity of the utopian impulse, but it does acknowledge material reality's "invisible hand." Against this sober recognition of the persistent drag of necessity, Hinkelammert's theology motivates human hope to push beyond the limitations of the present by offering it the assistance of a divine power.

The God of liberation theology, however, is not the hypostatized deity of traditional Christianity. Nor is it the obsolete image that Marx eliminated through his appropriation of Feuerbach's secularizing anthropology. In opposition to these hypostatized and alienated images of God, Hinkelammert offers a renewed image of the "Biblical God," for the deity that emerged in what Bloch called the atheist religion of the Bible is one that has abdicated absolute power through the historical covenants with Moses and Jesus. In these two covenants, then, *God is changed*. With the first covenant, God "ceases to impose divine will on the human being in any way" (231) and works in partnership "within the human praxis of liberation" (230). With the second covenant, "the human being becomes sovereign" (231), and God's will and that of the liberation of the human community "coincide completely" so that "the imperatives of human liberation indicate what God's will is" (231). As Hinkelammert suggests, the figure of the deity available for his Christian-Marxist discourse "derives from the liberated human being" (231).

In this rereading of Scripture, Hinkelammert's theology does not mechanically eliminate God, nor does it conflate humanity and God. Rather, as expressed in what Bloch would identify as the social space of religious discourse, God remains as the signifier of an Otherness that empowers humanity to reach beyond its own utopian aspirations. Standing outside humanity, but in partnership with it, the "God of the Bible" provides a symbolic source of radical non-identity that ensures the openness of the liberation process. This signifier of the ability of humanity to transcend its limits therefore provides the nexus between Christian and Marxist concepts of transcendence and freedom that facilitates the move to a stronger form of oppositional praxis.

However, to make that connection viable Hinkelammert must first surpass Marx's rejection of the image of God and the dilemma which resulted from that understandable and necessary theoretical move. The traditional Marxist concept of the deity is the medieval supreme being who is the surrogate of human reason, but this is a figure that can be dispensed with in modernity. For with the prospect of the journey to the new earth by means of human labor and reason, Marx can replace the other-worldly supreme being with a humanity that makes its own history. Therefore, the compensatory deity of the medieval Church no longer has a useful place in history. Yet, Hinkelammert notes that in rightly dismissing that God, orthodox Marxism faces a new dilemma. The realm of freedom called forth by historical materialism is still a transcendent goal, yet the theory provides no mediating bridge to join the present struggle to that hoped-for achievement which challenges humanity to exceed the limits of necessity. What is at stake is "the whole question of legitimating a human praxis of approaching the realm of freedom when one realizes that achieving it is a goal infinitely far off" (229). Without mediation, the gap becomes absolute, and any hope of crossing it is reduced to the status of myth. As Hinkelammert points out, this is a serious theoretical problem, but it is also a practical problem "found in socialist countries and socialist movements in the capitalist world." That is, "if utopian praxis is aimed at ends that cannot be achieved, why should there be such a praxis at all?" (229).

The solution Hinkelammert proposes for this legitimation crisis in the Marxist social vision is "to insert Christian faith into it" (229). This is not an act of opportunism but rather a serious contribution to creating the conditions for orienting human life toward the future, for without such hope, humanity faces the possibility pointed out by Teilhard de Chardin that "humankind might go on strike and refuse to work for its own survival" (229). Thus, in order to empower utopian praxis in its real forward movement, the God of liberation theology, the God that is now the externalized image of the liberated human being, can serve as the material signifier of Otherness which makes possible human movement across the apparently unbridgeable gap.

The human response to the God of the biblical covenants must therefore be understood in light of the radical reinterpretation of Scripture and Church doctrine undertaken by a liberation theology that is transformed by Marxist theory. For in following the covenant commandment of love of God through love of neighbor, the solidarity and mutual aid of the human community fulfills its side of the bargain, and in return the signifier of divine power motivates human effort far beyond its perceived limits. Thus, Christian praxis – based in suffering and exploitation and informed by a partisan faith, hope, and love – challenges secular revolutionary praxis never to rest content, never to say enough, never to close off possibilities. In its turn, the Marxist critique of fetishism challenges liberation Christianity to remain based in concrete material reality and not to fall into the trap of absolutizing values or actions, not to fall into the trap of closing off or totalizing reality in terms of abstractions unrelated to the historical situations of suffering people.

Thus, Hinkelammert correlates Marxism and Christianity in terms of the utopian function. However, in this correlation Christianity is not reduced to the "truth" present in Marxism, nor is Marxist analysis based in a material praxis of social analysis reduced to the insights of a liberated theology. Rather, in provocative interaction the two discourses transform and extend each other. As Hinkelammert argues, the fact that Christianity was unable to maintain its earlier message of liberation and – from the time of its fourth-century compromise with the Emperor Constantine – degenerated into a form of anti-utopian, institutional Christianity that was complicit with hegemonic secular power may be explained by its lack of a concept of praxis. Yet, as Marxism developed its concept of praxis it drew on the very tradition of transcendence that had been largely lost in the mainstream Christian tradition but which had been continued in the minority and heretical movements led by the likes of Joachim of Fiore and Thomas Münzer. Therefore, with the rediscovery of its own radical tradition of praxis, as carried forward in Marxism, Christianity can once more propose the liberation found in its origins, but it can also benefit from the progress of history and offer a methodological mediation that incorporates and legitimizes the Marxist goal of the realm of freedom.

IV

> Just as we cannot stamp Hegel as the philosopher of the Prussian state because he lets the development of the moral idea end in the Prussian state, we cannot reduce Bloch's thought, the philosopher in combat, to statements that he made about the Moscow trials, for these statements clearly contradict his entire philosophy.
>
> Oscar Negt[25]

As can be seen in the above survey, progressive theologies have been transformed by their encounter with Bloch's utopian Marxism. In return, Bloch's own theory of the utopian function has benefitted from its reception by these radicalized Christian discourses. The European and North American theologies of the 1960s stimulated a discovery of Bloch's utopian method that extended beyond religious circles into the political and philosophical imagination of sections of the new left, especially in West Germany and to a lesser extent in the United States. In a more direct intervention into the political struggles of their region, Latin American liberation theologians preserved and transformed Bloch's understanding of the utopian function for an emerging post-colonial oppositional discourse that goes beyond the limitations of the Western sacred and secular traditions.

That revitalization and transformation, however, did not come easily. Because of Bloch's failure to challenge his own hypostatization of the "concrete utopia" of a Soviet Union deformed by Stalinism long after his methodology should have warned him of his error, the emancipatory value of Bloch's work has regularly been questioned. There is, of course, no doubt that Bloch's silence on the obscenity of Stalin's actions represents a betrayal of his own utopian vision and opens the way for serious questions about the validity of his approach.[26] Reflecting on the criticisms of Bloch's position that appeared in reviews of the 1986 publication of the English translation of *The Principle of Hope,* Jack Zipes observes that what is most disconcerting about Bloch's utopianism is that "it simply labels other philosophical positions as bourgeois and irrational when they do not comply with the direction his own thought takes."[27] Zipes sees this tendency toward "rigid uncertainty" stemming from Bloch's "firm belief in the messianic telos of his philosophy" and his insistence upon holding to what he considered to be the correct positions of Marxist analysis (4–5). Although he recognizes the creatively negative side of Bloch's utopianism which attacks orthodoxy and seeks for ways to work through it, Zipes persists in asking if Bloch's utopian Marxism itself "prevented him from seeing reality" (6). He questions the extent to which Bloch's interpretation of the October Revolution as a step along the "red line of history" was the result of a flaw in his theory of utopian discourse, a flaw which prevented him from confronting the problems inherent in Stalinism. In other words, what Zipes and other contributors to a special 1988 issue of *New German Critique* explore is whether Bloch's blindness to Stalinism was due to a problem inherent in his very philosophical method – or to what extent it was due to a personal/political accommodation with the apparently leading edge of the communist movement of his time. In actuality, it seems to have been a combination of both. Although, as can be seen in the reception of Bloch by theologians and others since the 1960s, his utopian Marxism ultimately surpasses his Stalinist accommodations – and does so most effectively in his analysis of the radically subversive function of religious discourse. Indeed, as an examination of the dialogic tensions in *The Principle of Hope* indicates, Bloch's utopian method includes the necessary elements for preventing the sort of hypostatization that led to the tactical accommodation with Stalinism and thereby inhibited the further development of a utopian communist strategy in his time.

Jan Robert Bloch, Bloch's son, writing in the same issue of *New German Critique*, addresses these painful and complex contradictions in ways that uncover the more personal side of Bloch's accommodation with Stalinism. While the younger Bloch recognizes the value of his father's privileging of the "upright gait as the basic ethical rule," he also observes that the revolutionary history of the upright gait "contains the negation of human dignity, contains crimes, above all, the crimes of the avowedly upright on the basis of their law."[28] In a clear example of the anxiety of influence, he asks how it was possible that his father's "revolutionary-utopian Humanum went along with inhuman despotism" (15). In unlocking this riddle, however, the son does not seek to kill the father by invalidating Bloch's entire method. Rather, in a dialectical effort to salvage Bloch's work from its own worst tendencies, he seeks "to liberate the philosophical gold from the debris of a moral system which clung abstractly and therefore relentlessly to the upright gait, though humans broke under its force" (15).

Jan Bloch begins his analysis by explaining that in the face of the overt evil of fascism, Bloch "transfigured the USSR into a revolutionary emblem" (16) which prevented further criticism of that concrete utopia as long as the twin evils of German and US oppression existed.[29] He argues that this short-sighted political commitment prevented Bloch from further investigation of the wrong-doings of the "utopian" society

upon which he had placed all his bets. In the Soviet Union, for all of his
warnings of the dangers of conflating ideology and utopia, Bloch
described a utopia without darkness – or at least a utopia whose darkness
was less vicious than that which raged beyond its borders in Germany
and the United States.

Ernst Bloch's analytical skills failed him, then, at the point where
because of his personal commitment he neglected the critical strength
of his own method. His personal stubbornness combined with a privileging of his teleological principle of hope produced the ideological trap
that led to his uncritical support for the Soviet Union. As his son put it,
Bloch's

> heart ... was so much with the new Jerusalem, with Lenin, that until our
> times he shut his eyes to the victims of the "red tsars" of Soviet reality, whose
> existence he himself had suspected early on. He never grasped the scope of
> the disaster and was not able to: just as love makes one blind. [24]

Jan Bloch finds the flaw in his father's thinking in the gap between
"his long breath sweeping over eons" that expresses the utopian hope
in the telos of history and his myopic inability to see the real problems
in his Soviet utopia. Bloch was trapped not only by his loyalty but also
by a twofold error within his own method. On one hand, he adopted a
tactical tolerance of Stalinism that resulted from his strategic belief in
the power of the utopian telos to pull history forward, for he identified
what he considered to be the concrete utopian phenomena of Marxist
science and the Soviet system as necessary steps along a linear path that
ended with the classless society. On the other hand, because of this
slippage into ideological hypostatization and because of his persistent
focus on what he believed to be the greater evils of the Nazi and
American powers, he neglected the critical and negative aspects of the
utopian function that could have challenged and subverted even the
most apparently progressive of concrete utopias.

Here, then, is the dilemma of Ernst Bloch's utopian politics and of
his utopian method. Although a long-range vision enables humanity to
move beyond the darkness of the lived moment, unless that vision
includes an immediate critique of the ideological appropriation of the
"utopian" achievements along the way, that vision itself can betray the
very processes which are meant to lead toward it. If a given situation
produces an overemphasis on the long-range goal by either the arrogance of a triumphal Marxism or the fear of an impending defeat by
opposing powers – or, in Bloch's case, in a complex mixture of both –
that stunted application of the power of hope can easily destroy the
utopian function. In other words, unless both moments of the critical
dialectic of the utopian function are maintained – unless the negative,
denunciatory moment and the positive, annunciatory moment are both

employed so that each challenges the limitations of the other – the utopian method will fail through an acceptance of the provisional "success" valorized by short-sighted ideology.

Jan Bloch's critique of his father's work, therefore, is partly a response by the son to the stubbornness of the father, of the upright revolutionary patriarch who refused to be swayed by the contradictions of political history as he remained loyal to the October Revolution long after its agenda was betrayed. But it is also a recognition of the limitation of the utopian method itself if that method lapses into the sort of hypostatization that it was meant to oppose. If the utopian goal is valorized at the expense of the utopian project, the method fails. In this manner, at the very least during the years from 1934 to 1938, Bloch lost sight of his utopian dialectic and became a prisoner of his ideological allegiances.[30] That loss of perspective seems to have begun with Bloch's unwillingness to adhere to the critical unorthodoxy of his early years. From there, the political position that resulted from the combination of his hatred of fascism and what he saw as its North American counterpart with his theoretical proclivity to trust in the Soviet Union as a necessary station along the yellow brick road of communist progress became a stance which he could not easily abandon. In a Faustian bargain with the Stalinist devil for the promise of the hoped-for future, Bloch discounted the price that he had to pay for his capitulation to the "official" version of the revolutionary process. In so doing, he sacrificed the philosophical gold of utopia for the fool's gold of Stalinist ideology. Hence, the times in which Bloch lived, and the way in which he belonged to them, led him to refuse to engage in an effectively utopian critique of his own adopted concrete utopia, the Soviet Union.

At the end of his examination of his father's work, Jan Bloch argues that it "was almost inconceivable that Bloch would have renounced the Red October" because he "was too religious for that" (36). On the contrary, given Bloch's understanding of the persistent power of religious anticipation to pull humanity forward (especially after the meta-religious discourse has been liberated from its accumulated hypostatizations), the problem that Bloch faced was that, in his fatal attraction to the Soviet Union, he was not religious enough. Rather than holding to the dual strategy of negative dehypostatization and positive anticipation, he settled, at least until the late 1950s, for a tactically hypostatized vision. Even here, however, that tactical move paradoxically allowed him to carry on his own utopian strategy – for the benefit of many to come after him.[31]

V

Our ideological development is just such an intense struggle within us for hegemony among various available verbal and

ideological points of view, approaches, directions, and values.
The semantic structure of an internally persuasive discourse
is *not finite*, it is *open*; in each of the new contexts that dialogize
it, this discourse is able to reveal ever newer *ways to mean*.
                                                    M.M. Bakhtin[32]

There is, then, in Bloch's *Principle of Hope* a dialogic tension between a
historically entrenched orthodox Marxism with its strong belief in the
linear progression toward the communist telos of history and an
unorthodox understanding of the fragmentary and disruptive play of
utopia throughout human existence.[33] The major methodological difficulty in Bloch's philosophy of hope lies in his overemphasis of the
traditional Western category of the telos, the apparently powerful omega
point at the end of history that pulls human emancipation forward. To
the extent that Bloch privileges this totalizing telos in the name of
communism's triumph he dilutes the subversive power of the utopian
function as it wends its way through the cracks of everyday life.
Furthermore, to the extent that he emphasizes the purely rational,
scientific nature of his work as it grows out of Enlightenment thought,
he also devalues his discoveries of the persistence of the utopian
function in social spaces where the rational Marxist would no longer
look: in the culture of fascism, for example, or in religion, or in the
finality of death.

Bloch reveals his linear, teleological side throughout his work. In his
discussion of religion, he often presents a version of utopia that draws
on metaphors of *maturity* and *perfection* achieved at the end point of the
totality of history. In his discussion of the contribution that religious
founders make to the conscious movement "towards utopian reality"
Bloch makes the following statement:

> And the growing self-commitment [of the founder, such as Moses or Jesus]
> is finally grounded in that specific venturing beyond with which every
> religious act begins ... This specific venturing beyond, the *more mature
> religions become*, proves to be that of the most powerful hope of all, namely
> that of the Totum of a hope which puts the whole world into rapport with *a
> total perfection*. [1,192, my emphasis]

Here, the careful interpretation and appropriation of religious space as
a contested site for the utopian impulse collapses in a heavy-handed
imposition of images of maturity and totality that are part of the legacy
of Bloch's inheritance of the Western Enlightenment, with its
accompanying attitude of bourgeois arrogance and confidence.

One of the best examples of Bloch's reduction of utopia's creative
potential by means of his uncritical adherence to Soviet ideology and
unmediated teleological thought occurs in his discussion of ideology

and utopia in the first volume of *The Principle of Hope*. Certainly, he grasps the power of the anticipatory consciousness as it informs and exceeds the ideologies in which it has been enlisted as a motivating force throughout Western history. Yet, once he addresses the role of the utopian function within the Soviet socialist movement of his own time, he enters the dead end of his own hypostatization of history.

In his analysis of the symbiotic relationship between ideology and utopia, Bloch describes how ideology exploits utopian vision even as it restricts the potential of that vision to the requirements of a dominant class. He recalls Marx's comments in *The Holy Family* that the historically successful "interests" of a rising class produce a "cultural surplus" as their limited thoughts are phrased in terms of ideas that express the needs and aspirations of humanity in general, and he identifies that surplus vision as the "effect of the utopian function" (156). That surplus, he argues, can be revived for further movement forward. As he puts it, "these blossoms definitely can be removed from their first socio-historical soil, since they themselves ... are not bound to it" (155). He understands the utopian function as a dynamic social force that both motivates ideologies and carries human aspirations beyond their encapsulation within ideologies, and he understands that such aspirations can be enlisted long after their particular historical moment in the further movement of human emancipation.

However, once Bloch turns to the discussion of the role of the utopian impulse within actually existing socialism, he reduces the power of the utopian function to the status of a tool in the hands of the correct and inevitable masters of history who operate without the limitations of ideological mystification. To be sure, he rejects "merely abstract utopianizing" which is not rooted in the objective considerations of the material possibilities at hand, and he privileges the "power of anticipation" carried out within "*concrete utopia . . .* with its open space and its object which is to be realized and which realizes itself forwards" (157, my emphasis). Yet, the difficulty arises when he identifies the role within socialism of this "methodological organ for the New" (157) as one that simply reorganizes the surplus of utopian visions that have survived beyond their own ideological moments and have remained latent in the history of the Western consciousness. In its socialist manifestations, the utopian function awakens the utopian surplus of the past from its ideological slumber only to send it along "the attempted path and content of known hope" which has become synonymous with existing socialism.

The tension between the disruptively utopian and the teleologically utopian in Bloch can be more extensively seen in the contrast between the closing section of *The Principle of Hope*, "Karl Marx and Humanity: Stuff of Hope," and the penultimate section, "The Last Wishful Content and the Highest Good." In "The Last Wishful Content," Bloch cautions against the trap of false utopias whose contents have become ideologically fixed in an overconfident sense of what is better at the given moment. Recalling the proverb that "the better is the enemy of the good," he warns against foolish wishes and ideal value-images that prevent movement toward a utopia that, in the best sense of Bloch's work, is never fully achieved in terms of fixed content. He insists that the primary utopian drive rooted "in hunger, in need" (1,321) can be found as "surplus" in most of the idealized formations of ideology. In this light, he reads particular utopian figures such as the image of Jesus in the heretical sects of the middle ages or the revolutionary ideal of the bourgeois citizen as subversive signifiers which lead to versions of existence beyond what they mean in their own time. Even in this section, however, Bloch tends to explain the forward pull of these guiding images in terms of an "all-embracing purpose" of what is "humanly final" (1,317). Yet, as long as he maintains a balancing caution against ideological fixation, his use of the categories of totality and finality remain at a level of provocative utopian tropes rather than categorical imperatives that order all which comes before them. In the temptation to "stay awhile" which carries with it the danger of becoming encased in a given ideological matrix, Bloch still identifies a moment when one is on the edge of a "good" that goes beyond what is offered.

Bloch, therefore, understands the danger of hypostatizing the category of the "highest good." Utopian images, even of the highest order, provide not finished content but rather "relentless invariance of direction towards a content" (1,324) so that the highest good is the sliding signifier of a "goal which is not yet formed" (1,324). He recognizes that the key images of that highest good – the religious God, the atheist Kingdom of God, and the communist realm of freedom – are ideals that reveal tendencies but not finished constructs of what human existence must be. For the world is "a process" based in the materiality of existence which may be subjected to human intention and goals but which always remains a separate category, with its own "allied potential" (1,327). This process discourages human intentionality from exclusively determining the shape of things to come because "every formation of value is dependent on the tendency-latency in its material" (1,333) so that a hypostatized version of attainment alone cannot fully account for the process. Therefore, "the hope of the highest value or of the highest good, this last conceivable border-ideal, contains both Self and World, in a manner which points the utopian way" (1,333) but which does not reduce that utopian movement to one system of perfection. In the encounter of human aspiration and the materiality of the world, there is always a surplus; for "only the best still hungers" and resists whatever "attempted figures of perfection" are superimposed upon it. Consequently, utopian "ciphers" need to be understood by means of a "material theory of signs" wherein such ciphers are read as provisional encapsulations within "available meanings" but which also always already exceed those meanings. Although there is movement toward what is felt to be a "final figure" (1,345), at its best Bloch's philosophy of hope never rests satisfied with that absolute sign. Authentic utopian symbols are ones where "the thing signified is still disguised from itself," but they also are figures which have to be played through a concrete mediation with the possibilities of the given material world. They are not simply "attainable by a mechanical-levelling world picture" (1,346). Utopian symbols, in other words, are "solely *tension*-forms, dialectical material *process*-figures" which "have around then, before them, the *uncompleted-ness* of latency" (1,351). There may well be "utopian edges of meaning" around all signifiers, but they are not reducible to the content of those signifiers. Bloch therefore cautions against "mythical hypostases" (1,329) that reduce the images of the highest good to static accomplishments. He states that the authentically highest good

> dawns thus in the entire potential of matter ... This, its kingdom-figure which does not yet exist, governs throughout great dangers, hindrances and orbitings, all the other figures of the good path, and in it the Authentic, according to the intention, is formed like joy. *These are the frontier definitions of intention towards the highest good and the frontier concepts of every thought that moves toward the Absolute of human wanting.* [1,353]

At this juncture, Bloch is at his critical best. He insists that the utopian function includes both the power to define fulfillment as well as the power to resist *all* efforts to contain its potentially unbounded hope in any hypostatized definition.

Unfortunately, in the next section, the narrative telos of his entire study, Bloch violates this methodological strategy. In "Karl Marx and Humanity: Stuff of Hope," he commits the very act of mythical hyposta-tization that he rails against throughout the three volumes. Driven by the needs of his times and his inherited Enlightenment and Marxist arrogance, he puts the brakes on his utopian process by hypostatizing the Absolute Subject of Marx and the fixed communist project of a scientifically attained classless society. In this section, Marx becomes the "true architect" (1,354) who *finally* empowers humanity to actively comprehend itself. "Genuine Marxism," for Bloch, "in its impetus, its class struggle, and its goal-content is, can be, will be nothing but the promotion of humanity. And, in particular, all the cloudings and deviations along the way can only be really criticized, indeed removed, within Marxism" (1,358). Going further in this hypostatization, Bloch makes theory and not people the active agent of progress as he asserts that "in those countries *where Marxism took power* ... quarters are arranged for the future" (1,367). This, then, is the site of Bloch's methodological faultline and the source of his emotional blindness that found its outlet in his uncritical support of Stalinism. This is the deep flaw in the philosophy of hope: namely, that it settles for a teleological end point located in a militant hypostatization of those items which inspired its forward motion in the first place – reducing them to the limits of Soviet Marxism and the Soviet state. At the point where Bloch's method should be opening up to whatever historical developments may yet occur in the unknown future, he clings tenaciously to the communist achievements of his time and place and thereby denies the future potential of the communist movement and his own method.

Nevertheless, contrary to the dire assessments of either his anti-communist or his revisionist critics, even at this darkest moment of his work Bloch still argues against the closure to which he himself had fallen prey. For in the hypostatizing chapter on Karl Marx, Bloch provides future students and practitioners of the utopian function with the wherewithal to deconstruct his own worst failures – to turn the utopian Bloch against the ideological Bloch. That countervailing strand of dialogic energy begins with the epigram from Lessing that introduces the section: "It is not true that the shortest line is always the straightest" (1,354). In this quotational gesture, he makes an opening cautionary gambit against the temptation to take the simplest way forward, whether that be in the act of making history or of reading the chapter at hand. Thus, as he celebrates Marx and the communist goal, Bloch warns that "no dreaming may stand still" (1,365), and he wisely observes that people have "always been expected to cut their coat according to their cloth" even as "their wishes and dreams did not comply" (1,365). Even when he mentions the "legitimately expectable and attainable goal" of "socialist humanization," he cautions that such a goal can be approached only if it is "not obscured by the inadequate, is not bitterly led away down false roads" (1,372). For human emancipation, he asserts, can be decided only in "open history, the field of objective-real decision" (1,372). He argues that "the unfinished world can be brought to its end, the process pending in it can be brought to a result, the incognito of the main matter which is really-cloaked in itself can be revealed" only if the tendency-latency of those hopes is constantly held open. "Hasty hypostases" and "fixed definition" cannot serve utopian anticipation. Bloch clearly sees that there is "no pre-ordered" teleology at work "in the dialectical tendency-latency, open to the Novum, of material process" (1,373).

To be sure, in defining such pre-ordered teleologies, Bloch refers to "old teleologies" and ones that "are mythically guided from above" (1,373), and in opposing Marxism against those dated positions he again moves outside of the potential of his method. At this point, Bloch's critical utopian logic demands that he reject the orthodoxy and the pre-ordered telos of his communist comrades, for they too would lock the tendency-latency into a premature solution. His inability to do so, as I argue above, is the result of his teleological bent and his own tactical blindness, but Bloch's failure of nerve at this point does not bring down the entire structure of his utopian philosophy. Indeed, in his closing pages, he argues against that failure when he discusses the "ontic hypostasis" of pre-Marxist philosophies whose self-fulfilling method leads to a result which "becomes the palace which is already complete anyway at the end of the path" (1,374). In contrast to such self-enclosed outlooks, he offers the concept of "the process-world, the real world of hope itself" wherein the "dialectically aimed, systematically open view into tendency-shaped matter" is the authentic form of utopian expectation (1,374). At the end of his own work, then, Bloch gives his best advice to his readers – and ironically to himself had he heeded it. He cautions against absolute goals, and asserts that the "best still remains patchwork" (1,375). He understands that "every end again and again becomes a means to serve the still utterly opaque, indeed in and for itself still unavailable goals, final goal" (1,375). The "final goal" at the end of *The Principle of Hope*, therefore, is not an achieved or predicted end but rather a trope for that which is never fully attained. To settle for any goal "on the way" is therefore to pause fatally on the path to a homeland which still lies ahead.

Thus, Bloch ends his massive study by playing out the dialogic tension that runs all through the work. In so doing, he reveals the nature of his dilemma. As he asserts in his discussion of ideology and utopia, the utopian function serves as a critical and forward-looking force up to the point of socialism. Yet, within existing socialism the utopian challenge to the limits of any given definition of reality and its possibilities – especially as that reality is defined within the terms of a ruling ideology – is no longer required. Consequently, the utopian function under such conditions becomes a limited method for appropriating the lost visions of the past for the apparently clear-headed work of what is taken to be the new society. In the privileging of the inheritance of Western culture which stems from his European bourgeois background and in his political loyalty to the Soviet Revolution which stems from a combination of his philosophical belief in the correctness of Marxism and of his existential interpretation of both the United States and Nazi Germany as far greater evils, Bloch represses the most critical aspects of his utopian function precisely at the moment when they were most needed in his own time and place.

Throughout *The Principle of Hope*, therefore, Bloch fights against his own best insights. He articulates the critical power of the utopian impulse, and in so doing he teaches others to read against the grain of their time and to tease out the traces of human expectation. Yet, from the beginning to the end of his magnum opus, he regularly falls short of applying the power of that utopian critique to his own historical situation. Thus, Benjamin's advice returns. For what Bloch's principles of hope needed was an external challenge that would have exposed the dialogic contradictions of his work and set its best insights free. Or, as

Laclau and Mouffe would put it, his work required the rupture of its sutured integrity by means of an encounter with another radical discursive system in order to free it from its own discursive blindness. As the progressive theologians realized, a demystified and open-ended critical theology – rooted in present suffering and struggle and suspicious of all provisional teleologies – appears to have been Bloch's methodological way beyond this dilemma. Filtering the utopian function through the medium of theological critique and vision provided the needed mediation between political praxis and the hoped-for realm of freedom.

Obviously the discursive and political power of such an external challenge did not fully develop until after *The Principle of Hope* was completed, but then – echoing Benjamin's original advice – the theologians of the 1960s carried out such an operation in their appropriation of Bloch (and in doing so made Bloch's radical utopianism more readily available for the new secular left). Seeking ways to rewrite religious discourse so that it spoke to conditions of the modern world, European, North American, and Latin American theologians found a theoretical fellow traveller in this Marxist philosopher who both respected their own accumulated tradition and provided them with a method for dialectically transcending it. Unlike Bloch, however, they did not inhibit their thinking with an ideological hypostatization of their own theology. Instead, they turned Bloch's critical utopian Marxism against his limitations as well as their own and thereby generated a radical method that appreciates the signs of the times and constantly looks beyond them to newly emergent possibilities in human society.

In the work of the Latin American liberation theologians, especially, Bloch's articulation of the power of the utopian function resists closure by any ideological position – even one that occurs within the theoretical and pastoral structures of the liberation church itself. The liberation theologians have been able to "pluck the living flower" of Bloch's utopian function from the shortcomings and failures of his method and his own employment of that method. They have dialectically taken the utopian function to a new moment in the history of the human struggle for justice and fulfillment. Rather than simply exposing the failings of this unorthodox Marxist and cynically accepting the status quo of a world informed by anti-communism and dominated by transnational capitalism, they have dared to challenge that pervasive system in the name of a future that draws on the best of both Christian and Marxist praxis. Their critical strategy is not a backward, nostalgic opportunism, but rather an embracing of a revolutionary process that is still emerging from and beyond the limits of Western discourse.[34]

Notes

1. Quoted in Bloch, *The Principle of Hope*, trans. Neville Plaice, Stephen Plaice, and

Paul Knight (Cambridge, Mass.: MIT Press, 1986), 3 vols, p. 1,183. Unless noted, references to Bloch are to *The Principle of Hope*. I would like to dedicate this essay to Basil O'Leary, my teacher and friend, on the occasion of his seventieth birthday.

2. Walter Benjamin, "Theses on the Philosophy of History," *Illuminations*, trans. Harry Zohn (New York: Schocken, 1969), p. 252.

3. In the 1960s, influenced by liberal Protestant theologians such as Karl Barth, Rudolph Bultmann, and Dietrich Bonhoeffer, by the philosophies of phenomenology and existentialism, as well as by the activism of the Catholic Action movement, modern Christianity sought renewal in various ways. In the early 1960s, the Second Vatican Council was an attempt by the official Roman Catholic Church to open its windows to the world, but the Marxist-Christian dialogues in the mid-1960s engaged in a more radical level of interchange than that which had occurred on the contested terrain of the Vatican Council. See, for example, Roger Garaudy, *From Anathema to Dialogue: A Marxist Challenge to the Christian Churches*, trans. Luke O'Neill (New York: Herder & Herder, 1966). For an interesting example of work affected by the Marxist-Christian dialogues, see Terry Eagleton, *The New Left Church* (Baltimore: Helicon, 1966), and the *Slant Manifesto* produced by the group of left-wing Christians with whom Eagleton was associated in the early to mid 1960s. Although occurring later, there has also been a productive reception of Bloch within Jewish theology. See Marc H. Ellis, *Towards a Jewish Theology of Liberation* (Maryknoll, NY: Orbis, 1987); and Anson Rabinbach, "Between Enlightenment and Apocalypse: Benjamin, Bloch and Modern Jewish Messianism," *New German Critique*, 34 (Winter 1983), pp. 78–125.

4. This encounter between Christianity and Marxism can be understood in terms of the work of Laclau and Mouffe which describes the way in which a "sutured" or closed discourse can be opened to new possibilities of analysis and action through a process of "interruption" or subversion by an external discourse. As they argue, "it is only in terms of a different discursive formation" that the "positivity" of the categories of a given discourse can be challenged and changed. In other words, what is needed is a "discursive 'exterior' from which the discourse in question can be interrupted" (see Ernesto Laclau and Chantal Mouffe, *Hegemony and Socialist Strategy: Towards a Radical Democratic Politics*, trans. Winston Moore and Paul Cammack (London: Verso, 1985), pp. 152–9).

5. Gustavo Gutiérrez, *A Theology of Liberation: History, Politics, Salvation*, ed. and trans. Sister Caridad Inda and John Eagleson (Maryknoll, N.Y.: Orbis, 1973), p. 66. Douglas Kellner and Harry O'Hara ("Utopia and Marxism in Ernst Bloch," *New German Critique*, 9 [Fall 1976], pp. 11–35), rightly resist a simple co-optation of Bloch by theologians of any stripe and point out the important break with institutional Christianity that Bloch's work represents. However, I fear they fall into an orthodox Marxist trap of rejecting all revolutionary potential in the religious sphere and miss the subtleties of Bloch's refunctioning of religious space. As Gerard Raulet notes, "Bloch's thought rediscovers the meaning of Marx's statement that the critique of religion is the precondition of all critique" ("Critique of Religon and Religion as Critique: The Secularized Hope of Ernst Bloch," *New German Critique*, 9 [Fall 1976], p. 84).

6. Marx, letter to Ruge, quoted Bloch, p. 156.

7. Jürgen Moltmann, "Hope and Confidence: a Conversation with Ernst Bloch," *Dialog*, 7 (1968), pp. 42–55.

8. Kenneth Heinitz, "The Theology of Hope according to Ernst Bloch," *Dialog*, 7 (1968), p. 39.

9. Quoted in Gutiérrez, *A Theology of Liberation*, p. 240.

10. Ronald M. Green, "Ernst Bloch's Revision of Atheism," *Journal of Religion*, 49 (1969), p. 128.

11. For Bloch, Feuerbach represents the point at which "the final history of Christianity begins" (1,286). Feuerbach

> brought religious content . . . back to man, so that man is not made in the image of God but God in the image of man . . . As a result God as the creator of the world disappears completely, but a gigantic creative region in man is gained, into which – with fantastic illusion, with fantastic richness at the same time – the divine as a hypostatized human wishful image of the highest order is incorporated. [1,284–1,285]

The limitation of Feuerbach, however, is that he "knows man . . . only in the form of existence in which he has so far appeared, an abstractly stable form of existence, that of the so-called species of man ... above all man's uncompletedness is missing here" (1,285). Bloch therefore breaks with Feuerbach's mechanical materialism: "There is least place ... in Feuerbach's statically existent subject for status-shattering images of religion" (1,285). In Bloch's analysis, "religion as inheritance (meta-religion) becomes ... the act of transcending without any heavenly transcendence but with an understanding of it; as a hypostatized anticipation of being-for-itself" (1,288).

12. As Rabinbach puts it, Bloch "rejects the view accepted by Marxism, if not by Marx himself, that religion is merely a compensation for an unpalatable and painful existence. The paradox of the rationalized world is that it cannot contain the powerful forces within human beings which not only created belief and affirmation in the past, but also constantly emerge to challenge it in the present. Religion is not merely the expression of conditions which demand illusion, but a human potential that nourishes itself with illusion only insofar as it cannot fully find expressions in reality" ("Ernst Bloch's *Heritage of Our Times* and the Theory of Fascism," *New Germn Critique*, 11 [Spring 1977], p. 9).

13. An analysis of Bloch's treatment of religions other than Judaism and Christianity must wait for another time, but a consideration of Bloch's work from the perspective of Edward Said's critique of orientalism would be an enlightening project.

14. For more on messianism and its creatively destructive power by Bloch and Benjamin, see Rabinbach, "Between Enlightenment and Apocalypse."

15. For more on the implicit atheism of Judaism and Christianity, see Bloch, "Religious Truth," *Man on his Own: Essays in the Philosophy of Religion*, trans. John Cuming (New York: Herder & Herder, 1971); and Moylan, "Rereading Religion: Ernst Bloch, Gustavo Gutiérrez and the Post-Modern Strategy of Liberation Theology," *Center for Twentieth Century Studies Working Papers*, 2 (Fall 1988).

16. Franz J. Hinkelammert, *The Ideological Weapons of Death: A Theological Critique of Capitalism*, trans. Phillip Berryman (Maryknoll, NY: Orbis, 1986), p. 273.

17. Harvey Cox, "Ernst Bloch and 'The Pull of the Future,'" *New Theology No. 5*, ed. Martin Marty and Dean G. Peerman (New York: Macmillan, 1968), p. 201.

18. Ibid., pp. 201–2.

19. My summary and critique of Moltmann and Metz (see below) draws on their own work and on Gutiérrez's assessments. References to Gutiérrez's work are to *A Theology of Liberation* (1973 edn.): for Moltmann, see pp. 216–19; for Metz, see pp. 220–25.

20. See Johannes B. Metz, *Theology of the World*, trans. William Glen-Doepel (New York: Herder & Herder, 1969), pp. 110–14.

21. The influence of liberation theology can also be seen in those areas of the First World which now figure as "Third World" sectors of the economic and social machinery of global capitalism. These include, for example, Ireland, Spain, and the predominantly Hispanic areas of the southwestern United States (especially in Los Angeles and along the US–Mexican border).

22. For the history of liberation theology, see Phillip Berryman, *Liberation Theology*; Peadar Kirby, *Lessons in Liberation*; and Penny Lernoux, *Cry of the People*. For my analyses of Gutiérrez, see "Rereading Religion" and "Mission Impossible: Liberation Theology and Utopian Praxis," *Utopian Studies III*, ed. Michael Cummings and Nicholas D. Smith (Lanham, NY: University Press of America, 1990), pp. 33–65.

23. For more on Bloch's image of the "upright gait," see "Upright Carriage, Concrete Utopia," *On Karl Marx*, trans. John Maxwell (New York: Herder & Herder, 1971), pp. 168–73, especially.

24. For more on this section of Gutiérrez, see my "Mission Impossible."

25. Oskar Negt, "Ernst Bloch – The German Philosopher of the October Revolution," trans. Jack Zipes, *New German Critique*, 4 (Winter 1975), p. 9.

26. See "A Jubilee for Renegades" *New German Critique*, 4 (Winter 1975), pp. 17–26, for Bloch's defense of his support for the Moscow trials. For a historical perspective on Bloch's position, see Negt, "Ernst Bloch," and David Gross, "Bloch's Philosophy of Hope," *Telos*, 75 (Spring 1988), pp. 189–98.

27. Jack Zipes, "Introduction: Ernst Bloch and the Obscenity of Hope," *New German Critique*, 45 (Fall 1988), p. 4.

28. Jan Robert Bloch, "How Can We Understand the Bends in the Upright Gait?", *New German Critique*, 45 (Fall 1988), p. 10.

29. Bloch's criticism of the more subtle oppression perpetrated by US capitalism has yet to be addressed. As Jan Bloch suggests, the elder Bloch did not develop an adequate

dialectical reading of US society that identified the progressive potential as well as the exploitative dangers of the emerging consumer society; nevertheless, Bloch did anticipate the social failures of the postwar affluent society. In the light of his insights into the false promises of the "American utopia," Bloch's uncritical support of the Soviet Union is perhaps more understandable.

30. Zipes, "Introduction," p. 7.

31. For examples of Bloch's later repudiation of Stalinism, see "Upright Carriage, Concrete Utopia" and his interview with Landmann.

32. M.M. Bakhtin, *The Dialogic Imagination: Four Essays,* ed. Michael Holquist, trans. Caryl Emerson and Michael Holquist (Austin: University of Texas, 1981), p. 346.

33. I would be tempted to characterize the two strands running through Bloch's work as "anarchist" and "Marxist" if those words were not themselves subject to far too much ideological closure. Bloch's early political outlook is largely unexamined (as Rabinbach asserts in "Between Enlightenment and Apocalypse," p. 109), but Bloch's combination of anarchist, pacifist, expressionist, messianic, apocalyptic positions was radically unorthodox and appears to have fomented a deep strain of openness that never left his work and that constitutes one strand of his dialogic tension. Indeed, Bloch's later move into Marxism seems to have been prevented from becoming fully orthodox by his early sensibility. Contrary to Zipes's speculation that Bloch's early positions appear "to have prevented him from seeing reality" (Zipes, "Introduction," p. 6), it may well have been the opposite case that this radical base was the key factor that informed his method of reading utopia against the ideological grain and therefore the source of the attitude that kept him from totally adhering to the orthodox strand of his work.

34. For two examples of the critical post-Western discourse emerging from the indigenous cultures of Central America as they have been influenced by the intersection of Marxism and Christianity in liberation theology, see the essays of Tomás Borge, *Christianity and Revolution,* and the *testimonio* of Rigoberta Menchú. For an example of a theoretical effort to support such developments by a sympathetic Western intellectual (Australian, living and writing in the US), see Michael T. Taussig, *Shaminism, Colonialism, and the Wild Man: A Study in Terror and Healing* (Chicago and London: University of Chicago Press, 1987). In his chapter on "Magical Realism," Taussig discusses the ways in which the discursive strategy of magical realism (*lo real maravilloso* – the magically real) works not only in Latin American high culture but also in the popular culture of groups such as the Putumayo Indians of the Upper Amazon to subvert the sacred and secular colonial myths of conquest and redemption by reworking them into expressions of resistance and revolution. Taussig explains this discursive strategy in terms of Bloch's concept of "nonsynchronous development" in which images of the past are refunctioned to serve the hope of a better future (see pp. 165–6). For more on Menchú, see John Beverley, "The Margin at the Center: On *Testimonio* (Testimonial Narrative)," *Modern Fiction Studies,* 35: I (Spring 1989), pp. 3–11, and George Yúdice, "Marginality and the Ethics of Survival," in *Universal Abandon? The Politics of Postmodernism,* ed. Andrew Ross (Minneapolis: University of Minnesota Press, 1988), pp. 214–37.

8

Locus, Horizon, and Orientation: The Concept of Possible Worlds as a Key to Utopian Studies

Darko Suvin

In memory of Ernst Bloch

The truth is not in the beginning but in the end, or better in the continuation.

Lenin, *Philosophical Notebooks*

1. The Pragmatics of Utopian Studies[1]

Pragmatics has been much neglected in literary and cultural studies. In the semiotic sense in which I am using it, it was defined already by Charles Morris as the domain of relationships between the signs and their interpreters, which clarifies the conditions under which something is taken as a sign. From C.S. Peirce, G.H. Mead, and Karl Bühler, through Bakhtin/Vološinov, Morris, Carnap, and the Warsaw School, to, say, R.M. Martin, Leo Apostel, and John R. Searle, pragmatics has slowly been growing into an independent discipline on a par with syntactics (the domain of relationships between the signs and their formally possible combinations) and with semantics (in this sense, the domain of relations between the signs and the entities they designate). But what is more, there are since the late 1950s strong arguments that it is a constitutive and indeed englobing complement of both semantics and syntactics. The basic – and to any materialist, sufficient – pair of arguments for it is, first, that all objects and events are (only or also) signs and, secondly, that any object or event becomes a sign only in a *signifying situation*; it has no "natural" meaning outside of it (e.g. in More's Utopia gold is a sign of shame). This situation is constituted by the relation between signs and their users; a user can take something to be a sign only as it is spatio-temporally concrete and localized, and as it relates to the user's disposition toward potential action. Both the concrete localization and the user's disposition are always socio-historical. Furthermore, they postulate a reality organized not only around signs

but also around subjects, in the double sense of psycho-physical personality and of a socialized, collectively representative subject. The entry of
potentially acting subjects reintroduces acceptance and choice, temporal genesis and mutation, and a possibility of dialectical negation into
the frozen constraints of syntax (in fact, by the most orthodox structur-
alist standards, only such dynamics can make the – temporary – stability
of any structure meaningful). It also regrounds semantics: each and
every semantic presupposition is also a pragmatic one, effected by a
subject, whether atomic or collective, as a choice in a socio-historical
signifying situation.

Thus, pragmatics could also be taken as the mediation between
semiotics and an even more general theory of action or practice. Only
pragmatics is able to take into account the situation of the sign
producers and its social addressees and the whole spread of their
relationships within given cognitive (epistemological and ideological)
presuppositions, conventions, economical and institutional frames, etc.
The pragmatic presuppositions about the signs' possible uses by their
users, as argued above, necessarily inscribe historical reality – as understood by the users – between the lines of any text.

In this semiotic perspective, "text" is understood in the widest sense
of an articulated and recordable signifying micro-system, of a coherent
unit of signic work. Any spatio-temporal organization which can stand
still for such a recording qualifies for this sense of "text;" and in fact
semiotics began with ancient medicine taking the body for its text or
ensemble of signs (signifying health or various sicknesses). Yet there are
problems if this imperialistic sense of text is absolutized: against the
deconstructionists, I believe that bodies and objects (and subjects) are
not only texts, for I don't see how a text can experience loss, delight, or
indeed death. In other words, organic and inorganic molecules may be
no more or less material than signs, but they are material in different
ways from signs. Thus, even if the sciences are, no doubt, texts (though
not purely verbal ones), the book of science is also, for all its partial
autonomy, an interpretation of the book of nature, which is the
presupposition of all scientific propositions.

Furthermore, what exactly are the pertinent categories which constitute any object of investigation (in the widest sense, including a whole
discipline) in the first place? This delimitation, which constitutes not
only the cognizable domain but also the possible ways of envisaging and
cognizing it, cannot be established from the object alone but only from
its interaction with the social subject whose pragmatic point of view or
approach is defining the pertinence, and by that token constructing the
object's cognitive identity (though not necessarily the extra-signic pre-
existence of the object's elements, etc.).

Now in the light of such an approach, what is the first pragmatic fact
about utopian scholarship?[2] Let me take as emblematic the situation I

know best, in North America, which also has undoubtedly the largest number of scholars and investigations in the "utopian" field (Italy and West Germany probably coming a close second), who meet regularly at national or international conferences, often publish in the same journals, etc. The central fact about their activities, it seems to me, is that they encompass what is at a first glance two rather different foci and scholarly corpuses, namely utopian fictional texts and utopian movements and communities. While it is undeniable that there are certain overlaps between these two corpuses, mediated by imaginary projects and attitudes related to a fictional imagination but intended to be the basis or seed for empirical construction of a micro- or macro-society, the corpuses are usually subjects of different disciplines and rather different methodologies and discourses. In one case, literary and textual approaches are mandatory, in the other a spectrum of approaches about which I am too ignorant to pontificate, such as the sociological or geographical. Again, it should not be denied that psychology can be applied to authors of both corpuses, that philosophy is applicable to the first principles of anything and any activity, that everything happens within given social and political histories, etc. Thus, it is not only semioticians who can and do claim that their discipline can explain at least an important aspect of anything and everything: philosophers, historians, etc. have just as good a claim to mediate (indeed, it is my stance that unless semiotics is informed by philosophy and social history, as it is in a number of Italian scholars, it remains at best a sterile and at worst a dubious syntax, as in most Parisian versions). Nonetheless, for all the doubtless existing and welcome mediations, I hope not to encounter too much resistance if I note here that, for all the partial overlap in corpuses and for all the possibilities of fertile cross-pollination between the approaches to them, there are still two distinct "wings" to "utopian studies," which I shall in a simplified manner call "the literary" (or fictional) and the "sociological" (or factual).

This could be well documented by a glance at the agendas of various conferences on utopia/s, but I shall here substantiate it only with help of the *Directory of Utopian Scholars*, edited by the meritorious pioneer of our field, Dr. Arthur O. Lewis, and used in its May 1986 edition. It contains 349 names of scholars (of whom 62 are from outside North America) with a brief self-characterization of "utopian interests" and "related interests." Striving for a pragmatic and functional but loyal interpretation of the meaning of these interests, I find that they substantiate my above impression, for they are best divided into three large groups. The two opposed poles are a dominant interest in empirical utopian communities and movements vs. a dominant interest in fictional utopias. By my imperfect count (since the interests are not always clearly spelled out) the "empirical" pole accounts for ca. 45 per cent and the "fictional" pole for ca. 33 per cent of the entries. In between them is a dominant interest in utopian philosophy and thought which accounts for ca. 20 per cent, while 1–2 per cent of the entries do not permit any clear identification. Now I will readily concede not only that my interpretation of the scholars' interests may well not be final, but furthermore that for other purposes other groupings could be just as legitimate. Nonetheless, I find that the "empirical" group is professionally mainly in social science departments or indeed in political or social agencies outside of universities, with a few geographers, architects or art historians as well as a few teachers of religion and of literature or natural sciences who are breaking out of the discipline boundaries. Their "related interests" are usually history, political theory, planning, religion, ecology, and/or futurology, more rarely literature or science and technology, even more rarely philosophy or feminism. On the contrary, in the opposite "fictional" group, the most frequent "related" interests are science fiction, women's studies, literary theory, and various segments of literary history or political philosophy, more rarely fantasy literature, religion, or science. Finally, the "in-between" or "utopian philosophy" group relates most strongly in its interests to intellectual history (including political thought), but there is also a smattering of most diverse interests from computers through aesthetics and space to peace and mysticism.

Thus, in spite of a number of scholars with significant overlaps between two of the above three groups (ca. 15 per cent), in spite of the intermediate philosophy group, and finally in spite of the fact that utopian scholars as a whole are indeed a group with unusually and refreshingly interdisciplinary interests, I think that this little survey confirms a question that might occur to anybody who has assisted at one of the national or international conferences of utopian studies or who has read some of the volumes arising from their work: just what is the common denominator, in corpus or methodology, between the interest in New Harmony or the Shakers and the interest in Morris's or Wells's fictional texts? Now of course we all know that Bellamy's books started a political movement with partly utopian hues; that the Marxists call most writers of societal blueprints from More to Wells and further "utopian socialists," with respect accorded to people before 1848 and increasing impatience with regard to people after that, etc. I am not at all arguing that there were or are no good reasons for a scholarly group to be interested in what interests the "utopian scholars." But even if we conceded their corpus presented some continuities (which would still leave many discontinuities and problems), just what is the *methodological* common denominator in approaches to and discourses about Oneida "free love" and More's use of dialogue and satire? Personally, I must confess that I often think of being in the presence of a two-headed monster. And if this impression is justified, if centrally or predominantly utopian scholarship uses two (or more) different discourses or methodologies, is not this at least a radical pragmatic problem and perhaps even an intellectual scandal? In sum, is utopian studies one discipline or (at least) two?

It could be objected that there is in practice a common denominator which has been used to rationalize this budding discipline, namely the concept of "utopian thought" practiced by pioneering scholars as different as Mannheim, the Manuels, and Bloch. This is empirically correct but philosophically and methodologically (to my mind) quite inconclusive. I cannot discuss this anywhere near as fully as it deserves, but it seems fairly clear that psychologically, philosophically, or politically free-floating "thought" pre-existing to wholly different methodologies and largely different corpuses is a woolly concept that raises as many questions as it solves. If utopian thought created the universe of utopian studies, one must ask about this creator the same questions as about a monotheistic God: and who or what created God (or the idea of utopia)? If one stops at the notion of the creator or of the Platonic idea, this is an act of belief, not of scholarship. In sum: the touchstone and minimal requirement for a real unity of our field would be, I believe, *the existence of some common and centrally significant tools of inquiry*, ensuring the possibility of some common lines of inquiry. Can they be found? The rest of this essay is a much too brief and admittedly schematic attempt to answer this question in a cautiously positive vein.

2. Paradoxes and Ambiguities in the Denial of Utopia

In this section I shall make an only apparent detour into a consideration of central ideological objections to utopia which dominate present-day bourgeois and techno-bureaucratic attitudes in the "real world" and are not rarely interjected by scholars dealing with utopia. The detour is apparent because, as argued above, pragmatics subsumes – but also needs to be based upon – not only syntactics but also semantics (in this case, of utopian studies).

Without pretending to an even approximate survey of the state of the art in the burgeoning utopian studies (*Utopieforschung*), I shall postulate two related paradoxes within them. I call the first the "paradox of incoherent denial of utopia" – of both utopian fiction and empirical projects for utopian communities. Utopia is denied *in toto* and *a limine* as static, dogmatic, and closed. And yet this critique is incoherent because a lot of evidence exists, marshaled into arguments by Wells, Zamiatin, Bloch, and others since them, that utopian fiction and projects have historically not always been closed, that indeed theoretically they may be either open or closed, and that no easy (much less automatic) correspondence exists between utopia on the one hand and either openness or closure on the other.

I shall in this second section focus on verbal, predominantly fictional, texts, and only later see whether the argument can be extended to an approach to all fields of utopian investigation. In that perspective it seems, first, arguable that most of the significant utopian texts historically were *not* closed but subject to varying degrees of openness or opening. Secondly, I see no good (methodo)logical reason why utopian texts *have to be* closed.

This section could be called "true, but." True: historically utopias arose at least once (with More) as a secularization of the static millennium and projection of a final Paradise onto Earth, as a political version of Earthly Paradise. But: even in More there is change (the Utopians open up to Greek knowledge and Christian religion). Not to speak of non-fictional – i.e. doctrinal or what the French call "doxic" – texts such as Gioacchino di Fiore's or Condorcet's, in Bacon and Mercier the notion of a more or less ongoing evolution appears. True: there are notoriously dogmatic elements in these three texts too, and such elements grow almost seamless in such "cold stream" centralizers as Campanella, who delineated his utopian locus as an astrological prison, or Cabet, who expressly calls his locus "an Eden ... a new Earthly Paradise."[3] But: there was always a critique of such closure from within utopianism, from its "warm stream": Pantagruel's unending voyage balances Hythloday's arrival, Morris responds to Bellamy, the use of conditional tense and approach in Wells's *A Modern Utopia* throws into relief the weakness of most of his other utopian fictions. Often this dialectics between the cold and warm currents within the utopian ocean of possibilities that opposes the status quo is to be found within a single text – in More's ancestral dialogue, in the succeeding hypotheses of Wells's equally paradigmatic Time Traveller, or in the succeeding series of stations of Mayakovsky's *Mystery Bouffe* and Platonov's *Chevengur*.[4] This is also quite clear in the latest utopian fiction wave, the best US utopian science fiction of the 1960s–70s: *The Dispossessed* by Ursula K. Le Guin, the (highly unjustly neglected) *Daily Life in Nghsi-Altai* tetralogy by Robert Nichols, and *Woman on the Edge of Time* by Marge Piercy, among others.

However, even if we were to find that almost the whole past tradition of utopian fiction was in fact static, dogmatic, and closed, this would not answer the logical and methodological question of whether utopia as a genre and orientation is since Wells (or since tomorrow) *necessarily* such. As Ernst Bloch rightly noted, "utopian thinking cannot be limited to the Thomas More kind any more than electricity can be reduced to the Greek substance elektron – amber – in which it was first noticed" (*Prinzip*, 14). Following such methodological and historical leads, I have argued that utopia was "an 'as if,' an imaginative experiment" and that literary utopias in particular were "a heuristic device for perfectibility, an epistemological and not an ontological entity;" and I have concluded that "if utopia is, philosophically, a method rather than a state it cannot be realized or not realized – it can only be applied."[5] This argument of mine was based on a quite respectable philosophical tradition, perhaps first noted in Plato's dictum that "we have traced a *model* of a good city" (*Republic*, 472e, my emphasis), and continuing down to Bloch's discussions of fashioning models for an unfinished and open world-process.[6] The dogmatic and eschatological *forma mentis* found in all laicized religious psychologies – e.g. in those partisans and enemies of socialism who believed that a perfect, utopian state could be realized, such as Stalin and Berdyaev – is therefore fundamentally wrong. As Italo Calvino wrote in "Per Fourier": "utopia [is] as a city which cannot be founded by us but can found itself within us, can build itself bit by bit in our capacity to imagine it, to think it through."[7] I would today reaffirm my quoted claim that utopia is a *method* rather than a *state*, but I would add that it is a method camouflaging as a state: the state of affairs is a signifier revealing the presence of a semiotic process of signification which induces in the reader's imagination the signified of a possible world, *not necessarily identical with the signifier.*

In effect, "any true understanding is dialogic in nature . . . Meaning is the effect of interaction between speaker and listener . . ."[8] It follows from such considerations that "to apply a literary text means first of all (wherever it may later lead) to read it as a dramatic dialogue with the reader;" and that, therefore, "utopia is bound to have an implicit or explicit *dramatic strategy* in its panoramic review conflicting with the 'normal' expectations of the reader. Though formally closed, significant utopia is thematically open: its pointings reflect back on the reader's 'topia;'" and I cited Barthes *a propos* of Fourier to the effect that the utopian *écriture* must mobilize at the same time an image and its contrary.[9] Converging with this, in a rich essay on Russian utopias, Jurij Striedter has pointed out that the utopian state represented in a novel should not be confused with the function of that novel: "The explicit or implicit reference to the external context, the dialogue with this polyphonic reality, counteracts the isolation and the abstract idealism of the utopian 'polis' itself."[10] In other words, even in the case of perfect stasis and closure in the signifier, the signifying process inscribed in or between the text's lines, and finally proceeding to contextual reference, will make for a larger or smaller opening of the signified. Or, in a probably much more adequate terminology: whether the vehicle (Frege's *Sinn*) be open or closed, the tenor will finally be a more or less open meaning (Frege's *Bedeutung*). Any utopian novel is in principle an ongoing feedback dialogue with the reader: it leaves to the reader "the task of transforming the closing of the 'completed' utopia (and utopian novel) into the 'dynamics' of his [sic] own mind in his own world."[11] But conversely, if the reader is Stalin or Berdyaev, even the dynamic Marxian permanent revolution will for him freeze into an ossified stasis: "the application of utopia depends on the closeness and precision of his reading."[12] And if this bent reader's readings come to rule, they will destroy the method (the Way) in order to preserve the state (the supposedly final Goal).

Possibly the most sophisticated argument for this thesis can be found in a remarkable review sparked by a remarkable book, Fredric Jameson's "Of Islands and Trenches" apropos of Louis Marin's *Utopiques*. Jameson sees in Marin's stance a proposal to grasp utopian discourse as a process (in Humboldt's terms the creative power of *energeia* rather than the created piece of work or *ergon*, in Spinoza's terms *nature naturans* rather than *natura naturata*). This proposal is also the repudiation of the

> conventional view of utopia as sheer representation, as the "realized" vision of this or that ideal society or social ideal ... It is possible to understand the utopian text as a determinate type of *praxis*, rather than as a specific mode of representation ... a concrete set of mental operations to be performed on ... those collective representations of contemporary society which inform our ideologies just as they order our experience of daily life.

In this vein, the utopian "real" is not "something outside the work, of which the latter stands as an image or makes a representation." What is "real" or perhaps operative in a utopian text is rather a set of elements participating in an allegorical referentiality, "interiorized in [the text's] very fabric in order to provide the stuff and the raw material on which the textual operation must work."[13]

Thus, I claim that utopia is not necessarily static and dogmatic; that indeed it is at least as probable to suppose it may intrinsically not be such as to suppose the opposite. If so, what are the reasons for the paradox of incoherent denial of utopia? My hypothesis is there are two:

First, *the errors of utopophiles*, who stressed either the openness of texts considered as final objects of analysis and/or the ideas to be found in the texts, neglecting the real location of utopian fiction and horizons in a feedback traffic with readers. As against this error, my thesis is that *utopias exist as a gamut of Possible Worlds in the imagination of readers, not as a pseudo-object on the page*. It becomes evident here that (even without going into the complex formalizations of an Eco) we cannot do without some elementary but indispensable semiotic distinctions, such as the one between syntactics, semantics, and pragmatics, or between signifier and signified, or vehicle and tenor. As a Bakhtinian dialogue with contextual readers, utopian possible worlds are in principle not closed.

Secondly, *the errors of utopophobes*, who ab/used the (practical as well as – or more than – theoretical) errors of utopophiles to concentrate on the vehicle, the utopian text on the page, in order to impugn both the semantic meanings and the syntactic closure-cum-value hierarchy which is formally unavoidable in it. Omitting the pragmatic tenor, they identified, without much ado, both these levels of the vehicle with political repression. The best one can say of this procedure is that it oscillates between ignorance and bad faith.

This situation permits a very unhealthy ambiguity between objectors to utopian orientation as such (or in general) and objectors to closed utopias (in particular). To somewhat simplify, the first group objects to utopian orientation because that orientation radically doubts and transcends the bourgeois construction of human nature and the capitalist economico-political power system. The second group objects to utopias because they *did* not – or, in metaphysical hypostasis, because they in principle *can* not – find the otherwise necessary way out of backward-looking ideologies and out of a globally destructive system. A strange alliance has thus come about, it seems, between bourgeois conservatives and anti-Stalinist leftists understandably (but also inconsistently) shell-shocked from the three totalizing political experiences of fascism, Stalinism, and massified consensus capitalism spreading from the USA. Perhaps the best names for this alliance are on the one hand Karl Popper, Thomas Molnar, and C.-G. Dubois, and on the other hand Theodor W. Adorno and Michel Foucault. I wish I could enter into this at greater length, but this rather easily provable point must be left for documentation in another place. There is little doubt that it has powerfully contributed to the pragmatics of what one German scholar has called "the denunciation of utopia."

3. Locus, Horizon, Orientation, and Possible World

To help in disambiguating the pragmatic puzzles presented so far, I propose *more semiotico* to introduce the paired concepts of "utopian locus" vs. "utopian horizon." Since most of the present discussions around utopia are a mediated reaction to Marxist projects or to developments claiming to be Marxian, it might be appropriate to go back to the origins: "Communism does not mean for us a state of affairs that ought to be brought about, an *ideal* which reality will have to follow. We call communism the *real* movement which abolishes the present state of affairs."[14] This is a constant attitude in the classical Marxist tradition. On the one hand, it is pretty clear what communism should *not* be – a way of people's living together with war, exploitation, and state apparatus, so that from Marx's key notion of alienation a utopian horizon can be inferred by contraries[15] and so that Lenin can write perhaps the greatest utopian work of this century, *The State and Revolution*. Yet on the other hand in this vein, the same Lenin answered Bukharin's query about future socialism with a vigorous affirmation that "what socialism will be . . ., we cannot predict."[16]

As Bloch noted, ever since Plato used the term *topos ouranios* (heavenly space or place, the locus of Plato's ideas), a clear signal had been given that utopian location (*Ortung*) is only seemingly spatial, if spatial is to be taken in the positivistic sense of photographable places (*Abschied*, pp. 43, 45–6). To find this signal indicative and illuminating is quite indepen-dent from ideological agreement with Plato's notion that such a non-positivistic space is necessarily a transcendent or heavenly place for ideas: it ain't necessarily so. What is to be retained from Plato's intuition is that in the utopian tradition *the actual place focused upon is not to be taken literally*, that it is less significant than *the orientation* toward a better place somewhere in front of the orienter. In the most significant cases, furthermore, even the place to be reached is not fixed and completed: it moves on. It is thus situated in an imaginary space which is a measure of and measured as value (quality) rather than distance (quantity): "it is a true not-yet-existing, a novum which no human eye hath seen nor ear heard" (*Abschied*, p 46). The necessary elements for meaningful (and certainly for utopian) movement are, then: (1) an agent that moves, and (2) an imaginary space in which it moves. In this essay I have unfortunately had to bracket out the extremely important agential aspects, which would contain the properly political problematics of who is the bearer of utopia/nism. However, I hope that sufficient initial illumination may come from the pertinent aspects of space. They are: (a) the place of the agent who is moving, his *locus*; (b) the *horizon* toward which that agent is moving; and (c) the *orientation*, a vector that conjoins locus and horizon. It is characteristic of horizon that it moves with the location of the moving agent; but it is, obversely, characteristic of orientation that it can through all the changes of locus remain a constant vector of desire and cognition. As Musil was to formulate it in a self-reflection on writing ironic utopias in *The Man Without Qualities*, a text that is itself emblematic for its intended signification of permanent movement through various loci in a fixed direction which is also a movable, expanding horizon: "A utopia, however, is not a goal but an orientation."[17]

The use of notions such as locus, horizon, and orientation is predi-cated on an analogy with conceptions of the empirical world. The "possible worlds" (henceforth abbreviated as PWs) of utopian fiction, which exist in the imagination of given social types and implied addressees of utopian texts, take their structures, wherever these are not expressly modified, from "natural worlds" (i.e. dominant conceptions thereof). A highly important aspect is that for a PW "the term of 'world' is not a manner of speaking: it means that the 'mental' or cultural life borrows its structures from natural life,"[18] that "our *hic et nunc*" has "a preferential status."[19] In the same vein, Marin concluded (significantly, by advancing from an openly parabolic text) that

> the natural world, as an organized and perceptually structured spatiotem-poral ensemble, constitutes the original text ... of all possible discourse, its "origin" and its constitutive environment ... All possible discourse is

enunciated only against the ground of the perceived world's significant space, by which it is surrounded.[20]

The fact that we can meaningfully effect this metaphoric analogy, that we can transport these three notions into a discussion not of practice but of verbal (or of all signic) constructs, constitutes, therefore, itself a highly significant meta-meaning. My contention (developed at length in my essay "The Performance Text") is that the interaction between the fictional elements presented in a text and the presuppositions of the implied reader induces in the readers a specific PW. This PW is constructed by and in the reader's constrained imagination; it is a tenor (signified) to be clearly distinguished from the isolated text or the text surface which is a vehicle (signifier). As argued in section 1, an element (work, agent, shape, color, change, or indeed a whole corpus) that can help to induce and constrain a PW for the reader becomes a sign only in a signifying situation. In the particular case of reading fiction a specific, imaginary PW of a fictional text is constituted by complex and intimate feedback with the readers on the basis of its *not* being identical with, and yet being imaginatively supported by, their empirical world (or empirical PW). This interaction ensures (among other things) that, whatever the spatio-temporal and agential signifiers, it is always *de nobis* or, more precisely and significantly, *de possibilibus pro nobis* that the fable narrates. It is the tension between the finite, often closed texts and the multivalent (im)possibilities facing the reader that creates the fictional utopia's basic openness.

Let me pursue some consequences of what I argued earlier, so that they may be judged by their fruits. Since without a utopian orientation our field of inquiry does not exist, so that its discussion has to be left to the discussion of utopian agents, what are the mutual relationships – or indeed the combinatorics – of locus and horizon? Can they give rise to a typology which would be a useful grid for utopian studies as a whole?

My approach has been (for all my abiding demurral against his pan-utopianism) stimulated and largely shaped by Ernst Bloch, the most important philosopher of utopia. The concept of horizon comes from phenomenology (Husserl, Merleau-Ponty, Ricoeur), from which I believe we also have much to learn. But Bloch refunctioned it into a socio-politically concrete tool within a "warm stream" Marxism. As I have argued earlier following in his tracks,[21] imaginary space shifts into time with the industrial and bourgeois revolutions. Therefore, I shall here briefly discuss Bloch's late hypothesis on elastic temporal structure in history, on the analogy of Riemannian space. Riemann assumed that the metrical field is causally dependent upon matter and that it changes with matter: the field is not a pre-existent static and homogeneous fixity but a process of changeable material feedback. With all due caution toward analogies from natural sciences (e.g. the awful example of

Heisenberg's indeterminacy): historical matter is at least as unequally distributed as matter in relativistic physics. No doubt, history would have to add to this at least the latent tendencies possibly present and, in the form of dominant alternatives, most probably present, in its matter.[22] Adapting Bloch's final "Theses on the Concept of Progress," I would say that the goal of utopia is in principle not a defined, localized, or fixed humaneness but a not-yet-manifest type of human relationships, a "hominization" in Engels's or Teilhard's sense. This is "a depth dimension (*Tiefenbeziehung*) of the Onwards" (*Tübinger*, p. 147); from which it follows that there can be no final, "classical" or canonical locus of utopianism.

In my proposed terms, this can be systematized as *the dominance of Horizon over Locus*. Locus does not coincide with but interacts with Horizon: this makes for a dynamic, open utopia (e.g. Platonov's *Chevengur*, Le Guin's *The Dispossessed*). I shall characterize it in the words of a brilliant graduate student of mine: "The tension in *The Dispossessed* is not between a voyager from here and now (the familiar) and the utopian locus (the strange), but between the utopian hero and the utopian locus."[23] I would add that this is so because the hero or protagonist embodies here the orientation toward a moving (in this case, an anarcho-communist) utopian horizon.

The second possibility would be that *locus coincides with or swallows horizon*: this makes for a dogmatic, static, closed utopia (e.g. Campanella's *Civitas Solis*, Cabet's *Voyage en Icarie*):

A doctrinaire, or dogmatic, utopian text ... asserts the utopian focus as "ultimate" and drastically limits the possibilities of the utopian horizon; an *open-ended* text, on the other hand, portrays a utopian locus as a mere phase in the infinite unfolding of the utopian horizon, thereby abolishing the limits imposed on it by classical utopian fiction.[24]

The third possibility would be to have locus (by now to my mind a pseudo-utopian locus) alone, i.e. without a utopian horizon: this makes for heterotopia. The best theoretical example is of course Foucault, and the best fictional one his disciple Samuel Delany's *Triton*, also a direct polemic with *The Dispossessed*'s "ambiguous utopia" explicitly couched in terms of heterotopia. Both these science-fiction novels

[do away] with the doctrinaire identification of the utopian locus with the utopian horizon. Delany, however, goes one step further: he also does away with the utopian horizon itself. In Le Guin, too, the utopian horizon is not actual, solid; yet the utopian horizon, appearing as an urge towards certain actions, furnishes her narrative agents with a purpose; whereas in Delany, the horizon and the urge are ... absent, and that absence leaves his characters purposeless and confused.[25]

The final logico-combinatorial possibility is to have in a text horizon alone, without a utopian locus. This is where non-localized "utopian thought" belongs, all the abstract blueprints, utopian programs, etc. I have difficulty in seeing how a horizon without concrete locus – without Bakhtin's chronotope – can be a fictional narration in any strict technical sense (though it can of course be called both fictional in an ironic and narrative in a loosely metaphoric sense, both of which I would find irksome).

To resume the above locus/horizon combinatorics:

1. H >L: open-ended or dynamic utopia.

2. L = H or L >H: closed or static utopia.

3. L (H = 0): heterotopia.

4. H (L = 0): abstract or non-narrative utopia(nism).

Thus, there seems to be no obstacle to applying these terms (as well as further agential terms) as analytic tools to the whole range of utopian studies – fictions, projects, and colonies.

The interaction of locus and horizon in the case of the dynamic utopia constitutes it as not too dissimilar from, and possibly as a special case of, Eco's definition of a semiotic encyclopedia:

> It appears not as a finished object but rather as an open project: not a utopia as *terminus ad quem*, i.e. a state of perfection to be reached, but a utopia as a regulating idea, as a project *ante quem*, whose force stems precisely from the fact that it *cannot* and *should not* be realized in any definitive form.[26]

Let me add here, as an epistemological complement, that Eco himself is somewhat more agnostic or pessimistic (or "postmodern" or "weak thought") than I would be, since he identifies such an open utopia with a rhizomatic encyclopedia only, which I would in its "disorganized organization" rather liken to my possibility no. 3. I am very skeptical toward what Eco terms "shapeless shapes" (107), unless they are simply initial stages of our still partly inchoate understanding or construction of a new kind of organization and shape. While fully agreeing with Eco (and Deleuze) that it is an ideological illusion that knowledge could be organized in a definitive and permanent fashion, I would not share their distrust toward *global* (or indeed total) organization of knowledge (121) on the same presuppositions as those of utopia no. 1 above: on condition that this globality is conscious of itself as a synchronic crosscut for well-defined interests and with a limited pertinence, which yet does not prevent such an organization (e.g. a dynamic utopia) from defining strategically central cognitions necessary and available for action aimed at radical or global change.

4. Toward a Conclusion: Physician, Heal Thyself

I would like to conclude with some questions and open proposals of a partly self-critical nature, in light of further reflection (including further reading of Bloch) within our evolving ideologico-political situation. In my book *Metamorphoses of Science Fiction*, whose chapter 3, on defining utopia, was written at the beginning of the 1970s, I stressed the specificity of utopian fictions as *verbal constructs* (and of course this is readily extrapolated to other textual constructs in a wider acceptation of text, i.e. to paintings). I believe that such a stress was at that initial point mandatory. Indeed, it still seems to me the indispensable beginning, or A, of all wisdom when discussing utopian texts (and any description, verbal or pictorial, of a project or colony is also a text). Still, I would today advance from this position by saying that after A there follow B, C, etc., and that I was perhaps too narrowly focused when I claimed Blochian methodology for texts only. The dichotomy of the field of utopian studies into texts vs. practices, supposedly unified by "utopian thought" but in fact separated by a tacit gap, is *à la longue* untenable. It is also one of the utopophiles' errors, or at least areas of lack, that gives great comfort to the utopophobes, as mentioned in section 2 above. For, logically, either utopian texts and utopian practices are two fields, in which case there should be two disciplines and two professional organizations to study them. Or, on the contrary, we should attempt to establish at least some traffic across the existing gap. I have argued why the only present footbridge of "utopian thought," always flimsy, seems by now rather worm-eaten and not too *tragfähig*, unable to support much burden. The concept of "possible worlds," on the contrary, as adapted and humanized from a socio-historical and pragmatic semiotics of mainly Italian provenance,[27] and in particular its spatial categories of orientation, locus, and horizon, has some chances to become a real bridge. But, of course, this is only a hypothesis. It remains to be proven by further, if possible co-operative, exploration.

Allow me, nonetheless, provisionally to close this open-ended utopian modest proposal by reiterating, with Bloch, that we should hold a steadfast orientation toward the open ocean of possibility that surrounds the actual and that is so immeasurably larger than the actuality. True, terrors lurk in that ocean: but those terrors are primarily and centrally not (as the utopophobes want to persuade us) the terrors of the not-yet-existing, but on the contrary simple extrapolations of the existing actuality of war, hunger, degradation, and exploitation of people and planets. On the other hand, there exists a process and we people are at the advanced front-line of this world-process; it is given unto our hands to nurture the possibilities already pending . . . The seventh day of creation is still before us, the seventh day of which Augustine said: "dies septima ipsi erimus," we ourselves shall be the seventh day.[28]

But in order to understand how to approach such open adventist possibilities given into our perhaps feeble hands, I believe we have first to learn the lesson of the dynamic utopias, where locus constantly tends toward and yet never fuses with horizon. The best formulation I can find of this is in the stupendous close of Brecht's *Badener Lehrstück vom Einverständnis* ("Baden Learning Play of Consent," 1929):

THE LEARNED CHORUS
When bettering the world, you might have perfected the truth,
Now go on perfecting the perfected truth.
Give it up!

CHORUS LEADER
March!

THE LEARNED CHORUS
When perfecting the truth, you might have changed humanity,
Now go on changing the changed humanity.
Give it up!

CHORUS LEADER
March!

THE LEARNED CHORUS
Changing the world, change yourself! Give yourself up!

CHORUS LEADER
March!

And as Brecht added in his radio theory, "[i]f you deem all of this utopian, I beg you to reflect on the reasons which render it utopian."[29]

Notes

1. All translations, unless indicated, are mine. My thanks go to Prof.ssa Giuseppa Saccaro de Buffa, without whose help and patience this essay, first presented in an abbreviated form at the world conference of utopian studies she organized in Frascati in 1986, would not have been written. I also thank dr. Daniela Guardamagna and dr. Ignia Tattoni for their help in Rome. This essay was first published in slightly different form in *Utopia & Modernità: Teorie e prassi utopiche nell'età moderna e postmoderna*, ed. Giuseppa Saccaro Del Buffa and Arthur O. Lewis (Rome: Gangemi Editore, 1989), I, pp. 47–65.

2. For further discussion, see my essay, "Can People be (Re)presented in Fiction?", in

Marxism and the Interpretation of Culture, ed. C. Nelson and L. Grossberg (Urbana: University of Illinois Press, 1987), pp. 663–96.

3. Etienne Cabet, *Voyage en Icarie* (Paris and Geneva: Ressources, 1979), p. 3.

4. For more on Russian utopias, see my *Metamorphoses of Science Fiction* (New Haven: Yale University Press, 1979), ch. 10, as well as Jurij Striedter, "Journeys through Utopia," *Poetics Today*, 3:1 (1982), pp. 57–9.

5. See my *Metamorphoses*, p. 52.

6. Cf. the latest formulation in his *Abschied von der Utopie*, p. 131 et passim.

7. See *Una pietra sopra* (Turin: Einaudi, 1980), p. 252.

8. V. N. Vološinov [M. M. Bakhtin], *Marxism and the Philosophy of Language* (New York: Seminar Press, 1973), pp. 102–3. Cf. my "The Performance Text as Audience–Stage Dialog Inducing a Possible World," *Versus*, 42 (1985), pp. 3–20.

9. "The Performance Text," pp. 51–2.

10. Striedter, "Journeys through Utopia," p. 38. See as well the argument of Peter Ruppert's *Reader in a Strange Land* (Athens: University of Georgia Press, 1986).

11. Striedter, "Journeys through Utopia," p. 55.

12. Suvin, *Metamorphoses*, p. 53.

13. Fredric Jameson, "Of Islands and Trenches," *Diacritics* (June 1977), pp. 6–7.

14. Karl Marx and Friedrich Engels, *Die Deutsche Ideologie*, 3 (Berlin: Dietz, 1956), p. 35.

15. Cf. Bertel Ollman, *Alienation* (Cambridge and New York: Cambridge University Press, 1976).

16. Quoted by Striedter, "Journeys through Utopia," p. 36, from Lenin, *Sochineniia* (Moscow 1941–57), vol. 17, p. 1,922.

17. Robert Musil, *Der Mann ohne Eigenschaften* (Hamburg: Rowohlt, 1972), p. 1,594.

18. M. Merleau-Ponty, *Phénoménologie de la Perception* (Paris: nrf, 1945), p. 225.

19. Umberto Eco, *The Role of the Reader* (Bloomington: Indiana University Press, 1979), p. 223.

20. Louis Marin, "Pour une théorie du texte parabolique," in *Le Récit évangélique*, ed. Claude Chabrol ([Paris:] Aubier Montaigne, 1974), pp. 167 and 175.

21. See my *Metamorphoses*.

22. Cf. Bloch, *Tübinger Einleitung in die Philosophie*, p. 129 ff., in particular 133 and 136.

23. Bülent Somay, "Towards an Open-ended Utopia," *Science-Fiction Studies*, 11:1 (1984), p. 34.

24. Ibid., p. 26.

25. Ibid., p. 33.

26. Eco, "Quattro forme," p. 108.

27. A critical view of its sources can be found in my essay, "The Performance Text," and a development in "Can People be (Re)presented in Fiction?"

28. Bloch, *Abschied*, p. 63; see also p. 59.

29. Bertolt Brecht, *Gesammelte Werke* (Frankfurt am Main: Surhkamp, 1973), vol. 18, p. 30.

9

Paulo Freire, Postmodernism, and the Utopian Imagination: A Blochian Reading

Henry A. Giroux and Peter McLaren

For me education is simultaneously an act of knowing, a political act, and an artistic event. I no longer speak about a political dimension of education. I no longer speak about a knowing dimension of education. As well, I don't speak about education through art. On the contrary, I say education is politics, art and knowing.

Paulo Freire[1]

Introduction

This essay is a critical reading of the work of the radical Brazilian educator Paulo Freire. Highlighted in this reading is a discussion of Freire's concept of utopia as a crucial – yet generally overlooked – aspect of his pedagogy of liberation. We have been impressed by how much Freire's explicit and implicit indebtedness to a concept of utopia resembles the more nuanced and formally developed philosophy of utopia developed by Ernst Bloch. We think the comparison is both significant and instructive. We also believe that Freire's project of liberation can be more fully appreciated and deepened by rereading his work through a conceptual framework more directly linked to Bloch's monumental work on the utopian politics of hope. Our purpose here is fundamentally pedagogical. We have discerned in the work of these two dialecticians of the concrete a complimentary project of liberation that offers an unusually rich ground for self and social transformation. We also believe there are significant cultural, political, and theoretical aspects of postmodern social theory which can extend and deepen the emancipatory aspects of hope in the work of Freire and Bloch.

While Bloch is still a "relatively isolated figure,"[2] little known in Britain and North America and viewed by many Western Marxists as "a marginal oddity or at best a source of occasional insights buried in a welter of opacity,"[3] interest in his work is growing in North America. This is largely the result of the publication of the English translation of his three-volume work, *The Principle of Hope*. Freire, on the other hand, is more widely recognized and influential among a wide spectrum of social theorists and activists that include, among others, theologians, literacy workers, philosophers, social workers, and classroom and university instructors. Yet the work of both these writers on the topic of utopia remains largely untapped by educators and social theorists. In our opinion, Bloch and Freire's expansion of the concept of revolutionary hope offers provocative and important ideas for "keeping political work alive in an age of shrinking possibilities."[4]

Inserting the Political back into Postmodernism

The turn to postmodern social theory is rooted in an overall critique of materialism, the Cartesian concept of the unified human subject, and an Enlightenment notion of foundationalism. In part, postmodernism in its more critical forms rejects the Marxist assumption that consciousness is ultimately a refraction of matter, and that economic relations constitute the primary organizing principle of a social order. Arguing that reality must be read as a text, postmodernism reasserts the importance of language as a mode of representation that constitutes rather than merely expresses what counts as reality. At the same time, this is not a postmodernism that can be solely identified with the claim that nothing exists outside of the playfulness and irony of language; on the contrary, various postmodern theorists reaffirm Michel Foucault's insight that non-discursive forces have their own social and material gravity, but that they can only be understood within language and discourse. In this instance, power is seen as an attribute of discourse in its capacity as a signifying practice to actually construct reality. Central here is the presupposition that any viable notion of critical agency has to be conscious of how power and authority are secured in the languages through which individuals speak and are spoken.

But postmodernism does more than attempt to undermine theories of economic and material causality rooted in the legacy of Marxism. Equally destabilizing is its attack on the Cartesian notion of the humanist subject. Postmodern theorists have pointed to at least three major destabilizing forces. First, they have borrowed from Marx in arguing that history creates material and ideological conditions in the formation of individual and collective identities in which human beings have incomplete control and only partial understanding. Adding an important theoretical twist to this insight, history becomes less a search for a founding moment that will explain the present and the future than a text that needs to be interpreted and rewritten as an act of cultural recovery in which "one looks for meaning to the ongoing inner representations of experience, with current repetitions being seen as more significant than any 'original' moment."[5] Secondly, postmodernism has appropriated Freud's discovery of the unconscious in claiming that the self cannot completely know its own identity because its self-formation is never completely produced or revealed in consciousness. In this instance, rationality and consciousness provide only partial definitions of what constitutes human action and subjectivity. Thirdly, postmodernists have argued powerfully that the self is constructed within and against language and that identity, like language, is always contingent, shifting, and deferred. Within this formulation, the notion of an essentialized and fully transparent identity and universalized subject is replaced by one that is partial, decentered, and grounded in the particularities of history, place, and language. From this perspective, there is no subject or identity fashioned outside of its own history and contingency. Ernesto Laclau comments on the importance of this insight in claiming that identity is only meaningful through an assertion of its own history, the implication being that "if something is essentially historical and contingent, this means that it can always be radically questioned."[6] If identity can only be understood in political and historically relational terms this suggests that the entire modernist metaphysics of Western logocentrism is suspect, less as a civilizing discourse, as conservatives would argue, than as a colonizing practice that represses differences and the recognition of multiple identities. It is also important to acknowledge that the postmodern critique of the humanist subject is not tantamount to doing away with human agency or reducing human behavior to a function of shifting signifiers. What is at stake here is an attempt to interrogate how the subject is constructed, to more fully understand its constructed nature as the precondition of its agency, and to recognize that if the subject is constituted through a social grid of exclusions and differentiations that constitute multiple subject positions, the crucial political issue then becomes how such positions are actually negotiated.

Another important challenge that postmodernism has brought to bear on social theory and a number of other fields centers on its support of a radical anti-foundationalism as a precondition for politically engaged critique and practice. Arguing against essentialism, postmodernists have challenged versions of foundationalism and the illusion of a universality that masks the power relations inscribed in dominating claims for securing specific forms of authority, inclusion, and social relations. This is particularly true in the postmodernist refusal of totalizing narratives that subsume complexity, specificity, and contingency while simultaneously rendering its own discourse as unquestionable. At stake here is a critique of any principle which, because of its claim to universal status, denies human agency by foreclosing decisions about how it is constituted and how it is to locate itself in the grid of social reality. In other words, universalism is denounced because it demands reverence rather than skepticism, recognition rather than critical engagement, and transmission rather than suspicion.

For many postmodern theorists, the appeal to foundationalism undercuts the precondition for agency and political action. Agency in this case is undermined by being constituted outside of rather than within history. In a similar manner, it has been argued that the critique of foundationalism is not a surrender to relativism, but a willingness to view exchange, dialogue, and critique as a condition for the radicalization of democracy itself. Laclau points out that postmodern deconstructive practices

> accomplish the function of increasing our awareness of the socially constructed character of our world and open up the possibility of a foundation through collective decisions of what was before conceived as established forever by God, or by Reason, or by Human Nature – all those equivalent names that function by placing the destiny of human beings beyond the reach of their decisions.[7]

While there are any number of additional assumptions and practices that can be associated with the broad theoretical movement known as postmodernism, it is impossible for us to develop them in this essay. However, we do want to make a qualification regarding postmodern theory that might seem either ironic or contradictory to some. Postmodernism as a unified field does not exist. While there are central assumptions regarding language, identity formation, and representation that mark its theoretical borders, it is a diverse and fragmented collection of discourses that simply cannot be lumped together under a synthetic whole. Postmodern insights have been taken up by literary theorists, postcolonialists, feminists, critical educators, and a number of other academics and political activists. What is important to note is that postmodernism comes in a variety of forms, which are radical, liberal, conservative, or downright apolitical. As a method, it can be used to legitimate an interest in textual analysis that is as narrow as it is depoliticized. It can also be used to buttress an elitist, "clever" aesthetic formalism that erases institutional power and concrete social conflicts. But postmodernism is more than a retreat from politics and social engagement or an overbearing form of relativism. In the hands of different theorists, it has been used to highlight the representative spaces from which institutions construct dominant and subordinate voices. For example, feminists such as Judith Butler have used it to deconstruct gendered representations and to make visible strategic exclusions in dominant narratives, texts, and practices.[8] Moreover, many educators have drawn upon postmodern insights to deconstruct the

vanguardism of theory and the complex ways in which truth is produced
to uphold relations of domination in the schools and other institutions.
In all of these cases, postmodernism has attempted to make visible the
relationship between violence and discourse, to illuminate how social
groups are formed within relations of inequality, and to reveal how
cultural hegemony is secured and contested.

At stake here is a highly schematic rendering of postmodernism that
contests any attempt to position it under an artificially constructed
whole in order to then be summarily dismissed as another form of
theoretical nihilism. Postmodernism in this approach becomes an easy
target. Moreover, this type of criticism undermines the more difficult
task of appropriating those elements of postmodern discourse that
might be useful for expanding the possibilities of critical pedagogy and
cultural resistance.

One pressing task for radical pedagogy is to ensure that postmodern
perspectives now characterizing the work of various educational theorists are buttressed by the imperative of ethical reflection and subordinated to the creation of a viable, progressive political project. We
attempt to undertake this task at the end of our essay. But we want to
stress at the outset that part of our efforts in linking a politics of hope
to the cultural politics of a critical pedagogy is based on a continuing
effort to search for a critical language that will stress the primacy of a
politics of emancipation. For this reason, the work of Paulo Freire
provides an important focus of attention.

Paulo Freire and the Primacy of the Political
Viver e Lutar!

Positioning Freire's work within the foregoing discussion places him in
the front ranks of border intellectuals for whom liberation remains the
banner behind which to fight for social justice and transformation.
Freire's dialogic pedagogy, beginning with his goal of empowering
oppressed Brazilian peasants, has, over the years, assumed a legend-
ary and epoch-making status. Few educators have strode so knowingly
and with such determination along the crossroads of language and
culture.

Freire's internationally celebrated praxis began in the late 1940s and
continued unabated until 1964, when he was arrested in Brazil as a
result of a literacy program he designed and implemented in 1962. He
was imprisoned by the military government for seventy days, and exiled
for his work in the national literacy campaign, of which he had served
as director. Freire's sixteen years of exile were tumultuous and productive times: a five-year stay in Chile as a UNESCO consultant with the
Chilean Agrarian Reform Corporation, specifically the Reform Training
and Research Institute; an appointment in 1969 to Harvard University's

Center for Studies in Development and Social Change; a move to Geneva, Switzerland in 1970 as consultant to the Office of Education of the World Council of Churches, where he developed literacy programs for Tanzania and Guinea-Bissau that focused on the re-Africanization of their countries; the development of literacy programs in postrevolutionary former Portuguese colonies such as Angola and Mozambique; assisting the governments of Peru and Nicaragua with their literacy campaigns; the establishment of the Institute of Cultural Action in Geneva in 1971; a brief return to Chile after Salvador Allende was assassinated in 1973, provoking General Pinochet to declare Freire a subversive; and his eventual return to Brazil in 1980 to teach at the Pontificia Universidade Catolica de Sao Paulo and the Universidade de Campinas in Sao Paulo. These events were accompanied by the publicatin of numerous works, most notably *Pedagogy of the Oppressed, Cultural Action for Freedom,* and *Pedagogy in Process: Letters to Guinea-Bissau.* In more recent years, Freire has worked briefly as Secretary of Education of Sao Paulo, continuing his radical agenda of literacy reform for the people of that city.

Freire's previous work has been widely cited and evaluated elsewhere and we forebear to pursue a detailed summary of his ideas here. We do wish, however, to show how Freire's work constitutes an important contribution to critical pedagogy not simply because of its theoretical refinement, but because of Freire's success at putting theory into practice.

Based on a recognition of the cultural underpinnings of folk traditions and the importance of the collective construction of knowledge, Freire's literacy programs for disempowered peasants are now employed in countries all over the world. By linking the categories of history, politics, economics, and class to the concepts of culture and power, Freire has managed to develop both a language of critique and a language of hope that work conjointly and dialectically and which have proven successful in liberating the lives of generations of disenfranchised peoples. It is Freire's language of hope – what Giroux calls his "language of possibility" – that will serve as the focus of our discussion as we compare Freire's work with the recent trends in postmodern social theory.

We wish to focus our discussion on one recent book by Freire published in the United States, *The Politics of Education.* This book constitutes a formidable collection of essays which have been skillfully translated and arranged as a series of complementary themes dealing with such diverse topics as the act of study, adult literacy, the transformative role of the social worker, cultural action and conscientization, political literacy, humanistic education, and liberation theology. These themes are woven into the political design of the book, which attempts to lead the reader to an experience of "authentic conscientization" –

which Freire describes as "the revelation of the real world as a dynamic and dialectical unity with the actual transformation of reality."[9]

For Freire, speech and language always exist within a social context which, in turn, becomes the critical referent for the transformative possibilities of his work. This social context – which exists for Freire *both in and between language and the social order* – is comprised of the social relations obtaining among the material conditions of oppression, the exigencies of daily life, critical consciousness, and social transformation. Freire's sensitive grasp of the contradictions and tensions that emerge from such a volatile context is what eventually leads him to posit the need for a radical politics of liberation. As Florence Tager puts it:

> Freire's pedagogy insists on a deep connection between the culture of everyday life and radical politics. For Freire, critical consciousness and the dissection of themes from daily life is an ongoing process that grows out of praxis and leads to further praxis (Freire's term for action with reflection). Ultimately, education for critical consciousness leads to revolutionary politics. For Freire, radical pedagogy integrates culture and politics.[10]

Freire defines culture as a field of struggle over meaning, as a many-sided conversation that is never neutral. For Freire, language and culture are always trace-ridden with a plurality of values, voices, and intentions which are by their very nature dialogical. Such a perspective draws attention to the intensity of social contradictions within linguistic and symbolic systems. Freire's understanding of culture posits it as a terrain where discourses are created and become implicated in the struggle over meaning. Culture is never depoliticized; it always remains tied to the social and class relationships that inform it.

Within the Freirian cosmology, human subjects do not float aimlessly in a sea of signifiers; they are not "decentered;" rather, they are firmly rooted in historical struggle. Human subjectivity is never reduced to a hypothetical or abstract bundle of signs. Consequently, social agents never lose their capacity for suffering or their resoluteness for effecting social transformation. Freirian man and woman are very much alive and anchored materially in a multiplicity of social relations which provide the "stuff" out of which Freire fashions his particular brand of cultural politics.[11]

Freire's cultural politics combine both a language of critique and one of possibility. This permits his political project to be fundamentally directed toward a struggle over meaning, wherein meaning becomes both a product of and vehicle for power. In other words, education comes to represent "that terrain where power and politics are given a fundamental expression, since it is where meaning, desire, language, and values engage and respond to the deeper beliefs about the very nature of what it means to be human, to dream, and to name and struggle for a particular future and way of life."[12]

One of Freire's strongest insights is centered in his analysis of literacy and learning as an underlying political project – which he frequently refers to as "conscientization" – a process that invites learners to engage the world and other people critically; this project implies a fundamental "recognition of the world, not as a 'given' world, but as a world dynamically 'in the making'" (*Politics of Education*, 106). The ultimate goal of such a process is for learners to "exercise the right to participate consciously in the socio-historical transformation of their society" (50). Here Freire emphasizes the fact that human beings "have the sense of 'project,' in contrast to the instinctive routines of animals" (44). And, of course, it is Freire's attentiveness to the scope and quality of his political 'project' which illuminates the transformative and emancipatory dimensions of his work. Such a position of political attentiveness is not at odds with critical postmodernism, with its attack on foundationalism. On the contrary, by reaffirming the importance of taking politics seriously, Freire dignifies the notion of "taking a stand" while simultaneously interrogating all forms of foundationalism that make a claim to the universal. In effect, Freire mobilizes a project of hope without putting forth the theoretical baggage of elitism and vanguardism. Freire's dialectics of the concrete and his concern with human suffering and social practices have "grounded" him in a moral and political culture that is profoundly ethical in its concern with the relations between himself and others.

Rather than constituting a mode of critique devoid of human subjects, Freire's work problematizes the distinction between subject and agency. While recognizing that the humanist subject is untenable theoretically, Freire attempts to rework the implications of the subject as multiple and contradictory through possibilities made available in the processes of dialogue, identification, and choice. More specifically, Freire begins with a literacy process that grows out of the cultural capital of the oppressed and interrogates the very conditions that authorize experience, agency, and possibility. For Freire, the acknowledgement that the subject is contradictory and constituted provides the grounds for interrogating its construction as a basic tenet of literacy. In this case, the issues of how we are constructed, where one comes from, how one can intervene in one's own social and historical construction are fundamental to what it means to affirm rather than take for granted one's sense of individual and collective agency.

Critical Utopianism: Freirian and Blochian Perspectives

Ernst Bloch is largely responsible for the current rehabilitation of the concept of utopia and critical re-evaluation of this term in the social sciences. Writing in the 1930s, Bloch struggled to keep alive a redemptive and radically utopian spirit at a time when the Enlightenment tradition was being absorbed by the logic of fascism. Despite its often apologetic and triumphalist trappings and the strident militancy of its optimism, Bloch's work represents an extraordinary reconstitution of the meaning of utopia. Bloch dismantled arguments against utopia which criticized its other-worldliness and its unrealistic impractical, and illusory goals. Rejecting the idea that utopian thinking is a form of unbridled subjectivism which seeks to make objective reality conform to the abstract and often irrational ideals of irresponsible dreamers,[13] Bloch argued that "Utopia extends so far and inputs itself so powerfully to all human activities that every account of man and the world must essentially contain it. *There is no realism, worthy of the name, which abstracts from this strongest element or reality as something which is unfinished.*"[14]

His ontology of the "not yet" or "anagnorisis" (recognition) claims that one can ascertain figural traces of the future in remnants of the past. From such an extraordinary position one is compelled through Bloch's brilliant exegesis of hope to understand reality as fundamentally determined by the future rather than the past. Hope is given birth in a spectacular sea of possibility. In this view, only the infinitude of possibility can provide the necessary link among past, present, and future.

Bloch is fundamentally concerned with teasing out the elements of concrete utopia in an especially wide range of cultural forms that encompasses music, art, literature, philosophy, and even the cultural politics of fascism. "Concrete utopia" refers to the real, material conditions necessary to make utopia possible and for it to embody a critical praxis. Whereas "abstract utopian refers to utopia's formal, descriptive characteristics, 'concrete utopia,' attempts to locate a possible future within the real."[15] Reality, in this view, is engaged as both a subjective and objective experience, and due to its unfinished nature it is seen as something that is always in a state of becoming. Expectation, hope, and intention are always moving steadily – even teleologically – toward a possibility not yet realized.

Both mind and matter figure prominently in Bloch's concept of utopia. Utopia has both anthropological or subjective factors (that which is not yet conscious and which is always preceded by a dream) and ontological, objective factors (the real possibility of that which has not yet come to be). These factors are what Bloch refers to as the "subjective potency" and "objective potency" of utopia. When examined in the light of the dialectic of history, the "subjective possibility" of human consciousness and the "real-objective possibility" which is latent in nature produce a creative tension between historical conditions and the utopian imagination. The possibilities inherent in utopia cannot, claims Bloch, be traced to the repression of bourgeois ideology since there always exists a "cultural surplus" that "contains the spark that reaches out beyond the surrounding emptiness,"[16] and that can be directly linked to the utopian function which is expressed as both social and ontological states.[17] For Bloch, our collective dream needs to be translated into the material density of everyday struggle through a dialectical process and ontological unfolding in which "what is" is constantly being challenged in light of what "might be."

Utopian symbols are always supplementary, they always exceed what they point to. There are no absolute utopian images, only those that possess a latent power. In fact, Bloch "insists that the utopian function includes both the power to define fulfillment as well as the power to resist *all* efforts to contain its potentially unbounded hope in any hypostatized definition."[18] In this aspect, where Bloch stresses the multivalence of the symbol and the undecidability of signification, he sounds very much like a poststructuralist. Not surprisingly, Wayne Hudson likens aspects of Bloch's work to a "geography of desire" which could both extend and be extended by the works of such postmodern social theorists as Deleuze, Lyotard, and Derrida.

While both Freire and Bloch have revealed the process by which utopia can be seen as a form of orthopraxis, it is Freire who has teased out in greater detail the methodological features of this in his discussions of pedagogical dialogue leading to conscientization. Yet there is much in Freire's work that could benefit from a Blochian understanding of utopia. Bloch's theory of utopia is, in the words of Ruth Levitas, "the overcoming of antagonism between humanity and the world."[19] Utopian hope results from a "longing" and a "counter-emotion between anxiety and fear."[20] In fact, hope is much more than an emotion – it is a form of cognitive intentionality, of ontological assertion, and of anticipatory consciousness.

Bloch placed more emphasis on the concept of agency than did many of his Marxist contemporaries and predecessors. This is why the concept of intentionality runs so powerfully through his writings on utopia, as do his concepts of process and tendency, all of which play such significant roles in giving his socialist vision a human face. They also underscore the importance of utopia as freedom from alienation and the achievement of the fullness of humanity through solidarity and community and the liberation of the utopian "real possible." According to Roberts, Bloch offers humanity a "stark choice" between allowing the merely possible "to turn into nothing" or regarding the possible as "the real possible, the free and unconditional future, and turn it into Being."[21] Bloch's Marxism steadfastly mandates a "rebaptism" of the "living yesterday" by a revolutionary politics (*Principle of Hope*, 27).

The content of Freire's utopia places more emphasis on the role of democracy than does Bloch's Marxist vision. Yet in many ways, Freire's utopian imagination can be likened to Bloch's in the sense that real, radical democracy is understood by Freire as something latent in the present, something immanently future-bearing that can be grasped in the flickering moment of anticipatory consciousness. The utopian imagination for both thinkers drives forward the multiple levels of human desire while at the same time it is the result of an unconscious ontological pulling from the "not yet" of the still inarticulate future. The utopian imagination has, consequently, a subversive and emancipatory function. Unlike so many other critical social theorists, Freire and Bloch have not abandoned the utopian impulse in the struggle toward a praxis of liberation. In fact, by seizing from the totalized narratives of social life spaces of emancipatory possibility and making such spaces the centerpiece of their liberatory politics, both theorists develop a counter-hegemonic project of creating an historic bloc of liberated collectives.

Bloch's concept of passive-contemplative and active-participatory attitudes toward reality places the construction of everyday life on the side of utopian possibility. His idea of passive-contemplative attitudes bears a striking resemblance to Freire's description of the stage of semi-intransitive consciousness while his concept of active-participatory attitudes reflects an essential precondition to Freire's notion of conscientization – a state that involves learners' awareness of the contingency of their own oppression and the necessity of challenging specific forces of antagonism. Both Bloch's utopian praxis and Freire's critical consciousness begin with subjects' awareness of their own temporality. Awareness of the "limit situations" that confront them encourages learners to become subjects rather than objects of the historical process.

Another central idea in Bloch's work on utopia is that subjectivity is dialectically reanimating. For Bloch, "reality or 'being' is not a static or fixed entity but rather a dynamic potency involved in an ongoing process of development."[22] This notion resembles Freire's ontological project of becoming fully human through a dialectic of action and reflection, one that enables the awareness of our temporality to make us both historical and cultural agents. This process occurs as we realize that our subjectivity is the result of both human action in the past and a changed human reality in the future brought about by our own actions in the present. Freire writes:

> As men emerge from time, discover temporality, and free themselves from "today," their relations with the world become impregnated with consequence. The normal role of humans in and with the world is not a passive one. Because they are not limited to the natural (biological) sphere but participate in the creative dimension as well, men can intervene in reality in order to change it. Inheriting acquired experience, creating and recreating, integrating themselves into their context, responding to its challenges, objectifying themselves, men enter in the domain which is theirs exclusively – that of history and of culture.[23]

Another fundamental aspect common to the work of Bloch and Freire is their emphasis on the relationship between critique and hope. Adriana Puiggros brilliantly captures the mutually constitutive character of criticism and utopia in Freire's work:

> Utopia is linked to conscientization; conscientization implies utopia, because the more conscientized we are, Freire says, the more capable we will be of being announcers and denouncers, because all denouncement is an announcement, every conscious critique is infused with utopias. Consciousness is, at the same time, a process of breaking reality and demystification.[24]

Conscientization, therefore, contains hope as a constituent characteristic. Hope and critical consciousness are dialectically reanimating and together they produce "the shock" of new knowledge and new social and cultural configurations and possibilities for human transformation. Freire points out that "for this reason conscientization obliges us to assume a utopian position towards the world."[25] For Freire, utopia is not a form of idealism but rather "the dialectics of the acts of denunciation and annunciation, it is the act of denouncing the dehumanizing structure and of announcing the humanizing structure. For this reason, too, utopia is also a historical commitment."[26]

Freire's Utopian Project

To be committed to cultural action for conscientization means for Freire not only to engage in a vigorous form of ideology critique but also to take part in a utopian praxis. One of us has defined elsewhere the utopian and prophetic foundations of Freire's pedagogy:

> The *utopian* character of his analysis is concrete in its nature and appeal, and takes as its starting point collective actors in their various historical settings and the particularity of their problems and forms of oppression. It is *utopian* only in the sense that it refuses to surrender the risks and dangers that face all challenges to dominant power structures. It is prophetic in that it views the kingdom of God as something to be created on earth but only through a faith in both other human beings and the necessity of permanent struggle.[27]

Freire's utopian praxis is pitted against the oppressive relations of domination and privilege of the dominant culture. Freire writes that "cultural action for conscientization is always a utopian enterprise ... [which] is what distinguishes it above all from cultural action for domination" (*Politics of Education*, 86). He insists that education must always speak to the "annunciation of a new reality" which becomes not only a temporary "concrete reality" but a "permanent cultural revolution" (86).

Freire's utopian project addresses the need for a fundamental faith in human dialogue and community. In this sense, becoming literate is not just a cognitive process of decoding signs, but a critical engagement of lived experience in relation to others. Hence, literacy assumes a form of cultural action for freedom. "To undertake such a work," writes Freire, "it is necessary to have faith in the people, solidarity with them. It is necessary to be utopian" (63). The utopian dimension is natural to any revolutionary project dedicated to "transforming and recreating the world" (82). In fact, it is the very lack of any utopian dimension within the praxis of the right that defines the nature of its oppressive regime. According to Freire, authentic revolutionary praxis is utopian in nature, which means that it is dynamic, harmonious, creative, reflective, and dialogical. He writes:

> There ought to be a difference in the praxis of the right and of revolutionary groups that defines them to the people, making the options of each group explicit. This difference between the two groups stems from the utopian nature of the revolutionary groups, and the impossibility of the right to be utopian ... A true revolutionary project, on the other hand, to which the utopian dimension is natural, is a process in which the people assume the role of subject in the precarious adventure of transforming and recreating the world ... Revolutionary utopia tends to be dynamic rather than static; tends to life rather than death; to the future as a challenge to man's creativity rather than as a repetition of the present; to love as liberation of subjects rather than as pathological possessiveness; to the emotion of life rather than cold abstractions; to living together in harmony rather than gregariousness; to dialogue rather than mutism; to praxis rather than "law and order"; to men who organize themselves reflectively for action rather than men who are organized for passivity; to creative and communicative language rather than prescriptive signals; to reflective challenges rather than domesticating slogans; and to values that are lived rather than myths that are imposed. [81–2]

Freire's language of hope and his utopian vision are deeply ingrained in his identification with the prophetic new Church of Latin America. He assails the traditional church for presenting a world view that "satisfies the fatalistic and frightened consciousness of the oppressed" (131) while drowning them in a culture of silence. Freire articulates the birth of a new prophetic church that is at once at odds with both the traditional church and the modernizing church – both of which are characterized by "do-goodism," a defense of reforms which maintain the status quo, and an ultimate commitment to the power elite.

The prophetic church is occupied by "a critical analysis of the social structures in which conflict takes place" and demands of its followers "a knowledge of sociopolitical science" and ultimately "an ideological choice" (138). Accompanied by a theological reflection which is now commonly referred to as liberation theology, the prophetic church challenges the present historical situation in Latin America. Freire writes that "such a prophetic perspective does not represent an escape into a world of unattainable dreams. It demands a scientific knowledge of the world as it really is" (138).[28] This prophetic perspective put forward by Freire also demands that subjects not lose themselves in the militant drudgery of everyday life. Freire is worth quoting at length on this issue:

> [I]f I lose myself in the details of daily life, I lose, at the same time, a vision of the dramatic meaning of my existence. I become either fatalistic or cynical. In the same way, if I try to escape from the daily demands and details to take up my life's dramatic character – but without at the same time becoming historically involved – I can have no other destiny than to fall into an empty intellectualism, equally alienating. I shall then see existence as something impossible and hopeless. I have no other chance of conquering the alienating trivialities of daily life than by way of historical praxis, which is social and not individual. It is only insofar as I accept to the full my responsibility within the play of this dramatic tension that I make myself a conscious presence in the world.
>
> I cannot permit myself to be a mere spectator. On the contrary, I must demand my place in the process of change. So the dramatic tension between the past and the future, death and life, being and nonbeing, is no longer a kind of dead end for me; I can see it for what it really is: a permanent challenge to which I must respond. And my response can be none other than my historical praxis – in other words, revolutionary praxis. [129]

One important dimension of Freire's utopian vision calls for a restructuring of the nature of existing society in dramatic contrast to the oppressive aspects of everyday life; yet at the same time this utopian vision emerges from a concrete engagement in mundane reality. Freire's utopia does not speak to an idealized "transcendental signified" that can only be realized in the imagination and therefore is denied historical possibility. Nor is any immutable reference point for emancipation capriciously deconstructed. Rather, Freire's utopia is immanently realizable, but only in the process of conscientization and revolutionary practice. Suffering, and the historical memories of those who have suffered under the heels of the power elite, become, for Freire, the reference points that ground his revolutionary text. The task of liberating others from their suffering may not emerge from some transcendental fiat, yet it nevertheless compels us to affirm our humanity in solidarity with victims.

While it is important to recognize that Freire's work does not adhere to a language of freedom that exists outside of human engagement and struggle, it is also important to understand that it nevertheless speaks to an unequivocal and sovereign concern: the challenge and moral imperative to alleviate and eliminate the ideological and institutional basis of human suffering. In this instance, Freire seeks to unravel the concrete syntax of oppression and transform resistance to material and spiritual suffering into a revolutionary praxis dedicated to the establishment of a discourse of liberation and freedom.

If the sociology of knowledge originated by Karl Mannheim has taught us anything, it is that all theoretical assertions and conclusions are invariably and necessarily shaded by the evaluative preconceptions of the theorist. If values do indeed motivate particular types of research and govern the formulation of theory, then it becomes essential to ask of any social theory or body of research: what is the political project that informs it? What way of life does this theoretical discourse speak to? Freire's project has been and continues to be clear and unambiguous: a life-long engagement in the battle for emancipation and freedom.

Freire's struggle is both conceptually oriented and politically moti- vated. Like Foucault, Freire attempts to illuminate the social and political practices within specific texts. He is less concerned with understanding codes and significations for their own sake, that is, in isolation from their engagement by social actors. Freire is well aware of the power and peril of discourse, yet he nevertheless understands that discourse alone – that is, in isolation from the social movements that "carry" it – cannot usher in revolutionary change. While Freire's project makes no claim for historical guarantees, this does not affect the ground of his commitment, which is a preferential option for the oppressed. This commitment is echoed in the words of feminist theologian Sharon Welch, who writes:

> Liberation faith is conversion to the other, the resistance to oppression, the attempt to live as though the lives of others matter ... To honestly live and believe as universal the imperative of love and freedom is to hope that suffering can be ended, to hope that all lives without liberation in history were not meaningless, but it is to work for this hope without the guarantee that such meaning is possible.[29]

Welch captures the essence of Freire's liberating pedagogy when she speaks of truth as "conversation" rather than "reflection of essence." Rorty offers a position that is strikingly similar in his concern that rather than discovering truth, "the conversation should be kept going." True liberation, according to Welch, requires that definitions ascertained through one's own experiences of liberation need to be brought into dialogue with other interpretations, without assuming that the dialogue is to be one-sided or rhetorically manipulative.

Resistance Postmodernism and Critical Utopianism

Freire's concrete utopia can be further revived and deepened by bringing his utopian imagination into conversation with what Teresa

Ebert and others have described as "resistance postmodernism" and what Tom Moylan refers to as "critical utopianism." Ebert has proposed a transformative politics based on what she calls a "resistance postmodernism" as a way of forcefully contesting ludic postmodernism. She has described the latter approach as a "cognitivism and an immanent critique that reduces politics to rhetoric and history to textuality and in the end cannot provide the basis for a transformative social practice." Whether a form of poststructuralism, the "pastiche" of styles, or the deconstruction of modernist genres, "ludic postmodernism removes the ground from under both the revolutionary and the reactionary and in the name of difference effectively conceals radical difference." In effect, ludic postmodernism denies the gravity of the sphere of politics and criticizes and destabilizes dominant systems of representation through revealing the fragmentary and disruptive play of signifiers in the construction of social life. Yet while it helps to both "clarify the issues from the perspective of representation" and "effectively denaturalize and destabilize the dominant regime of knowledge and the naturalization of the status quo in the common sense,"[30] it fails overwhelmingly to articulate a historical, political difference, or a materialized, resisting difference. Our own view of postmodernism, as indicated in the beginning of this essay, reaffirms a political postmodernism, one that combines a sense of history, agency, and possibility.

Ebert challenges the ludic notion of difference as textuality and as a formal, rhetorical space in which representation produces its own lineaments of signification. She argues instead that difference is fundamentally social and historical. For instance, a ludic postmodernism criticizes the binary oppositions of logocentric or phallogocentric discourse and rather than reversing the hierarchy which privileges, for instance, white over black, or male over female, it effectively dehierarchizes or displaces these oppositions altogether by revealing that the binary Other is always its suppressed supplement. But a resistance postmodernism goes further than this by demanding that the power relations that are part of such hierarchical arrangements be politically challenged. In other words, difference is situated in social conflict and social struggle. Whereas ludic postmodernism destabilizes meaning by revealing the continuous dissemination of differences within the process of signification and exposing the undecidability of the signified and the non-representational character of language (in that language consists of a system of differences among signifiers), resistance postmodernism locates the sign in the materiality of social struggle. The sign does not float in some pan-historical space "of eternal ahistorical slippage and excess" (ibid.), but is "decidable" in the concrete arena of social conflict.[31]

Resistance postmodernism is geared to understanding totalizing systems of power such as patriarchy and capitalism as well as global structural relations of domination and the systematicity of regimes of exploitation. In this way it redresses some of the shortcomings that result from the emphasis ludic postmodernism places on detotalizing, Foucauldian micro-politics (Ebert). Ebert points out that difference is not adventitious or capricious but always linked to social contradictions. Difference is always *difference-in-relation* while totality must be seen as an *overdetermined structure of difference*. This emphasis on totality enables Ebert, like Freire, to challenge systems of difference that are organized into concrete patterns of domination and subordination. It enables them to directly challenge the imperial logic of the corporate capitalist marketplace in ways that move beyond ludic postmodernism's romantic anti-capitalism and abandonment of political strategic referents for establishing a utopian discourse.

It is easy to see why the writings of Bloch and Freire would possess a singular appeal for those who espouse a resistance postmodernism as a means of contesting the fashionable apostasy of ludic postmodernism with its attendant infatuation with a postoptimism discourse of political retreat. Not least is their shared idea of offering a trenchant criticism of the social totality while at the same time constructing a vision of the way things could be.

However sympathetic we might be toward the overall projects of Freire and Bloch, we do want to sound a cautionary warning that both Bloch's and Freire's work must be appropriated selectively and carefully so as to avoid some of its essentialist underpinnings. Ruth Levitas speaks to some of the limitations in current work in utopian studies when she argues that definitions of utopia solely in terms of content, form, or function should be avoided. She further claims such definitions elide important questions:

> If both the form and function of utopia vary with the social and cultural context, what are the conditions which prescribe particular forms and functions for utopia? When does utopia become pure compensation and why? How and when does it become the catalyst of change? And what is the relationship between form and function?

Defining utopia as "the desire for a different, better way of being,"[32] Levitas cautions that utopia cannot be conceived as an innate impulse, but rather must be understood outside of essentialist definitions of human needs and human nature. In other words, there exists no ideal universal standard utopia against which all utopias must be measured. Utopia is a "socially constructed response to an *equally* socially constructed gap between needs and wants generated by a particular society and the satisfactions available to and distributed by it."[33] Utopianism, in Levitas's view, "has as a precondition a disparity between socially constructed experienced need and socially prescribed and actually available means of satisfaction."[34] Levitas also argues, rightly in our view, that it is difficult to use a criterion of content in evaluating utopias because these can only be posited in the abstract outside of their concrete, specific manifestations. Any form of universal specifications can be construed as a form of totalitarianism – of constructing *particular* needs and matching them with "available satisfactions."[35]

Levitas argues that utopia needs to express and explore what is desired and also to hope that such desires may be realized while not limiting the subject matter to questions of form or the idea of utopia to a specific function. Whereas Levitas still sees the crucial problem of utopianism as searching for "that agency and the possibility of hope," we believe that Freire, in particular, has addressed this issue more concretely than has Bloch, particularly through Freire's work in literacy programs throughout the world. Freire's pedagogy supersedes the ontology–epistemology or theory–practice binarism since his work articulates both theory and practice as mutually constitutive and animating aspects of the process of becoming more fully human. His approach to becoming literate as an "act of knowing" encourages both action and reflection in the creation of critical/historical agency. The identities of historical agents are constructed, then, in the act of learning and in solidarity with others. Such identities are always provisional, and the alliances formed will be contingent upon the strategies, negotiations, and translations that occur in the act of struggling for both a common ground of alliance building (rather than a common culture) and a radical transformative politics.

While we respect Levitas's assertion that the content of any utopia cannot be prespecified, we take issue with ludic postmodern positions that attempt to challenge all principles that make some attempt at closure or root themselves in a form of foundationalism. We argue, instead, that foundational referents, when viewed as contingent, such as the discourse of justice and freedom, do not predetermine strategies or specific social or cultural practices. Rather, those foundationally contingent referents delimit the arena in which these provisional strategies may be undertaken without recourse to any transcendental justification or guarantees for exact knowledge of the outcome or consequences of specific actions. Foundationally contingent referents are important but only in the context of legitimating and enabling *particular* actions that need to be evaluated in the contextual specificity of their occurrence. We argue that the discourse of rights and freedom can be unifying without dominating and for this reason constitutes a "metadiscourse" rather than a totalizing "master discourse."[36] We believe this distinction is worth emphasizing.

We argue for linking the politics of hope with the need to insert politics within a discourse of strategic closure. In this case, the discourse of freedom and justice needs to be articulated as part of a broader meta-discourse in order to analyze the relationship among heterogeneous discourses – that is, the principles of justice and freedom provide a set of articulations for analyzing the possibility of politics, hope, and social struggle not only within specific contexts and social formations but also between the diverse constellations of differences that comprise a larger global totality. This is clear in Murphy's analysis of the function of meta-discourse – that of analyzing the relationship among the fragments of our pluralized and multi-dimensional world – and that of a master discourse. A master discourse "wants to impose itself on all the other discourses – it is progressive, they are reactionary; it is right, they are wrong."[37] A meta-discourse, on the other hand, enables the emergence of new possibilities in constructing what Murphy calls the "justice of multiplicity." Bloch's own dialectical materialism made great strides in understanding the treatment of particulars and universals in arguing for a theory–praxis that moves beyond an ontological materialism and remains open-ended, problem-directed, and unfinished.[38] Freire's problem-solving approach is similar in emphasis, although much more detailed in methodological terms.

Having said this, we recognize that inherent in the utopianism of both Freire and Bloch is a tendency to prespecify the *content* of concrete utopias. Not only is such a tendency marked by a "creeping" essential-ism, it also represents an incipient teleology in positing the worker or proletariat as the vanguard for social change. Of course, both theorists were products of their time and the language of the universal agent was barely contestable in Marxist circles. Moreover, in Bloch's work there is also a Eurocentrism that is characteristic of other neo-Marxist theorists such as Lukács and various members of the Frankfurt School. As Tom Moylan notes:

> In the privileging of the inheritance of Western culture which stems from his European bourgeois background and in his political loyalty to the Soviet Revolution which stems from a combination of his philosophical belief in the correctness of Marxism and his existential interpretation of both the U.S. and Nazi Germany as far greater evils, Bloch represses the most critical aspects of his utopian function precisely at the moment when they were most needed in his own time and place.[39]

A regrettable tendency of both Bloch and Freire is revealed in their tendency to essentialize experience. This is evident in their fundamen-tally phallocentric views of liberation which are located in the "practical mindfulness" of unalienated experience and the pursuit of freedom, which, in turn, are grounded in a notion of theory–praxis that "does not foreclose the nature of the world with premature ontological characteristics."[40] The not yet conscious is best expressed by Bloch as the realization of the classless society. At times such an emphasis in

Bloch's work can be linked to a crude economic determinism. For instance, it leads Bloch to privilege class over gender as the most significant form of oppression that needs to be addressed. Bloch's discussion of women's utopias would not be favorably received today by feminist critics. Vincent Geoghegan notes that "many modern feminists would find patronizing and sexist" Bloch's discussion of women through his work.[41] At the same time, Freire's early work has been criticized for ignoring the oppression of women,[42] but his later writings have made significant strides in trying to accommodate themselves to recent feminist concerns.[43]

Neither Freire's nor Bloch's utopianism sufficiently addresses the issue of race, and while the appearance of such lacunae is not to be considered excusable, we do understand it in relation to the geopolitical and historical conditions which influenced the development of Bloch and Freire's work. While some aspects of their work can arguably be considered idealist and romantic, it is not our place here to further mine these criticisms. In addition, the metaphysical aspects of their work would demand another paper.

Both Freire's and Bloch's excursuses into the meaning of possibility avoid the twin errors of linking hope to a past eschatological event, to a finite historical moment, or, on the other hand, to reducing hope to a future eschatological event – to a world outside of the fecundity of the concrete present, such that the now-time of humankind becomes a form of probation, an ineffable shadow world of what is yet to come. Bloch and Freire's utopian hope raises to axiomatic criteria the concept of self-transcending action made possible through a militant optimism. For both of these thinkers, hope co-operates with possibility in fashioning freedom as an eschatological reality, as a form of historical grace that is immanent in the synchronous and non-synchronous contradictions of a single present. Hope is understood and championed as a pulsating latency of possibility contained in the unity of the immanent and transcendent. As such, hope is to be conscripted by social agents in order to contest the gangsterism of the spirit so common in this era of consumer capitalism, and to fill the empty space of postmodern nihilism.

Both writers diminish the boundary between actuality and possibility – between ontological and social conditions – by positing the utopian impulse not as a fixed human essence but one of existential necessity for bringing about social transformation and freedom in reconstituted utopian forms within the political field. In so doing, they have created the conditions that would make cultural workers less likely to repress their own histories or confuse the act of knowing with passing over into the totalizing realm of explanatory certainty. Their stress on the awareness of temporality and their ability to supersede the ontological-epistemological binarism that plagues much of critical theory (by situating emancipatory praxis as both a way of being and a way of doing) makes their work exceedingly valuable to the current leftist social project.

For Bloch as for Freire, to find meaning in life and to find life in meaning can never result in utopia without first listening loudly and intently to the whispers of our dreams. Tom Moylan's work has further developed Bloch's concept of utopia in his recent discussion of "critical utopia."[44] For Moylan, a critical utopia is manifested in a micro-politics of autonomous social movements – but not the detotalizing micro-politics of ludic postmodernism. Rather, it consists of a political alliance *of the margins without a center* and is directed at creating new radical democratic values in both personal and political spheres. The old utopian periphery that so confidently demarcated and separated the past, present, and future has been blurred. The utopian vision of change that was underpinned by the articulation of teleological master narratives of a centralized and universal movement toward a prefigured and historically realized state has been fundamentally challenged. With a critical utopia, absolute meaning and sovereign power is jettisoned in favor of the power of a metaphorical engagement with Otherness and a displacement of the binary opposition of current metaphysical thinking responsible for constructing the hegemonic utopias of the past and present. This has been done in order to "create a yearning for what has not yet been achieved."[45]

Moylan's description of "critical utopia" both reflects and extends many of the characteristics of Freire's emancipatory praxis. He defines critical utopias as "metaphorical displacements arising out of current contradiction within the political unconscious" (213). Critical utopias are, first and foremost, self-critical, and their formation is designed to resist closure and an imposed totality by stressing "the contradictory and diverse multiplicity of a broad utopian dialogue" (210). We quote Moylan at length:

> The critical utopias give voice to an emerging radical perception and experience that emphasize process over system, autonomous and marginal activity over the imposed order of a center, human liberation over white/ phallocratic control, and the interrelationships of nature over human chauvinism – and they give voice to the seditious utopian impulse itself. The critical utopias still describe alternative societies, but they are careful to consider the flaws and insufficiencies of these systems. They still draw on the provocative mode of the fantastic, but they also mix in a realism that allows for fuller exploration of the activism required to move toward the better society. But beyond self-criticism at the symbolic level and generic discontinuities which help express the common ideologeme, these texts also call attention to their own formal operations in self-reflective gambits that identify the utopian form itself as a mechanism which makes such anticipations and activism possible. The critical utopias refuse to be restricted by their own traditions, their own systematizing content; rather, it is their own radically

hopeful activity as meaningful proto-political acts which they contribute to the current opposition. [211]

We believe Freire's utopian project contains the essential ingredients of Moylan's critical utopia. Like Bloch before him, Freire articulates the "real-possible" conditions necessary for the utopian function to take root in the concrete materiality of daily struggle, not simply as a negative force that challenges existing systems of intelligibility and relations of power, but as a dehypostatizing project that refuses accommodation to the leadership of an elite vanguard of bourgeois intellectuals and decries the conflation of ideology and utopia. Freire's utopian vision does not speak to a categorical set of blueprints, tactics, or strategies for human freedom, but instead remains attentive to the ideological and political dangers that follow from the practice of not challenging the discursive underpinnings of such a vision. Freire understands full well that a pedagogy of liberation has no final answers: radical praxis must always emerge from continuous struggle within specific pedagogical sites and among competing theoretical frameworks. Truth has no necessary closure, no transcendental justification. Even the God of History and the Oppressed can offer no final solution since history is, for Freire, "becoming" and is, furthermore, "a human event" (*Politics of Education*, 129).

Freire's ultimate utopian project constitutes a "counter-discourse" through which contestation stages its struggle and attempts its subversion.[46] As such, Freire's work reveals the necessary contingency of forms of societal domination, forms which through collective struggle and the exercise of human will can eventually be liberated. In this sense, counter-discourse becomes our necessary hope, and our struggle over domination "in which something like an authentic democracy might prevail."[47]

Freire's refusal to forfeit his political project and language of possibility could indeed serve as a means of resisting and hopefully transforming the current historical period through a pedagogy and politics that can be located at the border of modernist and postmodernist critique. This means combining those elements of political modernism that stress social justice, human rights, and collective struggle with a postmodern understanding of difference, identity, and representation. It means incorporating the historical and the relational with specific narratives that link difference with larger articulating principles. It is in this combination of elements that resistance postmodernism can be considered an extension of Freire's own project, one which provides a new model for public struggle by recognizing the imperative of border identities, border struggles, and border intellectuals.

Notes

1. Paulo Friere, "Reading the World and Reading the Word: An Interview with Paulo Friere," *Language Arts*, 62: 1 (1985), p. 17.

2. R. H. Roberts, *Hope and its Hieroglyph* (Atlanta: Scholars Press, 1990), p. xi.

3. Fred Dallmayr, *Margins of Political Discourse* (Albany, NY: SUNY Press, 1989), p. 159.

4. Larry Grossberg, *We Gotta Get Out of This Place: Popular Conservatism and Postmodern Culture* (New York: Routledge, 1992), p. 18.

5. B. Barrett, "Words and Things," in *Destabilizing Theory*, ed. Michele Barrett and Anne Phillips (Stanford: Stanford University Press, 1992), p. 203.

6. *Strategies* Collective, "Building a New Left: An Interview with Ernesto Laclau," *Strategies*, 1 (Fall 1988), pp. 24–5.

7. Ibid., p. 24.

8. See Judith Butler, *Gender Trouble: Feminism and the Subversion of Identity* (New York: Routledge, 1990); and Teresa Ebert, "Political Semiosis in/of American Cultural Studies," *American Journal of Semiotics*, 8: 1–2, (1991), pp. 113–35, and "Writing in the Political: Resistance (Post) Modernism," *Legal Studies Forum*, 15: 4 (1991), pp. 291–303.

9. Paulo Freire, *The Politics of Education: Culture, Power and Liberation* (South Hadley, Mass.: Bergin & Garvey, 1985), p. 169.

10. Florence Tager, "The Relation between Politics and Culture in the Teaching of Working Class Students," *Curriculum Inquiry*, 12: 2 (1982), p. 214.

11. Freire's concept of pedagogy and culture is not entirely unproblematic, and his work has certainly been criticized on a number of accounts. Not surprisingly, many of the arguments used to criticize Freire's work have had strong cultural-conservative instincts. C.A. Bowers's review of the *Politics of Education* (*Educational Studies*, 17: 1 [1986], pp. 147–54) is a case in point. In his review, Bowers attacks Freire for contributing to the reproduction of basic root metaphors or epistemes embedded in Western thinking, especially around the issued of individualism, critical reflection, and the progressive nature of change. Bowers's critique of Freire is informed by an understanding of Enlightenment rationality which lacks the benefit of being dialectical. To suggest that Freire's work celebrates an uncritical endorsement of Enlightenment rationality sets up a false dichotomy around it that pits individual judgement against communal wisdom, agency over collective action, and a nihilistic relativization of values over the time-tested truth of tradition. Furthermore, to claim that Freire possesses an oversimplified understanding of tradition, collective action, or the cultural assumptions inherent in his own pedagogy is to discredit the very strengths of Freire's pedagogy.

Certainly we are "positioned" as readers by language, as discourse theorists and thinkers such as Barthes, Bakhtin (Volosinov), Lacan, and Kristeva have taught us. But to criticize Freire for not deconstructing the text of his own pedagogy around this issue by engaging the ideas of Ong, Shils, Nietzsche, Heidegger, Vygotsky, Foucault, and others is to suggest that he remains unaware of the relationship between language and power. We would argue that Freire's position on language, culture, and power is equally as perceptive as that of Foucault.

12. Henry A. Giroux, "Introduction," to Freire, *Politics of Education*, p. xvii.

13. See Wayne Hudson, *The Marxist Philosophy of Ernst Bloch* (New York: St Martin's Press, 1982), pp. 50–51.

14. Quoted ibid.

15. Ruth Levitas, *The Concept of Utopia* (Syracuse: Syracuse University Press, 1990), p. 89.

16. Bloch, quoted in Anson Rabinbach, "Unclaimed Heritage: Ernst Bloch's *Heritage of Our Times* and the Theory of Fascism," *New German Critique*, 11 (Spring 1977), p. 11.

17. Levitas, *The Concept of Utopia*, p. 91.

18. Tom Moylan, "Bloch against Bloch: The Theological Reception of *Das Prinzip Hoffnung* and the Liberation of the Utopian Function," *Utopian Studies*, 1: 2 (Fall 1990), p. 44; reprinted here as chapter 7.

19. Levitas, *The Concept of Utopia*, p. 99.

20. Fred Dallmayr, *Margins*, p. 162.

21. Roberts, *Hope and Its Hieroglyph*, p. 122.

22. Dallmayr, *Margins*, p. 162.

23. Paulo Freire, *Education: The Practice of Freedom* (London: Writers and Readers Press, 1976), p. 4.

24. Adriana Puiggros, "Prologue to Freire, Paulo and Betto, Frei," *This School Called Life* (Buenos Aires: Legasa, 1988).

25. *Conscientization* (Bogota: Association of Education Publication, 1973), p. 83.

26. Cited in M. Gadotti, *Reading Paulo Freire: Life and Work* (Albany, NY: SUNY Press, forthcoming).

27. Giroux, "Introduction," p. xvii.

28. Freire's position on the role of literacy training, consciousness-raising, and the prophetic church shares similarities with numerous liberation theologians. See Juan Luis Segundo, *Our Idea of God* (Dublin: Gil & MacMillan, 1980). Also see Gustavo Gutiérrez, *A Theology of Liberation* (New York: Orbis, 1973), and his *The Power of the Poor in History* (New York: Orbis, 1983). Brazilian theologian Leonardo Boff discusses Freire in relation to liberation theology in *Church: Charisma and Power* (New York: Crossroads, 1985).

Freire's celebration of the prophetic church also shares much in common with the political theology of Johannes Baptist Metz (see Metz's *Faith in History and Society*, trans. David Smith [New York: Seabury Press, 1980]). In the case of political theology, theological reflection attempts to turn critical reasoning into practical action.

The current Vatican position on liberation theology is confusing, to say the least. On the one hand we have witnessed the Latin American Bishops' Conference meeting at Medellin, Colombia, in 1968, and at Puebla, Mexico, in 1979, where Christians were called to a radical commitment in the struggle for social justice. This new orientation of Catholic social teaching, often termed the "preferential option for the poor," was given amplification in John Paul II's encyclical, *Laborem Ecercens*, with the qualification that liberation was to be understood in more than purely economic and political terms. On the other hand, there are the actions of the Roman Congregation of the Doctrine of Faith (the former Holy Office) against Gustavo Gutiérrez and Leonardo Boff, two major liberation theologians, and the 1984 Instruction of the Holy Office, which warns Catholics of the Marxist threat within liberation theology.

It is significant here to remark that Bishop Jose Iro Lorscheiter, president of the Brazilian Conference of Bishops, offered a dramatic defense of liberation theology at the Extraordinary Synod of Bishops in Rome, 1985, one which "ranks as one of the most challenging statements made publicly to the Vatican by a high-ranking defender of liberation theology" (T.M. Pasca, "The Three Churches of Catholicism," *The Nation*, February 1986). Such a recent statement of support surely attests to the continuing desire among many Third World Catholics for the form of empowerment which Freire links to the role of the prophetic church.

29. Sharon Welch, *Communities of Resistance and Solidarity: A Feminist Theology of Liberation* (New York: Orbis, 1985), p. 87.

30. Ebert, "Writing in the Political," p. 293.

31. Mas'ud Zavarzadeh and Donald Morton, "Signs of Knowledge in the Contemporary Academy," *American Journal of Semiotics*, 7: 4 (1990), p. 156.

32. Levitas, *Concept of Utopia*, p. 181.

33. Ibid., pp. 181–2.

34. Ibid., p. 183.

35. Ibid., p. 184.

36. Peter Murphy, "Postmodern Perspectives and Justice," *Thesis Eleven*, 30 (1990), pp. 117–32.

37. Ibid., p. 126.

38. Hudson, *The Marxist Philosophy of Ernst Bloch*, p. 203.

39. Moylan, "Bloch against Bloch," p. 46.

40. Hudson, *Ernst Bloch*, p. 205.

41. Vincent Geoghegan, *Utopianism and Marxism*, London: Methuen, 1987, p. 93.

42. K. Weiler, "Freire and a Feminist Pedagogy of Difference," in *The Politics of Liberation*, ed. Peter McLaren and Colin Lankshear (London: Routledge, forthcoming).

43. Paulo Freire and Donaldo Macedo, "A Dialogue with Paulo Freire," in *Paulo Freire: A Critical Encounter*, ed. Peter McLaren and Peter Leonard (London: Routledge, 1993).

44. Tom Moylan, *Demand the Impossible: Science Fiction and the Utopian Imagination*, London and New York: Methuen, 1986.

45. Ibid., p. 45.
46. Richard Terdiman, *Discourse/Counter-Discourse: The Theory and Practice of Symbolic Resistence in Nineteenth-century France* (Ithaca: Cornell University Press, 1985), p. 338.
47. Ibid., p. 342.

Part III
Imagining the Totality:
Smaller Pictures

10

Utopian Projections:
In Memory of Ernst Bloch

Stephen Eric Bronner

Ernst Bloch is only now becoming known in the United States. For most of his long life, however, he was one of the best-known intellectuals in Europe. His extraordinary literary output, which always oscillated between art and philosophy, was marked by a unique style. His students revered him and, during the 1960s, he served as an inspiration. With the rise of neo-conservatism and the collapse of communism, however, his influence began to wane. Utopia became a term of derision. Nor is it legitimate any longer to speak of a "teleological suspension of the ethical" (Lukács). Alternative systems have lost their appeal; socialism and utopia can now only take the form of a regulative idea. But there is no denying the existential price for such philosophical moderation. Paraphrasing T.S. Eliot, people feel "hollow" in a modernity seemingly bereft of vision and purpose. Thus, it remains worthwhile to reconsider the legacy offered by undoubtedly the greatest of all utopian philosophers.

One idea preoccupied Ernst Bloch throughout his life: the ideal content and goal of humanity's striving to realize its "dream of the better life." The claim is basically simple enough: "everything existing retains a utopian glimmer and philosophy would be nothing were it not capable of furthering the intellectual solution to the creation of this crystalline heaven of a regenerated reality."[1] Bloch never surrendered this philosophical commitment. From *Spirit of Utopia* and *The Principle of Hope* to collections of stories, essays, and the last great works like *The Problem of Materialism* and *Experimentum Mundi*, his essential concerns remain constant.

Ernst Bloch was a prophet like Marx or Thomas Münzer. His work provides new content for an idea as old as humanity itself. Past utopias, especially of the political variety, were concerned with pacification, order, and symmetry; they were usually far more culturally conservative than most radicals would care to admit. But there was never anything

boring about Ernst Bloch's concept of utopia. Its free-flowing quality
became part of his expressionistic literary style. Its cosmopolitan character was reflected in his extraordinary intellectual range. Its inherently
unfinished quality left open the new experience of tomorrow.

Just like those others, of course, his utopian conception retained
residues of repression and confusion. Its teleological elements led Bloch
to identify with Stalin and often compromise his political judgement.
Seeking to build on the example of Marx, he wished to make his utopian
philosophy relevant for the present and a pre-figuration of the future.
Prophecy, however, is not the stuff of politics; indeed, from his lectures,
it was apparent to many that he had little real political insight, and
contemporary attempts to somehow preserve Bloch from his past are
dishonest. Nevertheless, it is an exaggeration for Jan Robert Bloch to
claim that the work of his father was constituted by nothing more than
a "philosophical and propagandistic cover for Stalin's terror."

The value of a work, as Ernst Bloch knew, is not exhausted by the
politics of the author. And, philosophically, Bloch was a maverick.
Communists considered him an outsider, an "idealist" and a "dreamer"
whose works might bring him honor, but who still could not be taken
seriously. Even within the Institute for Social Research, with which he
was loosely associated, Bloch's thought never jibed with the pessimism
of Adorno and Horkheimer. He was older. His thought harked back to
intellectual tendencies existing prior to the First World War when
cultural radicalism was defined by a commitment to the "new dawn"
foreshadowed by Nietzsche, the visionary communitarian socialism
identified with figures like Gustav Landauer, the concern with reification and alienation exhibited by neo-Kantians like Emil Lask and Georg
Simmel, the rebirth of interest in Jewish mysticism and Christian
chilianism, and the manifold experiments of the modernist avant-gardes.
Bloch's thinking incorporated elements from all these sources and
others as well. Indeed, the result would prove uniquely his own and jut
boldly into the future.   •

Utopia, in the thinking of Ernst Bloch, ceases to exist as "nowhere,"
as an Other to real history. It is a constituent element of all human
activity and, simultaneously, historical. It becomes manifest in the quest
for meaning, the thrill of sports, the desire for love, the daydream, the
wonder of a child, and the experience of lightness before a genuine
work of art. Each is a dim pre-figuration (*Vor-erscheinung*) of its existence;
the question becomes how to articulate and realize the hopes uncon-
sciously shared by humanity. And here, whatever the influence of neo-
romantic and mystical currents from the turn of the century, revelation
is inadequate to the task at hand since

the forward glance becomes all the stronger, the more lucidly it becomes
conscious. The dream in this glance seeks to make itself clear and the

premonition, the right one, quite plain. Only when reason begins to speak can hope, in which there is nothing false, blossom again. The 'not-yet-conscious' must become conscious in action, *known* in its content.[2]

Utopia is at the essence of human existence. But humanity appears in a variety of forms and so it follows that utopia will receive articulation in a variety of ways. It is no accident then that the gaze of this most European of thinkers should have extended to Zoroaster, Confucius, and the stories of the mythical Shararzad. Bloch retained what Kant termed a "teleology of hope," but considered material equality as the precondition for actualizing utopia. If this obviously led him to Marx, however, the recognition that various forms of experience provided a sense of the new also led him to medieval mystics like Meister Eckhardt and Jacob Boehme. A rationalist concerned with determining the "ratio of the irratio," he undertook the construction of an "underground" utopian tradition extending from Moses to Thomas Münzer to Marx.

Perhaps more than any other major philosopher of our time, Ernst Bloch was an eclectic. And so it makes sense that he should have been criticized from virtually every angle. Bloch was rigorous after his fashion. His cosmological theory of nature was built on a knowledge of physics and it anticipated what would become a new preoccupation with the "eco-system." Still, many of the technical and political criticisms of his work remain valid. His philosophical stance was never bound to praxis as he claimed and especially now, in an avowedly anti-speculative age, his utopian theory seems anything but "concrete." His claims were too often asserted rather than argued, and his categories generally lack precision. The religious, chiliastic-messianic strain in his work calls for a suspension of disbelief and few criteria are provided for the formulation of ethical or aesthetic judgements. He has little to say about the constraints on revolutionary transformation, the character of emanci-pated production relations, or the determinate institutions necessary for maintaining a realm of freedom. Indeed, when analyzing death and resurrection, daydreams and utopian symbols, the line between fantasy and logic often becomes blurred.

Bloch's daring attempt to reintroduce a radical telos into dialectical thought and ground it within an ontology of Being, however, extends the tradition of natural law and Marxism beyond purely economic or even regulative concerns. In this vein, whatever his own political commitments, the philosophy was a response to the manner in which goals commonly agreed upon were displaced into an ever more distant future by the communist vanguard. There is an inherently critical element to his way of thinking, which rests on a positive vision of emancipation. Its sophistication and quality have little in common with the dogmatism promoted by the communist states he supported. Never-theless, its willingness to unearth the moment of freedom and happiness in everyday experience also confronts what has become a deadening philosophical pessimism among intellectuals.

Ernst Bloch wished to provide an ontological foundation for utopia. His philosophy thus retained an eschatological view of history. But it was one without the certainty of salvation or redemption. Realizing utopia, according to Bloch, can occur only through the creation of conditions capable of guaranteeing humanity's reflection on what has been ignored.[3] It depends ultimately upon an act of will and the commitment to, in the words of his friend Walter Benjamin, "never forget the best." Categories for determining the "best" were, for Bloch, never forthcoming. It was enough to emphasize that the best will appear where it is least expected. Tolerance and civil liberties are thus immanently demanded by the philosophy of the man who once defended Stalin's show-trials. Unacknowledged works by the most diverse cultures, "traces" (*Spuren*) of forgotten lives, fragments of historical production, retain untapped perspectives on the "best life," which never simply "vanish" (Hegel) into immediate forms of practice. Indeed, "the waking dream everywhere feeds on what has been missed."[4]

Realizing the utopian *Novum* in the future depends upon tapping the potential from the past. And this, in turn, is dependent upon the degree of consciousness generated in the present. The future is thus no mechanical elaboration of the present; nor does it emerge from a series of "steps" or "stages" deriving in linear fashion from the past. The future is open; determining the "horizon" of the present is possible only through unearthing the "anticipatory consciousness" embodied in the cultural achievements of the past. Utopia is not an abrupt break with the past; thus, in contrast to critical theorists like Adorno and Horkheimer, history becomes more than the unrolling of "necessity" and "freedom" more than the affirmation of "negativity." That is why Bloch could say that

> [t]o the *Novum* there belongs, in order that it really exist as a *novum*, not only an abstract opposition to a mechanical renewal, but rather in fact a specific type of renewal: namely, the not-yet-realized total content of that goal which is itself meant and intended and processed out of history's progressive novelties.[5]

Of course, for all Bloch's claims to materialism, his is a fundamentally idealist vision. The "objective contradictions" within the existing order are not entirely forgotten. But the essential point, important enough, involves a commitment to *de-ideologize* ideology and the articulation of a utopian hermeneutic capable of building the content and furthering the realization of a "realm of freedom." Having said that, however, the philosophy of Bloch harbors a unique view of ideology which flies in the face of Leninism. Indeed, whatever the attempts to employ the language of communist orthodoxy, it inherently rejects any mechanical distinction between "true" and "false" consciousness.

The thinking of Bloch also rejects the popular idea that the potential within any form of social practice is exhausted by examining the historical context from which it arose. A reaffirmation of the dialectical relation between immanence and transcendence occurs as cultural products become more than mere "artificial social constructs;" they can also "jut beyond" the historical conditions of their emergence. And Bloch draws the theoretical consequences. A perspective takes shape in which, against all dogmatic forms of dialectical "stage theory," it becomes impossible to assume that a reconciliation of *all* the contradictions defining a given epoch will take place before the next appears on the scene.

Unresolved problems as well as unfulfilled hopes can carry over from one phase of history into another. And the form, no less than the function, of these "non-synchronous contradictions" will change within the dominant socio-economic and political structures of the new period. A single unresolved concern like salvation can manifest both positive utopian and negative dystopian characteristics in different ways in different historical epochs. The implications of Bloch's approach are important for analyzing manifold phenomena including racism, sexism, the "cult of the personality," and the role of atavistic classes like the peasantry and petty bourgeoisie. Indeed, even while Bloch considered the proletariat immune from "non-synchronous contradictions," the concept would prove crucial for his remarkable analysis of the triumph of fascism in Germany.[6]

The argument rests on the assumption that Marxism was being stripped of its utopian ideals in the 1920s while the Nazis were employing a corrupt and "false" interpretation of them in their quest for power. The claim with respect to Stalinism is questionable and Bloch never did clarify an alternative approach from within the existing communist model. Nor is it clear how Bloch's categories of "false" and "true" utopia are ultimately grounded in anything more than taste and goodwill. But he surely hit on something very real since the Nazis, no less than Stalin, did reap enormous propagandistic value from mutilating the past and establishing their particular forms of utopian symbolism. It becomes as apparent in the marching songs as in the films of Leni Riefenstahl and the torchlight parades. Nor is it an accident that Moeller van der Bruck should have taken the notion of a "third reich" from the humanist and utopian vision first articulated by the medieval philosopher Joachim di Fiore.[7]

Ideology, for Bloch, thus becomes a fungible concept. It is neither fixed nor finished. Ideology may obscure and justify the oppression of the status quo. But, since human practice inherently retains a teleological component, it will also retain an emancipatory moment. A ruling ideology is for him, in more concrete terms, the ensemble of ideas of a ruling class. But a universal interest, generally articulated while a class is on the rise, can coexist with a particular one in any given work. "Liberty, equality, fraternity" is an example; "we the people" and "the right to life, liberty, and the pursuit of happiness" is another. Every articulation of a universal interest projects the desire for justice, harmony, freedom, and the like. Most likely the dominant class will become alienated from the radical implications of its ideals by its oppressive activity. Nonetheless, without the existence of the utopian element within ideology, it becomes impossible to explain why they work and transcend the context in which they arose.[8]

Radical analysis is then not just a matter of sociological analysis or explaining the "immanent" historical roots of ideas. It is a matter of unearthing their "transcendent" potential as well. The ideology of a given period is subsequently never entirely "false," as in "false consciousness," since a set of "not-yet-realized" utopian possibilities remains "latent" and waiting for self-conscious appropriation. The new society, in short, will not just "objectively" appear. "Subjective" action is necessary to reshape the repressed needs of humanity as they appear in the manifold set of cultural products through which history is understood.

Gone is the determinism of "scientific socialism" and the willingness to ascribe an inflexible class content to a given idea or work. The sober emphasis on modernization gives way before the mission articulated by the young Marx and the Lukács of *History and Class Consciousness*. Visions of anthropological transformation, the employment of dialectics as a critical method with a humanistic intent, the creation of a fuller, richer, more meaningful existence becomes the purpose of the socialist enterprise. The aim is

> to lift the world and inwardness, in their new interaction, out of their alienation and reification. Marxism is thoroughly realistic, but definitely not in the sense of a banal schematic copy of reality; to the contrary, its reality is: actuality plus the future within actuality. Through its own concrete change, which it ever holds open, Marxism demonstrates: that there is still an immeasurable amount of unused dream, unfinished content of history, unsold nature in the world.[9]

Just this, the "unused," the "unfinished," and "unsold" − in its humanistic potential − is what critical inquiry must clarify. Grounding itself within the tradition of emancipation, in theory and practice, becomes a crucial concern. Reflection and critique never lose their primacy in the work of Bloch. But the importance of fantasy, and the experience which explodes the constraints of the given, is never lost either. Dealing with such concerns, in fact, becomes obligatory for the cultural critic. Aesthetic criticism subsequently cannot remain content with either political or sociological pronouncements. Nor will purely formal judgements get to the heart of the matter. Art, for Bloch, is a mode of enjoyment and of experiencing the world in a new way.

And the implication of his position is clear enough; chaining either cultural production or criticism to the traditions of the past is inherently illegitimate. Art, for Bloch, *must* experiment with new forms of expression which overcome the limitations of the past. The value of art, in fact, appears in its simultaneous ability to serve as a "utopian laboratory" and a "feast of elaborated possibilities" for the future.[10]

There is no stasis. The possibilities of a work, in his view, change through its interaction with a changing public. Bloch subsequently considers it necessary to judge even "unpopular" works, which might initially appear as irrationalist and fragmented, with an eye on the new and the unexplored. Bloch thus does not see "decadence" in the surrealist and expressionist attempts to merge dream and reality, perceive the world in a new light through distortion, or juxtapose dissimilar objects through montage. He looks for more. He delights in the new color of the fauves, the fantastic imagery of the surrealists, the irreverent fun of the dadaists, and the free play of the expressionists. The Stalinist always remained a modernist. And he wasn't a snob either. Indeed, just as he took exception to the "realist" position favored by Lukács in the famous set of debates between them during the tail end of the 1930s, his interest in a variety of popular forms ranging from the detective novel to nursery rhymes placed him in opposition to the stance usually associated with the Frankfurt School.

Experimentation with new forms and the aesthetics of fantasy make for, in the view of Bloch, a "dream which looks ahead" (*der Traum nach Vorwärts*) and confronts the "way things are." This dream is defined neither by regression nor a retreat backward into childhood. And so, in contrast to Freud, Bloch refuses to concentrate upon the "night-dream" whose truth emerges in memories of the past or the "no-longer-conscious." He instead emphasizes the role of the "day-dream" with its projection of the "new," the "not-yet-conscious," and its loose connection with the situation in which the individual finds himself. Hope appears in the "day-dream;" happiness is envisioned "as the shape (*Gestalt*) of things to come." The daydream, for Bloch, is capable of surmounting the censoring qualities of the super-ego and thus inherently retains a utopian kernel.[11]

Arguably, in analyzing the subjective presentiment of utopia, Bloch ignores how social repression is interjected into the very substructure of the individual and the freeing of rage that can occur once objective referents are exploded. Also, in his emphasis on the "anticipatory consciousness," the "day-dream," and the "not-yet-conscious," he rips the concept of possibility from any determinate analysis of existence and turns it into the property of pure consciousness. This would obviously place him in opposition not only to the followers of Marx and Lenin, but also to adherents of Martin Heidegger and Jean-Paul Sartre.

Phenomenology and existentialism had gained in popularity during the 1930s. They emphasized the "concreteness" of individual existence and drew a connection between the concept of "possibility" and death. The central category of "authentic" experience was "anguish" or "dread." Bloch was aware, however, that hope is as legitimate a fundamental mode of experience as anguish once a "possibility" is encountered. With any "concrete" possibility, after all, there is the hope of its being fulfilled as well as the anguish at the thought of its remaining unfulfilled.[12] Death is unavoidable; only through a philosophical sleight of hand does it become a "possibility." And so, once again, Bloch draws the consequences. Real possibility, for him, "does not reside in any finished ontology of the Being of that which is already existent, but rather in that ontology of the not-yet-existent (*noch-nicht-Seienden*) which is continually grounded anew as it discovers the future in the past and in all of nature."[13]

An openness to the possibility of utopia remains. Bloch's ontology is neither fixed nor finished. And, precisely for this reason, the unfulfilled promises of the past and the untapped sources of consciousness in the present prevent any *absolute* denial of utopia in the future;[14] indeed, once again, a line from Walter Benjamin comes to mind: "every second of time [is] the strait gate through which the Messiah might enter." And so, a "militant optimism" comes to define Bloch's worldview. Optimism of this sort bears no relation to the passive and naive variant so often encountered. Rather, it assumes the existential commitment to make good on the "latent" possibilities existing in the present and help in actualizing a new world for the future.

Now, Sartre once wrote that the question of whether history has a meaning is foolish, for the real question involves what meaning is given to it. Perhaps Bloch was too quick in dismissing the contribution realism might make in determining the concrete conditions wherein the "new" can serve as an "interruption." But he was correct when he wrote that "man does not live by bread alone – especially when he doesn't have any." Idealism is essential for the emergence of any political movement. And the fact is that the idealism of the intellectuals and the masses has dissipated with the collapse of the communist experiment in the East and the simple identification of social democracy with technocratic reform in the West. The reaffirmation of ideals is no small matter in today's world.

But that does not call for the suppression of the unpleasant, or for a self-imposed blindness regarding the mistakes of the past. This was a point of which Bloch was aware; human nature may be malleable, but the evil runs deep. And yet, "in the negative there are also constructs of the unconstructable, the absolute question: there are unbearable moments of wonder."[15] A Kafka who describes the existential no less than the bureaucratic nightmare with such precision thus makes a utopian contribution precisely insofar as he defines what must be overcome. Nor would his work lack an "anticipatory consciousness." Indeed, Brecht captured this when he said that Kafka "saw what was coming without seeing what was there."

Of course, it is highly debatable whether the "anticipatory consciousness" of utopia is inherent within every cultural construct. Bloch, in his ontological justification of aesthetic claims, may well have overstated his case. But he is willing to address the unacknowledged question. What is the worth of art? And his answer juts beyond the immediate effects of a work. He knows that every great work of art remains,

> beyond its immediate manifestation, imprinted upon the latency of the other side; that is, upon the content of the future which had not yet appeared during its own time, if not upon the content of a yet unknown final state. For this reason alone, the great works of all times have something to say and, in fact, a far-reaching *Novum* which is not noticed in any of them by the previous age.[16]

A project, inherently new, presents itself in the philosophy of Ernst Bloch. Embracing it militates against provincialism and against certainty. This project is founded on hope and a willingness to recognize that the potential for emancipation breaks the constraints of every fixed and finished system. It is the same with art and philosophy; of all the philosophers within the tradition of critical theory, Bloch is the most generous when it comes to aesthetic experience and so perhaps best understands what it means to speak about the integrity of an art work. His is an essentialism which does not exclude; it doesn't serve the purposes of sexism, racism, or any other form of oppression. His thinking refuses to accept anything as simply given; the articulation of what it means to strive for the "best life" can be found in a hundred rivers and a thousand streams. It calls for a cosmopolitan frame of mind and a refusal to chain the meaning of a work to any set of political aims or particular experiences. Critical interpretation breaks the chains of dogmatism and that enterprise, no less than the quest for utopia, is unending. Thus, following the African sages, Ernst Bloch would maintain toward the end of his long life that "if a story is nothing then it belongs to him who has told it . . . but it is when it is something that it belongs to all of us."[17]

Notes

1. Ernst Bloch, *Geist der Utopie* (Frankfurt am Main: Suhrkamp, 1962), p. 217.

2. Ernst Bloch, *Das Prinzip Hoffnung*, (Frankfurt am Main: Suhrkamp, 1973), 3 vols., I, p. 163. All translations from Bloch are my own.

3. Ibid., II, p. 620.

4. Ernst Bloch, *Verfremdungen* (Frankfurt am Main: Suhrkamp, 1964), p. 181.

5. Bloch, *Das Prinzip Hoffnung*, I, p. 230.

6. Ernst Bloch, *Erbschaft dieser Zeit* (Frankfurt am Main: Suhrkamp, 1962), pp. 104–60.

7. Bloch, *Das Prinzip Hoffnung*, II, p. 590.

8. Ibid., I, p. 170.

9. Ernst Bloch, *Die Kunst, Schiller zu Sprechen* (Frankfurt am Main: Suhrkamp, 1969), p. 67.

10. Bloch, *Das Prinzip Hoffnung*, I, p. 249.

11. Ibid., I, p. 101.

12. Ibid., I, p. 285.

13. Ibid., I, p. 274.

14. Ibid., I, p. 226.

15. Ibid., I, p. 351.

16. Ibid., I, p. 143.

17. Ernst Bloch, *Spuren* (Frankfurt am Main: Suhrkamp, 1969), p. 127.

Utopia and Reality in the Philosophy of Ernst Bloch

Ze'ev Levy

1. *Urgrund* and *Endziel*

Ernst Bloch was one of the most original and least dogmatic Marxist thinkers of our time. In addition to the impact of Marx, especially the early writings, one can discern in his oeuvre salient influences of classical philosophy – Kant, Hegel, Schelling – as well as of neo-platonism. In the latter one also encounters many traces of Christian and Jewish mysticism. Bloch met Jewish mystical trends in the Zohar, the magnum opus of the kabbala, with which he became acquainted through the writings of Gershom Scholem. All these different components gave birth to a worldview which conceived of the utopian endeavor as an elementary activity of the human mind: yearning, anticipation, and fantasy. In this sense he frequently spoke about "dreams as wish-fulfillment" and "anticipatory consciousness,"[1] and viewed the world as a "laboratory of possible good" ("*laboratorium possibilis salutis*"), i.e. something that has not yet been completely realized.[2] He thus strove to lay down the "blueprints" (*Grundrisse*, alluding to Marx's famous first draft of *Capital*) of a better world. The world comprises unlimited possibilities which have not yet been actualized. In this consists the significance of utopia.

Bloch deduces his notion of utopia from his all-encompassing philos-ophical conception. Following Hegel, he conceives of reality as a "mediation" between subject and object. The whole of being takes place between two poles. One precedes the process of mediation; it is its "primordial cause" (*Urgrund*) which existed before the dichotomy of subject and object, of matter and spirit (mind). The second pole is the "final goal" (*Endziel*), the ultimate merger of subject and object. However, what distinguishes Bloch as a philosopher is his almost prophetic vision which is perpetually turned toward the future: the veritable act of creation was not in the beginning but will occur at the end. This is the genuine meaning of "utopia" in Bloch's thought, namely a typically religious experience, although without God. This end he often designated as *Ultimum*, i.e. the embodiment of ultimate reality and ultimate meaning. Unlike the traditional trend of philosophy, inaugurated by the pre-Socratics, and recently taken up again by some thinkers in the aftermath of French structuralism (e.g. Michel Foucault), Bloch asserts that life and existence cannot be understood by the question "where from?;" it is incumbent upon us to understand them by asking "where to?" and "what for?" Leaning on the erstwhile Christian theologian Marcion and his modern counterpart Adolf von Harnack, he reaffirms their conclusion that, despite God's alleged intention ("And God saw everything that He had made, and, behold, it was very good" [Gen. 1: 31]), the present world is nevertheless not yet the best and most perfect world. It still waits for its forthcoming full redemption.[3] (Bloch, of course, does not accept Marcion's and von Harnack's apologetic principal thesis, that the New Testament is completely independent of the Old Testament, and that Christianity did not absorb any influences from ancient Jewish sources.)

Although Bloch's thought focuses on the "final goal," he does not neglect the role of the "primordial cause." It also has its proper place in his concept of utopia. It is motivated by a more or less hidden cosmic drive which Bloch designates as "hunger," and counterposes to Freud's concept of libido (*Prinzip*, 71). There exists an essential difference between the two concepts. Without gratification of the sexual drive, an individual will still stay alive, whilst non-gratification of hunger leads to death. This "hunger," in the wide and metaphorical sense that is Bloch's, is a flagrant manifestation of reality; it concerns the innermost essence of the subject as well as of the object. Its full and adequate satisfaction remains, however, for the time being still a matter of the future. But what is of the essence, for Bloch, is that there is already, at least *in potentia*, the "possibility" (on this category see below) to overcome this hunger.

This was undoubtedly one of the most startling conceptual intuitions of the young Bloch: to describe the history of the world, or more exactly, human history, as a totality that ought to be conceived and explicated by its end (in the twofold sense of this word). What I mean here by "end" is, obviously, not the "end" of all movement and development, but "end" as a future which opens up "endless" new possibilities. This is more or less the core of Bloch's all-embracing philosophical system as he developed it over the years, a historical-philosophical conception of utopia as a potential realization of the possible. This theme represents the nub of all his inquiries, and attains its grandiose and most systematic crystallization in his magnum opus, *Das Prinzip Hoffnung*.

2. The Logical Category of "Possibility"

From all this, it follows that the logical category of "possibility" fulfills a central role in Bloch's thought. The primordial hunger that activates the (human) subject puts before humanity two possibilities: desire and hope. This is where the concept of utopia makes its entrance, because hope appears in the beginning as something utopian. Hope, indeed, expresses the vision, or the foresight, of the possibility to realize something which is not yet anywhere. This is the literal meaning of the word "u-topia" – a nowhere which can be reached *in potentia*. What is ruled out a priori is impossible; it cannot even become an object of hope, and will never become a utopia. It would be no more than an illusion or, to use a Freudian term, a delusion. Hope, Bloch's principal notion, embodies the tendency and the tension toward the future, toward the *Novum*. In this sense he characterizes the utopian future as "dawn forwards" (*Dämmerung nach Vorwärts: Prinzip*, 129). The singular characteristics are not yet bright because the sun which radiates its light on everything has not yet risen; it is still dawn, but no longer dark. The direction which one ought to follow is already visible. All this metaphorical rhetoric is intended to show that hope is not merely a projection of reason, a "mental creation" of human thought, but an expression of what is *really possible*. This future possibility, which looks to us today like a distant dream, is not simply a dream, but a "daydream;" it results from conscious thought. Bloch insists on the essential distinction between daydreams and night-dreams. In line with Freud's interpretation, he characterizes night-dreams as the effects of unconscious and repressed desires and drives, usually relating to one's own personal problems. Daydreams, on the other hand, represent a free "expedition" forwards, rich in fantasy, but this time the "dreamer" is conscious. These dreams manifest the inclination "to mend the world" (*Weltverbesserung*). (Perhaps Bloch borrowed this term from the kabbalistic term, *Tikkun Olam.*) It is one of the many metaphorical speculations in Bloch's philosophy. The result is a very complicated system of relationships between subject, object, reality, and possibility.

Reality holds within itself the anticipation of a possible future. Bloch was perhaps influenced on this issue by the Jewish philosopher Franz Rosenzweig; in the 1920s he belonged, with Erich Fromm amongst others, to Rosenzweig's circle. Rosenzweig emphasized, in his *Star of Redemption*, the idea (which he formulated in religious terms) that the individual's task consists in transmitting God's love of humanity to others. But the main point to be underscored in this context is the following: according to Rosenzweig's argument, the redemption of the world consists of the transformation of the good, looming in the future, into a reality of the present. Both philosophers conceive of true reality as the reality of something imminent which, for the time being, is still absent but can come into being. Only Bloch elaborated this idea explicitly. Rosenzweig expressed it by the Schellingian formula of *Nicht-seiendes Sein*, whilst Bloch preferred the ontological category of *Noch-nicht-Sein* (*Tübinger*, 210 ff.). As an objective possibility the future represents a reality today. This is, according to Bloch, the essence of utopia. But now he introduces another important distinction: theoretical versus real possibility.

Theoretical possibility means that the object concerned is not yet realizable. It is a possibility, but a theoretical one only, a sort of fantasy, of longed-for dreams. It lacks a real relationship with existence or history. As against this, real possibilities (without going here into the inherent logical difficulty of this notion) exhibit a practical relation to the future. They are concretely linked to the hoped-for utopia. In this case utopia is no empty, merely theoretical, possibility, but a very real one. As such it is not only edifying and convincing, but – this is the crux of the matter – it also displays the ways and means for its realization. Utopia is a striving toward the "real possible," since present reality already contains the elements for its possible future changes (i.e. possibilities that do not exist *in actu* but are at hand in potential). Humanity's creative capacities which are still dormant can be aroused and realized; this is implied by the idea of utopia. Utopias embody these possibilities. Therefore they play an essential and decisive role in human consciousness.

But now, suddenly, Bloch introduces one more surprising, unexpected idea. Utopia is a real possibility, but its essence consists in that, notwithstanding being anchored in the present as a "real possibility," it is at the same time *unconditioned*. In this idea, Bloch's outlook differs from that of vulgar Marxism, though perhaps not so much from Marx's thought. The laws of social development, contrary to the simplistic and dogmatic versions of Marxism, are not necessary in the same sense as natural laws. Let me illustrate this point with an example which has been popular with dialecticians since Hegel. The seed already contains, as a *real* possibility, the plant, tree, or animal which will grow out of it or be born from it (it is irrelevant to our problem that not every seed will bring forth fruit). What ought to be underscored here is that nobody would define the tree which grows here as a utopia. The very term is out of place. In other words, what is conditioned (i.e. stems from predetermined conditions) cannot be included in what Bloch calls utopia. It certainly was not coincidental that vulgar Marxism denied the significance of utopia. According to its pseudo-"scientific" conceptions, socialism would grow out of capitalism by necessity (although revolutions are likely to accelerate the process), due to the "inevitable contradictions" between the forces and relations of production. This will happen in the same way that capitalism evolved from feudalism. Such a mechanistic view left no place for the concept of utopia. The proclaimed ideal was, according to Engels's famous slogan, to transform socialism from a "utopia into a science." Bloch, who repudiates this simplistic view, rehabilitates at the same time the "lost face" of utopia. This implies a dialectical process too: neither to conceive of utopia as a "theoretical possibility" (see above), as preached by the pre-Marxist utopian socialists; nor to adopt the allegedly "scientific" antithesis, preached by traditional Marxism; but to conceive of utopia as a synthesis that overcomes the regrettable one-sidedness of the two former versions. Utopia can become an objective and real possibility only when it is not bound by predetermined conditions. Only an unconditioned utopia can become a realizable utopia.

Bloch did not recant his Marxist outlook. He intertwined into his worldview the two chief philosophical components of Marxism: dialectical and historical materialism. He added, however, an original layer to each of them. In order to overcome the platitudes of the vulgar versions of *dialectical* materialism, he introduced the notion of "primordial hunger" (*Urhunger*) which serves as a more or less natural motive (*agens*). It remains questionable, however, whether this can be considered as an ordinary materialist conception, as Bloch wishes to affirm. The notion of primordial hunger as a natural motive makes sense only when it is directed toward some end. But then it is no longer a matter of nature but a human affair. Vico (whom Marx held in high esteem) asserted that history differs from nature because the first is performed by humans whilst the second is not. Similarly, in order to overcome the platitudes of the vulgar versions of historical materialism, Bloch added the central concept of his whole philosophy, the concept of hope. Here again one encounters the religious dimension of Bloch's Marxism, although it is an atheistic religiosity.

In this context it is also important to stress the following point. Bloch conceives of utopia as some kind of merger between subject and object, which impromptu reduces the problems of nature to human history: first, to the yearning of romanticism for a better world; secondly, to the messianic expectations which draw their inspiration from Jewish and Christian mysticism. Although he declares himself to be a Marxist, he presents his thoughts in an entirely different garb to that of common Marxist reasoning. The unusual force of his argumentation is also very much reinforced by his impressionistic and idiosyncratic manner of writing, which is quite unique in contemporary philosophical and scientific literature. This evidently engenders many difficulties for readers who wish to come to grips with his philosophy, which often looks almost esoteric. He describes, for example, utopia in a quasi-religious style as "the Kingdom of the children of God," borrowing the expression from Thomas Münzer, the revolutionary theologian of the Reformation.[4] But he conceives of this "Kingdom of the children of God" at the same time as the "realm of freedom" (*Reich der Freiheit*),

employing the renowned expression of Marx. Then all exploitation of
people by one another will disappear. He therefore acclaims the Bible
(including the New Testament), and in particular the books of prophecy, as the first announcement of this great future without exploitation
and oppression. This endows the Bible with its unique significance
amongst all the religious scriptures of humankind. (This view perhaps
expresses some kind of inadvertent ethnocentrism, but this is irrelevant
in the present context.) When he draws inspiration from the Bible,
Bloch is evidently less concerned with the God of Job, who answers Job's
questions as a God of nature, than with Isaiah's God of justice. Only the
latter is a worthy source of authentic religiosity. The Bible is, therefore,
not to be considered as a particular property of the Jewish people, for
its humanist and universal message belongs to the whole of humanity.
In line with his own philosophy, Bloch interprets the Bible, perhaps a
little bit arbitrarily, as the proclamation of a utopian better world for
all. The Bible on the one hand, and the humanist principles of Marx's
theory on the other, thus form together the two fundamental corner-
stones of Bloch's utopian vision.

Freedom – the ultimate end of hope – is not an abstract, empty
freedom, but one that is concrete and real. This means that it is possible
to reach and realize it. It will be freedom from hunger and distress,
from fear and anxiety; at the same time it will be the freedom to
develop, without restraints, the manifold inclinations, capabilities and
potentialities concealed in humanity's inner being, which embody truly
human nature. (Well-known ideas from Marx's work, including the
early writings and the *Critique of the Gotha Programme*, reverberate here.)
The realization of the true identity of subject and object which Bloch
tries to elaborate in his book on Hegel (*Subjekt*) relies, therefore, on
Marx's idea of humanization of nature and naturalization of humanity.
Naturalization implies that people are capable of achieving optimal
fulfillment of their inherent human nature. Unfortunately this still
remains a utopia because until now such a reality has nowhere come
into existence. But it is a real possibility; it is unconditioned and
depends ultimately on free human activity.

Bloch inverts the traditional Marxist theory of knowledge. It is not
enough to reject the vulgar "mirror" theory (which predominated in
Marxist thought for so long, triggered mainly by Lenin's *Materialism and
Empiriocriticism*). Many Marxist thinkers had already done this before
Bloch. He, however, changed the very assignment of epistemology; no
longer dealing with cognition of the "become" (*Gewordenen*), but of the
"becoming" (*Werdenden*), focusing attention once more on the "not yet."
This opens up far-reaching opportunities for both epistemology and
ontology: the first manifests "anticipatory consciousness" (the title of the
second part of *Das Prinzip Hoffnung*) whilst the second is concerned with
Noch-nicht-Sein (*Tübinger*, 210). Bloch pursues the same idea, which

appeared for the first time in Schelling's later philosophy and was then taken up by Rosenzweig. Notwithstanding these striking influences, one ought not, however, to overlook one decisive difference. In his *Star of Redemption*, Rosenzweig distinguished between *nicht Sein* and *nicht seiend Sein* (it is impossible to render this distinction into English), in order to accommodate the biblical conception of creation with his own philosophy, whose three fundamental elements – God, world, humanity – he apprehended as being completely distinct and independent from each other. He was concerned with a theological problem, namely to explicate a cosmic event of the past in line with his own religious belief. Bloch, on the other hand, although he was also fascinated by certain mystical and messianic ideas, dealt with a philosophical problem, in order to explicate a foreseeable event of the future. But this too does not yet exhaust the whole difference. According to Rosenzweig *nicht seiend Sein* is a *Sein* ("being") which has not yet become *seiend* ("extant"). According to Bloch, *Noch-nicht-Sein* is a possible being; although not yet extant, its possibility imposes on humanity, not on God, the urgent task to do everything to bring it into existence. Utopia thus embodies the good and the commendable, which for the time being is still wanting. It does not only express the longed-for positive being which has not yet come into being, but reflects and entails the negation of the negative being that prevails at present. The famous dialectical concept of "negation of negation" which has been so strongly jeopardized by dogmatic abuses and misinterpretations since Marx and Hegel, thus recovers some of its erstwhile dignity. It helps Bloch to give an adequate expression of the relationship between the idea of utopia and true reality.

What fascinates Bloch more than anything else is, perhaps, the following. He attempts to elucidate why people are attracted to something which is not yet there. How can this strange phenomenon be accounted for? Why do people engage in fantasies and daydreams of this sort? What is the peculiar drive that generates hope? Since thinking the possible has no limits, one can always suppose and postulate new possibilities. There will always be utopias. People will never cease to ponder over possibilities that are not yet realities. Utopian yearning is an inseparable part of human consciousness. This leads Bloch to the surprising conclusion that, in contradistinction to customary belief, the true roots of utopia have to be looked for not in the social tier but in the anthropological. It is the will (based on humanity's latent creative capabilities) to liberate oneself from one's immediate factual surroundings, in order to create new "possibilities" such as have not even been "dreamed" of. It belongs to the very concept of utopia, not merely to predict new possibilities, but to discover those possibilities with which the present reality is pregnant (i.e. already comprehends *in potentia*). By nursing them, people change the reality in which they live. This is the "principle of hope." Hope must derive from something given, and at the same time imply an active attitude to it. There ought to be a clear linkage between exposition of possibilities and scientific investigation of such possibilities; this must include *ex tempore* ways for their realization.

This entails an interesting mutual relationship of the kind explored by modal logic. Since the relevant possibilities for the improvement of the human condition are necessary, they are indeed possible. In this connection Bloch enlarges his earlier dichotomous distinction between "theoretically possible" and "really possible," and speaks about four "layers of the category possibility" (*Prinzip*, 258–88):

1. The "formally possible": this is the naive optimistic position which disregards the given reality; it brings forth an abstract and irresponsible idea of utopia. Moreover such a utopian idea is no more than the thought of one singular person. Such persons formulate the content and goals of the utopian idea as a corollary to their negation of the existing reality, but do not take into consideration how to bring the new reality into being, and by what means. They are also unaware of those possibilities of change which, as we have seen, are already concealed in the existing reality. For this reason all the famous classical utopias were doomed to failure. Bloch devotes much space and attention to their analysis. They came too early, and were therefore severed from the real possibilities of the social reality of their time. Such was the predicament of Owen, Saint-Simon, and Fourier, and before them, Thomas More, Bacon, Campanella, and the like.

2. The "cognitively possible" (259 ff.): this means reflecting on new problems, as well as proposing new solutions. It leans on reason, but, like the former position, remains stuck in the limited frame of subjectivity. It is also still incapable of becoming a social program.

3. The "objectively possible" (264 ff.): this is more or less the same as the "theoretically possible" whose shortcomings Bloch had criticized. Although it springs out of the social reality itself, it nevertheless lacks practical usefulness because it restricts itself to theoretical aspects only.

4. The "dialectically possible" (271 ff.): as one would expect, this kind of possible is what Bloch most cherishes in his concept of utopia. It expresses most strikingly the dialectical bond between the utopia which possesses a firm relationship with reality and reflects its progress, and the utopia which embodies human freedom. This means that it is unconditioned (see above) and not subjected passively to objective reality. A propos, this conception of the "dialectically

possible" has been further developed by the sociologist Zygmunt Baumann, who characterized utopia as a group of "ideal possibilities"; its opposition to the existing social reality exposes those possibilities which can be found there *in potentia*. This sounds perhaps a little bit strange, but it engenders the vision – Bloch would probably say "the hope" – of novel formations of human reality.

The utopian vision grows out of the present reality. It is not something hovering over it. It manifests ideas which (can) function in the present, and belongs therefore to the reality which it endeavors to transform. Bloch infers from all this that no profound social changes can occur without taking into account the significant role that the utopia fulfills as a guiding visionary principle.

3. Utopia and Ideology

There looms, however, another danger, namely that all the multiple meanings bestowed upon the concept of utopia will leave it ultimately without any fixed and definite meaning. If I may use a current term of poststructuralist literary criticism, the concept of utopia runs the risk of "deconstruction." Bloch tries to evade this danger by his "principle of hope." Hope forms the link between theory and praxis. The fact that it judges the existing reality critically demonstrates that hope always transcends the existent. Otherwise it would be useless as well as meaningless to hope for anything. Everything would become hopeless. By definition, hope relates to something which is still absent. So, by explicating utopia through the concept of the possible, by establishing it on the principle of hope, and by linking it to the future, Bloch distinguishes it from the concept of ideology. This ought to prevent its devaluation. It seems, however, questionable whether this intention, to remove the concept of utopia from the realm of ideology, does not impair after all the proper understanding of ideology. Bloch defines ideology, quite caustically, as the maid-servant of the ruling class. He conserves Marx's idea of "ideological superstructure" but does so in a much more simplistic form. According to his argument, utopias, unlike ideologies, can never represent or serve a ruling class. Is this really the case? Moreover, what happens on the other hand to a concept such as "socialist ideology"? Would it be no more than a meaningless *contradictio in adjecto?* Bloch is certainly right in saying that every ideology comprises certain forms of deceit and falsity. It is most often meant to conceal the true intentions of its spokespersons. Ideology indeed turns, as shown very convincingly by Roland Barthes, into a "myth." It might, nevertheless, still make some sense to speak of a utopian ideology. Bloch indeed does so. It should focus on the humanly "possible"; it should also include the "principle of hope." But such an ideology is, by Bloch's own criteria and definitions, not an ideology but a utopia.

Perhaps this issue can be resolved in the following manner. Every single utopian category ought to be judged by the yardstick of criticism of ideology. If after such a critical scrutiny of the utopia there remain substantial utopian components, it gains more value *qua* utopia. This would be no mere "wishfull thinking" or abstract expectation; it would truly establish the foundation of a concrete utopia.[5] Bloch did not restrict himself to an analysis of Marxism as a critique of prevailing social conditions and ideologies, supplementing it, as it were, by some utopian surplus value; he conceived of it as a realistic scrutiny of the future, based on firm relations between theory and praxis (see above). This is what Bloch calls "future-latency in the present" ("Zukunfts-Latenz in der Gegenwart") which ipso facto indicates a "future-tendency" (*Zukunfts-Tendenz*), i.e. a real possibility (188). Instead of dealing with ideologies by categories, one ought to treat categories without ideology (he had, of course, in mind the category of possibility). Then the utopia will represent a "pure utopian surplus without ideology" ("lauter utopischer Überschuss ohne Ideologie") (189).

With regard to this last point, I should like, at the end of this article, to venture another definition of the concept of ideology; this is to overcome its simplistic identification with the interests of the ruling class, which regrettably remains part of Bloch's analysis. It seems to me that the following distinction between ideology and utopia is preferable. Utopia manifests the program of an ideal and perfect social order which does not yet exist anywhere. This order differs substantially from the present existing reality. Ideology, on the other hand, is a thought-system which does not necessarily manifest or proffer a perfect social order. Therefore it can *also* serve the existing social order. This does not contradict, however, the assumption that there are ideologies which express the striving for a better world order. After all, as we have seen above, Bloch himself had no qualms about employing the term "utopian ideology." Ideology as such is not to be condemned, for it depends on what it stands for. One could therefore recapitulate: utopia is always struggling for the realization of the possible best; it is motivated by hope for the "*optimum.*" Ideology is something different; it can fulfill three different roles which must not all be disparaged:

1. A covert defense of the existing order and its ruling class. This is Bloch's conception of ideology.

2. A call for changes in the present order. This does not mean support of the "ruling class" (I do not deal here with the question of to what extent the notion of a "ruling class" is still applicable).

3. To strive for a better social order in the future, guaranteeing a dignified life for all human beings.

This third role of ideology shares much with the concept of utopia. It alone can be designated as "utopian ideology." According to these criteria, Plato's *Republic* could be apprehended as a utopia *par excellence* (it is again of no concern in this context whether Plato's state ought to be also judged critically for displaying totalitarian features, etc.). On the other hand, Plato's last book, the *Laws*, which he wrote after his failure to realize his blueprint in Sicily, could then be apprehended as some kind of ideological platform. The simple identification of ideology with the defense of the interests of the ruling class certainly cannot be upheld any more.

Notes

A similar, though not identical, version of this article has appeared, in German, in *Bloch Almanach*, 7 (Ludwigshafen: Folge, 1987), pp. 25–51, and, in Hebrew, in the "Introduction" to *Ernst Bloch: Selected Writings*, Tel-Aviv: Sifriat-Poatim, 1987, pp. 5–29.

1. *Das Prinzip Hoffnung* (Frankfurt am Main: Suhrkamp, 1968), chs. 14, 21, 22.

2. "Zur Ontologie des Noch-nicht-Seins," *Tübinger Einleitung in die Philosophie* (Frankfurt am Main: Suhrkamp, 1970), pp. 212–42.

3. *Atheismus im Christentum* (Frankfurt am Main: Suhrkamp, 1968), pp. 236–42.

4. *Thomas Münzer als Theologe der Revolution* (Frankfurt am Main: Surhkamp, 1969).

5. "Herausbringen, unverfälschtes Ordnen – Über die Möglichkeit eines Systems, aber eines Offenen," *Der Mensch als geschichtliches Wesen – Festschrift für M. Landmann*, ed. Klaus-Jürgen Grundner (Stuttgart: Klett, 1974), pp. 186–91.

12

The Mystery of Pre-history:
Ernst Bloch and Crime Fiction

Tim Dayton

It begins cryptically, glances at social determinants, echoes with rever-berations from the remotest past and most eccentric metaphysics: Ernst Bloch's "A Philosophical View of the Detective Novel"[1] features many of its author's abiding and most central concerns. That Bloch bestows such attention upon the detective novel, trivial subliterature to some and a component of a repressive culture industry to others, is itself, of course, typical of his wide-ranging interests and sympathies. The essay may thus be seen to concentrate its author's concerns into an almost predictably unlikely package. Yet, for all of its typicality, the essay is not of course comprehensive of Bloch's concerns; indeed, it fails to extend the analysis of its immediate object, crime fiction, as far as Bloch's work elsewhere would seem to recommend. In this essay, I will first examine "A Philosophical View of the Detective Novel" in relation to Bloch's larger concerns, revealing how the essay resonates within Bloch's "open system." I will then interrogate Bloch's analysis by comparing it to Franco Moretti's functionalist reading of detective fiction, and, finally, explore some possible lines of argument with regard to the broader field of crime fiction that Bloch opens up in *The Principle of Hope*, but fails to pursue in his detective-novel essay.

1. "A Philosophical View of the Detective Novel"

"A Philosophical View of the Detective Novel" explores four principal aspects of its subject: (1) its primary sociological determinant; (2) the nature of the suspense it generates; (3) the centrality in it of unmasking and discovery; and (4) its characteristic of beginning at an origin that is "unnarrated." Of these four, the last is "the most characteristic of the detective novel," and the one that leads most fully into Bloch's larger concerns. I will take up each in turn.

The detective novel poses a historical question of the critic: given that crime figures prominently in literature and mythology, stretching back to, say, the Fall of Satan or the slaying of Abel by Cain, through *Oedipus Rex*, to the brink of capitalist modernity in *Macbeth*, how may one differentiate these earlier stories of crime from what is generally recognized as the modern detective novel? Bloch finds the sociological origin of the detective novel to lie in a single feature of the bourgeois social revolution: the development of the trial by evidence. As Bloch notes, the need for an exhaustive search for evidence – the basis of much of the form and content of the classical detective novel – depended upon the advent of the trial by evidence. This legal procedure represents (justifiably, it would seem) for Bloch the progressive side of the bourgeois revolution in its struggle against the feudal order, displacing the previous legal procedure, in which confession by the accused was central – and often extracted through torture. In this light, the detective novel represents a literary manifestation of an aspect of the bourgeois social revolution with a largely progressive function in the development of Western culture (246–7).

The first *formal* feature Bloch investigates is that of suspense. He correctly distinguishes the peculiar nature of detectivistic suspense as that which concerns the discovery of clues, as opposed to the fate of the characters. (Clearly, Bloch has in mind classical detective fiction here, produced by such figures as Edgar Allan Poe, Arthur Conan Doyle, and Agatha Christie, and not the hard-boiled detective novel of a Dashiell Hammett or a Raymond Chandler, to say nothing of the crime/suspense novels of, for example, David Goodis or Harry Whittington. In these later forms, the hard-boiled detective novel especially, the concern for clues is linked to a concern for the fate of the characters that does not cancel out, but rather – as we will see – complicates the application of Bloch's assertions.) This seemingly obsessive focus on clues leads to the second formal feature, and one that Bloch will develop to good effect, the element of exploration, discovery, and unmasking characteristic of modern crime fiction.

In the detective novel, the smallest, the most incidental of details can be crucial; the detective hero becomes involved in a process of discovering and "appreciating" materials, perceptions, and characteristics that are passed over by the mainstream of bourgeois society or its institutional representatives, the police. Standing outside the channels of normal police routine and evincing an interest in seemingly incidental detail, the detective hero cuts a bohemian figure, outside the utilitarian calculus of bourgeois society. Often explicitly an artist in the conventional sense (Poe's Dupin writes poetry, Doyle's Holmes plays the violin), the detective *qua* detective is also an artist. As a bohemian and an artist, the detective enjoys a certain distance from respectable society, a certain alienation, and this alienation suits the detective form's process of

unmasking the falsity of this society. This process of unmasking constitutes a destabilizing narrative within the detective story: it uncovers the
corruption and violence lurking behind society's smiling appearance.
This feature the detective story shares with the procedures of the most
distinguished intellectual figures of the nineteenth century: Ibsen,
Freud, and Marx. For Bloch, the generalized hypocrisy of bourgeois
society calls into being these "detectivistic" unmasking methodologies,
each of which operates on different terrain, to different effects.

But it is with his third category that Bloch moves most truly and
recognizably into his own, where he describes the "*most decisive* criterion"
of the detective novel as a narrative form: the centrality to it of an "*unnarrated factor* and its *reconstruction*" (255). Here Bloch refers to the
structure of the typical detective story: it begins with a crime which
constitutes the central event of the story but which takes place prior to
the narrative proper. This priority differs from that found in any
narrative that, beginning *in medias res*, narrates previous – but not
properly mysterious or hidden – incidents at a later point because the
detective form is marked by "darkness before the beginning" (255), a
darkness presented as *resistant to elucidation*. But while this unnarrated
factor presents the distinguishing feature of detective fiction, it does not
distinguish it in such a way as to seal off detective fiction from all other
literary forms; indeed, it is this principle precisely that relates the
detective novel to, especially, pre-modern stories of crime found in
literature, mythology, and metaphysics.

The classic literary example of "darkness before the beginning" is, of
course, *Oedipus Rex*, which presents "the *primordial detective* theme per
se" (257). Bloch introduces – in a characteristically "negative" fashion –
his utopian thematics at this point: the situation of Oedipus, the
foundling, is that of "everyone on earth whose world is not of his or her
own choosing" (258). Thus the Oedipal theme is that of life in a world
not truly adequate to human beings (or rather, a world "not yet"
adequate). The Oedipal mystery, then, narrates the life of those whose
lives are drastically other than they would have them be, and who do
not know why this is. This "why this is" presents itself as the "unnarrated," the "darkness *ante rem* [before the event]" (261) which
figures the opacity of all relations in an insufficiently humanized world,
in the world of "pre-history."

Bloch quickly moves the discussion from literature to mythology and
philosophy, and in so doing moves also from a social to an ontological
level. In much mythology and some philosophy, as in the detective
novel, *uncovering* prevails, as does the "presupposition that a veiled
misdeed precedes the creation of the *world itself*" (258). This notion
often takes a reactionary form: rebellion against just authority (the Fall
of Satan, or of Adam) precedes the destruction of an ideal world, or as
Bloch puts it, "the den of gangsters erupts into the world of the

righteous" (260). Yet, as Bloch notes, non-reactionary forms of this are also available in Boehme and in Hegel. In any case, detectivistic investigation becomes linked to ontology here in that the "unnarrated" refigures those accounts of the origin of the world that emphasize the nullity – the Not – from which the world springs. The unnarrated, then, is another form of the Not that "lies in origin as the still empty, undefined, undecided, as the start of the beginning" (*Principle of Hope*, 306). The drive to elucidate the unnarrated in the detective novel plays out a story remarkably similar to that in at least some folklore and metaphysics: both reveal an origin in *privation*. Thus the detective novel provides accessible narrative formats for the popular appropriation of the story of "darkness *ante rem.*"

Interesting as it is, however, Bloch's analysis of the detective novel remains merely one way among many to theorize this literary form unless one plugs it into its author's larger system, for this essay on a humble object, the detective novel, opens onto the broadest vistas of utopian desire. There are two different directions by which to approach this utopian dimension, two directions which must not be seen to contradict one another, but especially in Bloch's view, to complement one another: the subjective and the objective.

Subjectively, the experience of detectivistic investigation, leading into the uncovering of the omitted beginning, figures the opacity of immediate experience, as Bloch indicates when he asks the question, "Is the reader of these mysteries not caught in the darkness of his undisclosed momentary being continually renewing itself?" For Bloch the darkness of the undisclosed origin reproduces itself in the human experience of the lived moment as incomplete and incompletely knowable, with the two elements joined on the ground of privation, that is, both signify a lack. Bloch explains that this "darkness of the lived moment" emerges from the inadequate relationship between subject and object that manifests itself in the greater availability of experience to foresight or recollection than to immediate consciousness: "Only what is just coming up or what has just passed has the distance which the beam of growing consciousness needs to illuminate it" (*Principle of Hope*, 287). The immediate, the nearest, stands in a relation of unknowability, and of inexperiencability to the subject, and *the knot of the riddle of existence is to be found in this nearest* (*Principle of Hope*, 292). While such an explication of this "darkness" appears to be primarily existential, Bloch's entire system argues that it is also historically grounded. An explanation that (at the risk of oversimplifying) makes more lucid the nature of this subjective darkness finds expression in a question: "Did Caesar, did most men of action of the class society, which means here of *unfathomed* history, . . . grasp the moment when they acted in terms of its historical content?" (*Principle of Hope*, 294). Thus the darkness of the lived moment correlates to the impenetrability of the historical – or rather the pre-historical, since this is what "unfathomed" history is – insofar as this unfathomed history is driven by the operation of a necessity alien to human wishes and human control. Thus the detectivistic investigation into the origin reveals a Not that "is in fact not a far removed, not an immemorial darkness at the beginning of time ... But on the contrary: the darkness of the origin remains, as immediate darkness" (*Principle of Hope*, 307).

On the objective side, the narrative of investigation and uncovering is linked to the subjective insofar as the darkness of the moment corresponds to the darkness of the world ("The darkness of the lived moment is depictive for the darkness of the objective moment" [*Principle of Hope*, 292]). Objectively, Bloch's notion of the unnarrated corresponds to his (refunctioned) category of ground.

For Bloch, ground, or that out of which things arise, is in fact a non-ground, a Not; that is, what distinguishes it is not that it contains potentially everything that is later to come, but rather that it fundamentally *lacks* itself. This lack contains within it a drive to completion. Like the unnarrated, the Not exists prior to any beginning, and it is also distinguished by its nullity: it is "empty" and "dark."[2] By positing a negative ground, Bloch enables his philosophical system to remain open, rather than to enumerate the unfolding and foreknown potentials already extant in a positive ground. This open character of the system is meant to correspond to the open character of the world itself, and this openness is one of the bases for Bloch's optimism: all possibilities are not yet apparent, to say nothing of realized, and the world as it exists does not tell us everything there is to know about the world as it might be.

It appears, then, that the detectivistic narrative functions for Bloch as evidence of a long-running and widespread awareness – on a certain level – of the nullity of the Not, of the openness to rational investigation of the question of origins. The problem, Bloch suggests without explicitly stating, is that by its very form the detective story fixates on the past, since its structure is such that an entire novel becomes the edifice within which a single moment in the past is reconstructed. So that while the non-narrated character of the *alpha* of the detective story expresses adequately the nature of the non-ground, the backward-looking character of such narratives suggests the ultimate inadequacy of this prior moment: that human history, while it is open because of this primordial nullity, may only be fulfilled in an equally open future, a future which it is beyond the provenance of the detective novel to imagine. This formal, structural limit to detective narratives imposes the form's ultimate cognitive limit.

2. A Counter-model: Franco Moretti's "Clues"

For Franco Moretti, whose Marxist and largely functionalist approach provides a sharp counterpoint to Bloch's utopianism, detective fiction may (or perhaps must) be explained strictly within the confines of the nineteenth-century bourgeois culture in which it was born.

> It is an extreme example of liberal bourgeois ideology according to which society must "self-regulate" on the impersonal and automatic mechanisms of the market economy ... The detective is the state in the guise of "night watchman," who limits himself to assuring respect for laws – in particular, for economic laws ... In this light, detective fiction is the swan song of the Manchester ideals.[3]

Moretti demonstrates convincingly that Arthur Conan Doyle's Sherlock Holmes stories figure for their mass audience a world of "total scrutability" (of which Jeremy Bentham's panopticon is the by now famous symbol), in which modern methods of communication and transportation make criminal anonymity impossible and bourgeois stability unshakable.

Thus crime fiction allays the anxiety of bourgeois society about the effect of the forces it unleashes: that the decay of older "organic" Christian pietistic society will lead to the total erosion of social restraint and governability, and that massive and teeming conurbations will provide a cover of anonymity to those who (illegitimately) profit from this dissolution. The Holmes stories reassure – and warn – their bourgeois readers that, whether by their choice in footwear, taste in tobacco, or the pattern of wear on their clothing, all individuals may be singled out and that the modern conveyances and channels of communication that accompany the birth of the industrial city ensure the possibility of social control. Yet at the same time, detective fiction prefigures the self-referential world of mass culture and late capitalism that will mark the end of liberal capitalism. In detective fiction reading becomes literally a waste of time, something you do only because you have been taken in by the false clues deliberately placed in your way. (Here the classic example must be Edgar Allan Poe's "The Purloined Letter," in which Dupin solves the mystery before it is even properly put before him, before the story really begins.) A waste of time – but a socially sanctioned one, for we have entered now into the world of self-referential culture, whose connection to reality is tenuous, and whose coherence is not related to the external world.[4] Thus, for Moretti, detective fiction may be adequately understood purely in terms of its functional role in late nineteenth and early twentieth-century bourgeois culture.

Moretti's reduction (and here I use the term in a descriptive and not a pejorative sense) of detective fiction to its social function in Victorian bourgeois culture is broadly consistent with the findings of John Cawelti, Stephen Knight, Ernest Mandel, and Dennis Porter. While these critics, unlike Moretti, do not explicitly formulate functionalist theories, their work may easily be integrated into a functionalist framework. Such a framework, of course, stands opposite to Bloch's utopianism (although one might want to refer to Moretti's as a *negative* and Bloch's as a *positive* functionalism). Thus it remains to be seen whether or how one might reconcile such functionalism with a utopian reading. But such a project, whatever practical difficulties it poses, is not alien to that of Bloch, since, as he puts it, Marxism itself may be seen to be a radical detective methodology, and "detection techniques, when correctly understood and applied, have the effect of nitric acid in the testing sense: they dissolve false gold, rendering that which remains of the genuine element" ("A Philosophical View," 255). According to Bloch, then, an initial functionalist reduction of the text is necessary precisely to unlock the utopian content. Theoretically, then, we ought to be able to integrate Moretti's (or any other valid) sociological reduction with Bloch's utopian recovery in order to test this recovery and to supplement Bloch's incomplete reduction in the opening pages of "A Philosophical View of the Detective Novel."

A more complete locating of detective fiction within its origins in bourgeois society finds Bloch inadequate when he identifies the sociological origins of the detective novel as the advent of the evidentiary trial. Rather, we must see the detective novel based also, for example, in the tendency of the bourgeoisie to become increasingly favorable in their disposition toward the legal system as their power becomes increasingly stable in the course of the nineteenth century, and as the working class comes to be seen increasingly as a dangerous class, whose organization takes on for the bourgeoisie an increasingly "criminal" cast. Here one need only think of the passages in *Culture and Anarchy* where Matthew Arnold portrays the English working class in criminal or quasi-criminal terms. The members of the working class "are beginning to assert and put in practice an Englishman's right to do what he likes; his right to march where he likes, meet where he likes, enter where he likes, hoot as he likes, threaten as he likes, smash as he likes."[5] To be sure, Arnold is here concerned primarily with attacking the limits of "doing as one likes" as a social ideal, but the figure he paints of the working class is revealing, especially when he cites the dangers of "the man who . . . breaks down the park railings . . . or delivers a lecture made of 'words' says the Home Secretary, 'only fit to be addressed to *thieves and murderers*'" (430–31, my emphasis). As Raymond Williams points out, this is pure bourgeois fantasy, or perhaps nightmare, because "the most remarkable facts about the British working-class movement, since its origin in the Industrial Revolution, are its conscious and deliberate abstention from general violence, and its firm faith in other methods of advance" (*Culture and Society*, 136). Thus the objection of Arnold, the bourgeois critic, is not so much to any particular method of class advance, but rather to such advance itself, which could not help but appear to the stabilizing bourgeoisie as an incursion, an assault on their well-being, and hence as a fundamentally criminal act.

In addition to a particular class politics underlying the advent of the popular detective story, geo-politics intrude themselves rather directly into the Sherlock Holmes stories,[6] many of which feature a displacement of criminality from England to the rest of the globe. In such cases Sherlock Holmes sets out to solve a crime that has occurred within England, but whose solution finds that the crime committed in England has been preceded by a prior crime committed elsewhere. For example, in the first two Holmes stories, A Study in Scarlet and The Sign of Four, a mysterious murder occurs in or near London which baffles the police. Holmes arrives on the scene and in the course of his investigation discovers that the murder in question resulted from some prior act of criminality that transpired in the USA and India, respectively. Thus crime in these stories is something that *originates* elsewhere, but is *solved* in England, the seat of order and reason. The precise nature and import of this spatial displacement becomes clear if we compare, say, The Sign of Four to a story such as "The Musgrave Ritual," which would appear not to conform to the pattern of displacement, since the originary crime in "The Musgrave Ritual" occurs within England. Yet closer examination of The Sign of Four reveals that in it the originary crime occurs not only in India, but also during the Sepoy Rebellion. Thus the crime transpires *without* the administrative control of England in a spatial-historical sense. In "The Musgrave Ritual," the originary crime, the beheading of Charles I, occurs within England but during the historical rupture of the English Civil War. Thus while the originary crime is not spatially displaced, it is historically displaced. That is, the crime, again, occurs outside the routine administration of English history.

The classical detective novel, then, fixes the limits of social mobility, making the intrusion of the working class into active social agency a crime and displaces criminality outward from the bourgeois social order of England to the unruly sectors in time and space. This argument, of course, appears to be at the farthest remove from Bloch's evaluation of the detective novel, and yet it seems to me ultimately reconcilable in the following way: detectivistic narratives perform functions oppressive with regard to those who are other to the English ruling class, and comforting to those within it. But, significantly, the preferred tool for doing so itself activates in popular form narrative patterns with impressive lineage (*Oedipus*, the Bible) that figure a notion of origin as privation. This notion, like the detective novel on the whole, while manipulable by bourgeois hegemony, also retains an irreducible element that is open to and preserves utopian vision. Here then we would see that, even as the dominant culture constructed an apparatus more or less strictly suited to the conditions of its hegemony, it also activated utopian images over which it could not and cannot exert complete control, however much their hegemony must depend on the manipulation of such imagery. Thus the utopian argument and the functionalist argument prove ultimately to be mutually supporting – or at least mutually correcting. To put it somewhat narrowly, the functionalist argument explains why the bourgeois social order would produce a form such as the detective novel, while the utopian argument explains why vast numbers of readers would find these narratives appealing. While one must stray beyond the argument developed in "A Philosophical View of the Detective Novel" to draw such a conclusion, it is consistent in form and character with, for example, Bloch's important analysis in *Heritage of Our Time* of the Nazi appropriation of popular imagery and mythology, as well as with any number of Bloch's methodological pronouncements.

3. "Streets Dark With More Than Night": Anxiety Dream and Hard-boiled Crime Fiction, or, Bloch Beyond Bloch

In any conventional sense, the world of hard-boiled crime fiction is hardly the place of utopia, less so even than is the world of the classical detective story, where the concern with murder and death is at least not compounded by a pervasive atmosphere of brutality and boredom. The problem that such an intensely negative form presents for a resolutely positive method such as that of Bloch is obvious: if all cultural material records in some way the trace of human hope, then how do we account for the "hopeless" forms? Of course, to pose the question in this way is nearly to answer it, for the form of the question runs parallel to that posed by Freud when, in the course of laying out the great hermeneutic system of *The Interpretation of Dreams*, he faces the problem of dreams that would appear to contradict the principle of wish fulfillment, or anxiety dreams.

Freud's resolution of this problem through the mechanism of distortion is rearticulated by Bloch in *The Principle of Hope* along social lines. Bloch argues that Freud's basic insight is that anxiety and wish are not simple, but rather dialectical, opposites. Thus, the child's fear at separation from the mother is the negative trace of the positive attachment to the mother. But here Freud locates the source of desire and anxiety solely in the past, in the earliest relationship to the mother. Against this Bloch insists on the importance of the future for the interconnection of wish and anxiety:

> [W]aking anxiety culminating in the fear of death does not go right back to the beginning to find its explanation in the vanishing libidinal object of its own ego, that is, of the transposed mother. It is precisely this anxiety which cannot be explained chiefly in narcissistic regressive terms, but rather in terms of the axe which will cut life short in the future, in terms of the pain and horror of an objectively expected night. [85]

However, Bloch insists, one can reject Freud's "libido-subjectivisms of anxiety" and still find the connection he establishes between anxiety and the wish valid and meaningful. The anxiety dream may well have its origin in parturition, but anxiety finds its particularly human content not in the biological destiny of the creature to die, but in "*social* blockages of the self-preservation drive. In fact, it is simply the *annihilated content* of the wish, *a content actually transformed into its very opposite*, which causes anxiety and ultimate despair" (85). Precisely this dynamic operates in much hard-boiled crime fiction.

Dashiell Hammett's first novel, *Red Harvest*, generally acknowledged as the first hard-boiled crime novel, reveals the anxious quality of this type of fiction. The textual signs of hard-boiled fiction's anxiety abound, and in this, as in so many ways, Hammett sets the style for the genre: the world of the novel is fraught with danger uncoupled, often, to adventure; the action occurs at night, or in the dark spaces of the urban underworld; the hero finds himself (or, in the work of such recent writers as Sara Paretsky or Sue Grafton, herself) captured by his antagonists, bound, detained, and drugged; or merely slugged, sapped or pistol whipped, and left on the ground, only coming to slowly, and realizing that his is not the only body in the room. These obsessive returns to a strangely mundane danger, to night scenes, and to states of unconsciousness serve as the textual signs, eruptions onto the surface of the text, and into the formula itself, of the anxiety typical of hard-boiled fiction, an anxiety often figured by the nocturnal.

But, following Bloch, this negative, nocturnal quality, that is, its identity as an anxiety dream, is also the location of hard-boiled fiction's specific utopian dimension: *the hope of the hard-boiled novel is to be found in its despair at the fate suffered by hope at the hands of the present.* Thus hope often appears most powerfully in these novels as its opposite, a situation with which Bloch is comfortable indeed. As Fredric Jameson puts it,

> for Bloch . . . horror and the black emotions are infinitely precious insofar as they constitute forms of that elemental ontological astonishment which is the most concrete mode of awareness of the future latent in ourselves and in things . . . Bloch wishes . . . to locate the positive *within* the negative itself.[7]

The plot of *Red Harvest* is based on an originary crime underlying the dark present of the novel which may, with little departure from the explicit content of the text, be termed capitalist exploitation, since it is Elihu Wilsson's desire to maintain his power over the workers in his mine that leads him to bring in the band of rogues that Hammett's anonymous detective hero, the Continental Op, battles against. The Op sets out to "clean up" Poisonville, but entertains few illusions about the viability of such a project. He calls Wilsson an "old pirate"[8] and hopes to take him down along with the other hoodlums; when he fails to do this exactly, he tells Wilsson to call in the national guard. "Then you'll have your city back, all nice and clean and ready to go to the dogs again"

(187). The originary crime, which thwarts the hope of the miners, rules out all hope from the novel, so that the Op depicts his "victory" in terms that avoid despair only through irony: he tells us that martial law was transforming Poisonville "into a sweet-smelling thornless bed of roses" (199).

Thus *Red Harvest* as a whole may be seen as an "anxiety dream;" this narrative level provides the overarching context for other negative and nocturnal elements in the novel that are entirely of a piece with anxiety and despair. Here we may place many fragmentary aspects of the novel, digressions within the anxiety dream's narrative progression: the story of Ike Bush, the boxer trapped between arrest by the police and murder by the mob, Myrtle Jennison, the young woman dying of Bright's disease whose bloated body – a corpse not yet dead – horrifies the case-hardened Op, and the crooked lawyer Charles Proctor Dawn, whom the Op finds dead, "huddled among two brooms, a mop, and a bucket, in a little alcove formed by the back of the stairs and a corner of the wall" (167). A cheap con artist found dead in a broom closet: it is an identity or at least a fate the novel offers to all its readers.

Looking at the novel as a whole, *Red Harvest*'s negativity is premised upon the thwarted hope of the miners whose defeat is the precondition for all that follows. This thwarted hope provides the novel's utopian dimension, the dialectical opposite to the novel's intense negativity. *Red Harvest* evinces this negativity on two levels. The first level is that of narrative progression, which essentially concerns plot, and is tra-ditionally referred to as the level of narration. The second level is that of imagistic digression, which concerns those elements in a narrative that function not to advance the plot, but rather to detail the world within which this plot takes place, and is traditionally referred to as description. (The best account of digression in crime fiction may be found in Dennis Porter, although he perceives no utopian dimension in it.[9]) These two levels correspond to a distinction implicit in Bloch between two primary forms in which the utopian impulse reveals itself: the narrative, which may be seen most clearly in rationalist utopias, explicitly utopian novels, or the disguised and inverted utopia of anxiety dreams, and the imagistic, which may be seen in wishful actions or landscapes, anticipatory ciphers, or the inverted figures of despair (for example, *Principle of Hope*, 158–78). This distinction helps to elucidate the utopian dimension generally, and pertains especially to hard-boiled crime fiction, much of the power of which resides in the atmosphere within which its plots unfold. A brief glance at the hard-boiled fiction writers Mickey Spillane, Harry Whittington, and Jim Thompson illus-trates the utility of Bloch's distinction.

An example of the utopian finding (distorted) expression through the narrative aspect of fiction may be found in Mickey Spillane's *I, the Jury*.[10] In this, one of the best-selling novels of all time, a pervasive misogyny mixes with a less visible, but still present, hostility to the ruling class and at least some aspects of capitalist social relations. Admittedly, Spillane's novels are, on an immediate level, utopias only for the most reactionary, misogynist readers, yet there is also a profoundly emancipatory and utopian undercurrent to *I, the Jury*. But this undercurrent is articulated with, and only analytically separable from, the real misogyny of the text. The utopian narrative of *I, the Jury* sees Mike Hammer, whose name associates him with manual labor (if not, indeed, with the artisanal labor that often figures a kind of utopia in its own right) and many of whose characteristics label him as working-class, solve the mystery surrounding the murder of his friend and wartime comrade Jack Williams.

Hammer's investigation leads to his romantic involvement with Charlotte Manning, an alluring and wealthy psychiatrist. Much is made of both Manning's sexuality and her upper-class status throughout the novel, but it is at the novel's famous conclusion that these two dimensions of Manning collide. Hammer discloses simultaneously to Manning and the reader that he has discovered the murderer to be none other than Manning herself. When Manning shot Williams she stayed behind to watch him die, not out of sadism, but in order to "make a psychological study of a man facing death." Here as elsewhere the novel presents Manning as a figure of the ruling class. In this particular instance Manning figures mental labor – psychiatry – and a sharp (if melodramatic) form of reification: Manning wants to turn the human content of Williams's death agony into data. But this revelation occurs while Manning attempts to divert Hammer's attention and sway him from his purpose by performing a striptease before him. Thus Manning is figured simultaneously as the ruling class and as the female Other, and when Hammer executes one he executes both. *I, the Jury*, then, is both deeply misogynistic and utopian in that it figures the elimination of the ruling class, and with it the reifying logic of capital; and this utopian element articulates itself through the narrative mechanism of plot, where we see the crimes of the ruling class displayed and punished.

In addition to the relatively large-scale dynamics of the utopian narrative, crime fiction also presents certain, perhaps typical, forms of fragmentary figuration of little utopian moments lodged within the larger edifice of the anxiety dream. These moments can occur in even the darkest of fictions, and are probably most powerful there, where they provide not so much relief from as contrast to the overarching night of the world of the text. But even where the utopian moment does not stand in utter contrast to the anxious and unredeemed narrative, the fragments of utopia can set up intersecting patterns of interference with the larger narrative structure.

For example, in Harry Whittington's *The Woman is Mine* (a misleadingly titled novel), Jeffrey Patterson and Paula Whitcomb find themselves on the run from Dexter Glissade and Dr. Stuart Cosof, who claim that Paula is Glissade's wife and Cosof's patient, escaped from a mental institution. The police also become Patterson's and Whitcomb's antagonists when Patterson is framed for the murder of a nurse who helped Whitcomb in her escape from Cosof's sanitarium. The function of the hero, Patterson, in this novel is to defeat the corruption of Glissade and Cosof and to reconcile the relationship between himself, Paula Whitcomb and a mistaken but tractable society represented by the police; thus, his mission is to correct the social world.

This need to correct the social world is made evident in typical fashion: after he has been framed for the murder of the nurse, he finds himself an innocent man on the run, a well-nigh archetypal figure in this kind of fiction. Interestingly, and again typically enough, this fugitive sequence is initiated with a "nocturnal" sequence in which Patterson is knocked out, and comes to only to find a corpse in the room and the police at the door. On the run from Glissade, Cosof, and the police, Patterson and Whitcomb at one point steal a car and drive into the countryside, where Patterson, the narrator, tells us:

> I saw this house in a weed-grown field. A battered sign on it was illuminated in a flare of lightning. "Meadowfield Farms – Farms – A Home for the Rest of Your Life."
>
> I slowed down, waited until the lightning blazed again. There were no houses anywhere, no signs of farms. This was somebody's real estate idea that hadn't panned out.[11]

While Patterson and Whitcomb hide out in the abandoned real-estate office, "Lightning flared and touched her face softly, showing it to me. She was looking up at me, my hand against her cheek, and in her eyes I saw all any guy would ever want to see" (104).

Here we have a fragmentary utopian moment that stands in contrast not only to the plight of the two characters but also to the inevitably ironic backdrop of the failed development. Here, in this shed, love, warmth, pleasure may be had in a way that would not have been possible in the houses that would have been built had the development succeeded. Such a utopian moment is then fragmentary in a double sense: in that it stands out, as we will see, within the narrative as an irreducible moment, and also in that it is enabled by the fugitive condition of the characters, so that the utopian experience and the social condition of the characters parallel one another.

This fragmentary condition stands out finally not against the darkness of the novel as a whole, but rather against the "world-improving" daydream that frames it. The conclusion of the novel sees the triumph of the regular guy Patterson over Dexter Glissade and Dr. Cosof: the social world is brought into line with the needs of the individual. This narrative we might call utopian in a minor sense, because while it figures a world in which the institutions of power are made responsive to the needs of the individual, no real transformation of those institutions is imaginable within the constraints of the genre. Yet the moment in the shed stands out as something that may not be reduced to the ultimately consensual master narrative of the text. The social world of the text, to which Patterson and Whitcomb are reconciled, offers no pleasures so keen as they found in their fugitive moment.

However, utopian moments sometimes do gain their power strictly from their contrast to the surrounding night. In Jim Thompson's *A Hell of a Woman* (an even more spectacularly misleading title than *The Woman is Mine*), Frank Dillon suffers from a severe estrangement from himself and others, an estrangement produced by his adaptation to the demands of what the novel presents as a particularly naked and brutal sector of the American marketplace, door-to-door sales and collections. Dillon lives out a form of alienation whose ultimate object the novel declares to be the self fully as much as others. *A Hell of a Woman* sees Dillon plot and execute the double murder of a laborer, Pete Hendrickson and the supposed aunt of a young woman he has met, Mona. The aunt, who deprives and abuses Mona, has $100,000 stashed away in her basement. Dillon plans to take Hendrickson out to the aunt's house and make it appear that the day laborer beat the old woman to death, but that before she died the aunt managed to shoot Hendrickson. While this initial stage of Dillon's plot works, later events lead Dillon to commit a further murder, and to his and Mona's flight – without the money. Mona, in despair at Frank's increasing hostility – to him this is just another deal gone sour, which he takes out on a woman – kills herself; and, at novel's end Frank castrates and kills himself in a drug-supplemented frenzy that is surely one of the strangest endings to a novel in any genre. *A Hell of a Woman* is perhaps the darkest novel in the oeuvre of a profoundly dark novelist.

And yet at one point in the novel, while Dillon is keeping Hendrickson around his house prior to murdering him, a strange moment occurs: he and Hendrickson play cards and drink. And as they do so, Dillon tells us, Hendrickson "began to hum, to kind of mumble sing. The first thing I knew I was doing it with him. We grinned and came in on the chorus together: it was 'Pie in the Sky,' as I recollect."[12] Dillon and Hendrickson sing the old IWW (Industrial Workers of the World) standards and Dillon comments that it "wasn't so strange" that they should both know them from having been in the Pacific northwest: "guys like us would just naturally travel around a lot; we wouldn't do the same kind of work but we'd land in a lot of the same places. It seemed funny, though; strange, I mean. And when I could make myself forget – the other – it seemed kind of good" (81–2). The other, of course, is that he is soon going to kill Hendrickson. But for an uncanny moment, Frank manages to escape

the individualist self that determines his life, and manages to feel
solidarity with another.

In *A Hell of a Woman*, such a utopian fragment stands in a different
relation to the larger narrative of which it is part than in Whittington's
The Woman is Mine, since here the novel as a whole never emerges from
the anxiety dream, and the fragment is lodged within the dark night of
a world that sees not even the false dawn of an obviously ideological
closure. And when we consider that Dillon and Hendrickson sing a song
written by Joe Hill, who had been dead for over thirty years, and
associated with the IWW, which was effectively crushed shortly after
Hill's execution, then the notion that the anxiety dream expresses the
annihilated content of hope finds further evidence and resonance. But
here, too, the utopian fragment offers a momentary glimpse of a world
that could be otherwise than this one is, but which this one decidedly is
not – at least not yet.

4. Conclusion: Bloch and Crime Fiction as Popular Literature

Rather than summarizing the main points of this essay, I will conclude
with two observations about the usefulness of Bloch for the study of
popular literature. The first of these will be of a methodological-
theoretical character, and the second of a narrower, more empirical
character. First, I think sections 1 and 2 of this essay make it clear that,
as others have noted (for example Levitas[13]), additional attention to the
internal discipline supplied by (negative) functionalist approaches provides a necessary corrective to Bloch's emphasis on the utopian. *But*
what emerges on the other side of this functionalist moment of analysis
finally supports the utopian thesis more powerfully than does an
insufficiently mediated utopian approach.

Secondly, Bloch offers a uniquely valuable perspective on crime
fiction as a form of popular literature. Crime fiction has been a
persistently popular form: within the confines of modernity, the
Newgate Calendar and last testimonies of condemned prisoners attest
to the popularity of the form before the development of the detective
novel, while the dime-novel detectives (so ably analyzed by Michael
Denning[14]) attest to the mass readership which narratives of detection
could claim in the nineteenth century, up to the continuing centrality
of detective and criminal narratives – in television and film as well as in
fiction – in the present. While these narratives no doubt serve to some
extent the ideological function of affirming the current social order,
Bloch permits us to see the ways in which this form – which often
legitimates a "law and order" perspective, or figures insistently a
darkness that would appear to be at the farthest remove from conven-
tionally conceived utopias – activates at the same time utopian registers
of various kinds. Thus in the analysis of popular literature that he makes

possible, as in his other work, Bloch offers tools by which to wrest away from a less than utopian present the utopian contents of the past and the future.

Notes

1. In *The Utopian Function of Art and Literature*, trans. Jack Zipes and Frank Mecklenburg (Cambridge, Mass.: MIT Press, 1988), pp. 245–64.

2. Wayne Hudson, *The Marxist Philosophy of Ernst Bloch* (New York: St Martin's Press, 1982), pp. 120–21.

3. Franco Moretti, "Clues," trans. Susan Fischer, in *Signs taken for Wonders: Essays in the Sociology of Literary Forms* (London: Verso, 1983), pp. 154–5.

4. Ibid., pp. 149–50.

5. Matthew Arnold, *Culture and Anarchy: Poetry and Criticism of Matthew Arnold*, ed. A. Dwight Culler (Boston: Houghton Mifflin, 1961), p. 430.

6. Arthur Conan Doyle, *Sherlock Holmes: The Complete Novels and Stories* (New York: Bantam, 1986).

7. Fredric Jameson, *Marxism and Form: Twentieth-Century Dialectical Theories of Literature* (Princeton, NJ: Princeton University Press, 1971), p. 133.

8. Dashiell Hammett, *Red Harvest* [1929] (New York: Vintage, 1982), p. 140.

9. Dennis Porter, *The Pursuit of Crime: Art and Ideology in Detective Fiction* (New Haven, Conn. Yale University Press, 1981).

10. Mickey Spillane, *I, the Jury* [1947] (New York: NAL, 1968). I pursue more fully the analysis outlined in "The Annihilated Content of the Wish: Class and Gender in Mickey Spillane's *I, the Jury*," *Clues: A Journal of Detection*, 14: I (Spring/Summer 1993), pp. 87–104.

11. Harry Whittington, *The Woman is Mine* (Greenwich, Conn.: Gold Medal, 1954), p. 103.

12. Jim Thompson, *A Hell of a Woman* [1954] (Berkeley, Cal.: Black Lizard/Creative Arts, 1984), p. 81.

13. Ruth Levitas, *The Concept of Utopia* (Syracuse, NY: Syracuse University Press, 1990), p. 105.

14. Michael Denning, *Mechanic Accents: Dime Novels and Working-Class Culture in America* (London: Verso, 1987).

A View through the Red Window:
Ernst Bloch's *Spuren*

Klaus L. Berghahn

For Axel Stein

Preface

At a time when I was still contemplating my topic for this essay, I was asked: "What are you working on?" "I am struggling very hard," I answered, "I am preparing my next error." Of course, this is a well-known Keuner story, which Bertolt Brecht aptly called "hardship of the best."[1] This short text has a double function here. It serves as a *captatio benevolentiae*, and it leads into the subject matter of this essay. Brecht's story belongs to a cluster of texts written or published around 1930. Authors and texts that come to mind are: Walter Benjamin's *Einbahnstrasse* (One-Way Street, 1928), Siegfried Kracauer's *Die Angestellten* (The White-Collar Workers, 1930), Ernst Bloch's *Spuren* (Traces, 1930), Bertolt Brecht's *Geschichten vom Herrn Keuner* (Stories of Mr. Keuner, 1926–34), Robert Musil's *Nachlass zu Lebzeiten* (Literary Estate While Alive, 1936), and, as a latecomer, Theodor W. Adorno's *Minima Moralia* (1944). What characterizes these "stories without a story," as Musil once called them, is a combination of observation and reflection, a rare cross between literature and philosophy. They seem to be cognate to Kafka's parables and they border on the essayistic philosophy of the Frankfurt School. Often it is not clear which is more important, the poetic narrative or the didactic commentary, as we can observe in the following example by Brecht:

A Good Answer
A worker was asked in court whether he wanted to use the secular or the religious form of oath. He answered: "I'm unemployed." – "This wasn't just distractedness," said Mr. K. "By this answer he let it be understood that he was in a situation where such questions, indeed perhaps the entire court procedure as such, no longer make sense."[2]

Here the balance between anecdote and commentary tips in favor of the interpretation; the terse shrewdness of the "good answer" gets buried by the heavy-handed explanation.

What we have, then, is a simple prose form with a prevalence for a moral, call it a parable or a fable; not much to it, or so it would seem. But there is more to it than we see at first glance. As an example I have chosen to discuss Ernst Bloch's *Spuren* (Traces), one of the best, yet least-known, texts in modern German literature.

Traces, Criss and Cross

"The title *Spuren* mobilizes primary experiences like reading cowboy-and-Indian stories for philosophical theory," Adorno noted in his review.[3] Indeed, the book contains a remarkable collection of stories that combine story-telling with philosophizing, in keeping with Bloch's *bon mot*: "I know only Hegel and Karl May; everything in between is an impure mixture of both."[4] And there is room for more associations: the trapper and the philosophical pathfinder are joined by a detective: "Something is uncanny, that is how it all starts."[5] The world seems to be full of traces, and the petty details of everyday life in particular contain evidence that something is going on, anticipating things to come. Those things have their meaning, and their stories are part of history, making us aware of an ongoing process. Insignificant things and petty details especially attracted Bloch's attention; as he relates in the only autobiographical piece of *Spuren*, "Spirit, which just forms itself," in which he tells us about experiences of childhood. One image, that is as inconspicuous as it is mysterious, stands out – the red window:

> Eight years old, and the strangest experience was the sewing kit in a shop window on my way to school; it stood between wool and quilt next to feminine needlework, which didn't mean anything to me. But on the sewing box something was painted, with many color dots and spots on the smooth surface, as if the image were coagulated. It showed a cabin, lots of snow and a moon high and yellow on a blue winter sky, in the windows of the cabin glowed a red light . . . I have never forgotten the red window.[6]

An insignificant red window, painted on a sewing box, becomes the orientation and vanishing point of his life; it expresses a longing for something that has no name yet, a boy's daydream that points to great things to come. Whatever the meaning of this symbol may be – and Bloch is careful not to explain it – it is evidence of a process of self-awareness and self-cultivation that started with the sudden recognition of that image.

The genesis of the book offers another clue to understanding the title, *Spuren*. The work belongs to the oldest formation of Bloch's philosophy. (In a footnote to the table of contents of the 1969 edition of *Spuren*, Bloch remarked that these stories originated between 1910 and 1929.) It can be traced back to the essay collection with a Karl May title, *Durch die Wüste* (Through the Desert, 1923), and more importantly to *Geist der Utopie* (Spirit of Utopia, 1918). Many paralipomena of these two books ended up in *Spuren*, which was published in 1930. It had no impact whatsoever upon its first publication, was not reprinted until 1959, and was finally published as the first volume of Bloch's *Complete Works* in 1969. As is typical for Bloch, he changed the work in its 1969 edition by adding twenty-one stories and altering the introduction. During his lifetime, all of his books were works in progress, and they all contain an introductory section similar to a group of *Spuren* texts that leads into the book and gives it a perspective. The short prose form of *Spuren* seems to be a style as well as a thought process. Even his magnum opus, *The Principle of Hope*, is introduced in this way. Its five famous questions (Who are we? Where do we come from? Where do we go? What do we expect? What expects us?) are followed by *Spuren*-like texts. Since *Spuren* is closely connected with *Spirit of Utopia* and the same narrative structure is used to lead into *The Principle of Hope*, it can be safely assumed (as Adorno does) that the stories in *Spuren* – despite their diversity and colorfulness – have only *one* perspective: they follow and read the traces leading to utopia, which never comes into sight.

Tracing: Mark the Detail

It is one thing to find traces, but quite another to read and understand them. Bloch does not provide an introduction on how to interpret his texts. These after all are descriptions and stories that can stand on their own and do not need the support of a philosophical tract. Only at the end of the first section is there one text that can be viewed as a preface, since it offers some general advice on how to read the traces in the sand of reality or in the rubble of history. The text is called "Das Merke," which can mean: take note. "It is the small things one should pay attention to, pursue them," is his advice. "A matter which is simple and unusual will often take one the furthest."[7] Bloch's *objets trouvés* include the contents of his pocket when he was a child as well as things that surround us every day. Siegfried Kracauer once observed that Bloch was especially attracted by the "phenomena of indistinct life,"[8] obscure and curious things, the life of fairs and carnival booths. Like his friend Benjamin, Bloch was a *flâneur* and collector who paid attention to minute detail. Even the trash of history interested him, and there is a lot of trash in our culture; but at the same time Bloch did not want to leave the kitsch and tinsel of the culture industry unnoticed.[9] In this regard, Bloch's *Spuren* is closely connected with his contemporary socio-political analysis, translated as *Heritage of Our Times*. *Spuren* can also be viewed as an example of Bloch's understanding of the literary heritage. He seems to prefer simple and popular forms of narration such as fairy tales, anecdotes, almanac stories, and, above all, pulp novels (*Kolportage*). The pieces of literature that he found and used in *Spuren* are mostly products of low or popular culture. Likewise, he observed with curiosity the disintegration of bourgeois culture. In contrast to Lukács, who smelled the rat of bourgeois decadence in expressionism, Bloch defended the modernist techniques and popular tendencies of this movement. In good old stories and in bad new forms he discovered dreams of a better life and a gleam of hope. He was not willing to yield this heritage to the Nazis for their exploitation.

The meaning of the *objets trouvés* or found stories in Bloch's *Spuren* is not easy to decipher. If Bloch's short prose pieces have a moral, it is not his intention to tell a story for the sake of its moral. Bloch's narratives certainly have a philosophical essence, but they are not the ornament for his philosophy. He describes a thing, or observes a situation, or simply tells a story, and while he talks the listener/reader takes notice without being forced to accept a *fabula docet* solution. His philosophy is part of the narration: he thinks in fables, and he fabulates while thinking. As he follows the traces, he starts a narration of which thinking is a part, as we can see in the following simple story:

> *The Poor Woman*
> What are you doing? I asked. I am saving electricity, said the poor woman. She had already been sitting in the dark kitchen for a long time. It was easier than saving food, after all. Since there is not enough for everyone, the poor come to the rescue. They work for the big shots even when they are at rest and left alone.[10]

We have here a simple description of an almost idyllic situation that renders transparent the problems of a class society. The quiet rest in the dark kitchen is evidence of a social process that lies outside the kitchen, overshadowing it. What could be a natural situation becomes unnatural under the conditions of capitalism. The absurdity of the situation is that the poor serve their masters even when they rest.

Emblematic Traces

But what do we call these stories? Bloch himself does not give any clue. His book does not have a subtitle that would indicate a genre. It is not organized as an anthology of short stories, nor can its stories be categorized among traditional forms. Granted, many of Bloch's stories are remakes, so to speak, and they remind us of such traditional forms as fairy tales or anecdotes. Bloch, who is not the inventor but merely the narrator of stories, changes their content and form drastically. He uses the found stories as material to work with, and in the process they are given a new meaning. On the part of the critics there is uncertainty as to what to call them: philosophy, or literature, or both? Hans Mayer proposes "philosophical fables," a form of narration that seeks to make a practical philosophy poetically palatable.[11] Traditionally a didactic form like this would be called parable. But these stories are not one-dimensional, nor do they have a moral. They are at best parables without a moral that make the readers notice something, make us aware. Or to adopt a term coined by Lessing: these stories are *fermenta cognitionis*, they stimulate thinking.

Because of their dual nature, narrative/descriptive and reflective, they seem to require an allegorical reading. Traditionally this would mean that the image, the situation, or the story can be reduced to one idea. We have already noticed that this is impossible. But there is another understanding of allegory, defining not just a representation or personification of an abstract concept, but rather a metonymic relationship between image and meaning. For Bloch, as for Benjamin, the allegorical method lies not in projecting a meaning onto a thing; instead, it is discovered in the thing, as a quality that has to be interpreted. In our still unnamed genre, the subjective activity of narration and interpretation corresponds to an objective quality of the world. The narrator finds the world as it is or has become; through narration and commentary he disrupts the normal order of things, letting us see them in a new light.

For this allegorical narrative I cannot think of a more appropriate name than *Denkbild*, thought-image, a term coined by Walter Benjamin. In his review of Benjamin's *One-Way Street*, Adorno explains this neologism as an invention of Stefan George, and later in the same text he observes that these prose pieces are riddles that shock the reader into thinking.[12] This is as convincing as it is far-fetched. There is, however, a rather simple solution to this riddle: the new genre is as old as the emblem, for which *Denkbild* seems to be an apt German translation. Benjamin, who was an expert on Baroque literature and its imagery, knew what he was talking about when he named his short prose pieces in *One-Way Street* "thought-images." They indeed combine *inscriptio* (title), *pictura* (thing, description, image), and *subscriptio* (commentary, interpretation), as is required of an emblem.[13] The tripartite structure and the combination of image and text that constitutes the form of the emblem can also be found in two more recent examples, Benjamin's *Angelus Novus* and Brecht's *Kriegsfibel* (War Primer). Benjamin's famous angel of history received his name and image from a rather insignificant drawing by Paul Klee. The drawing is the *pictura* and the title is the *inscriptio*, while the *subscriptio* can be found in Benjamin's "Theses on the Philosophy of History," the ninth of which reads as follows:

A Klee painting named "Angelus Novus" shows an angel looking as if he were about to move away from something he is fixedly contemplating. His eyes are staring, his mouth is open, his wings are spread. This is how one pictures the angel of history. His face is turned toward the past. Where we perceive a chain of events, he sees only one single catastrophe which keeps piling wreckage upon wreckage and hurls it in front of his feet. The angel would like to stay, awaken the dead, and make whole what has been smashed. But a storm is blowing from Paradise; it has got caught in his wings with such violence that the angel can no longer close them. The storm irresistibly propels him into the future to which his back is turned, while the pile of debris before him grows skyward. This storm is what we call progress.[14]

The text as a whole has become a thought-image. Under the title *Angelus Novus* it combines a short prose description of the drawing with an interpretation. The angel of history looks back on the ruins of history while being driven by a storm, which blows from paradise, into an undecided future he cannot see.

Brecht's *Kriegsfibel* can be regarded as a modern emblem book.[15] It consists of war photographs from *Life* magazine (*pictura*) to which Brecht added a caption (*inscriptio*) and an interpretive four-line verse (*subscriptio*). Brecht wanted his "photograms," as he called them, to be used as didactic material to teach the art of reading pictures and deciphering the hieroglyphs of photojournalism, as we can see in the following example: The picture shows the skull of a Japanese soldier that was propped upon a burned-out tank. Brecht's *subscriptio* reads as follows:

> Alas poor Yorick of the jungle tank!
> Your head has found no burial plot.
> You died by fire for the Domei Bank,
> But still your parents owe it a lot.[16]

The picture does not speak for itself; it is ambiguous and needs an interpretation to give it a political and tendentious meaning. For Brecht, it is not enough to be morally indignant about the image; he asks in whose interest Yorick died. The image of horror is transformed into a political statement.

Benjamin's own thought-images are part of his book *One-Way Street*, where the short prose pieces have titles that seem to be lifted from reality, such as "Construction Site," "No. 13," "For Men," "Lost and Found Office." He sketches the physiognomy of places and things and then adds his reflections, which do not explain but rather illuminate the situation and shock the reader into thinking. Bloch was one of the few who reviewed *One-Way Street* and the first to notice the emblematic quality of his prose. He characterized Benjamin as someone who observes and reads the world as if it were a script, a "book of nothing but emblems."[17]

Bloch shared with his friend an interest in objects and allegorical narratives that had to be decoded as if they were hieroglyphs. For both, the
world was full of traces, which for Benjamin led from the now to promises
of the future in the past, while for Bloch they led to a better future.

Now that our stories have a name and a familiar structure, everything
seems to be in order. The unfamiliar new forms have been traced back
to an old tradition; the new is never as new as it first appears. But it is
new nonetheless, for despite formal similarities between emblem and
thought-image there are important differences that make the thought-
image an expression of modern experience. Emblems make use of a
pre-established harmony between image and interpretation; the poet
contemplates the meaning that God has inscribed in nature. This
harmony cannot be found in thought-images, nor is their imagery based
on nature. The material for thought-images is chosen from city life or
everyday experiences in a modern society, and it is presented in such
manner that tensions and contradictions become apparent. Bloch
observes that only such stories make us notice that something is wrong,
since we or society are out of balance.[18] Looking back on our examples,
we can see how the contradiction within a situation can be amplified by
the commentary: the almost idyllic image of a woman sitting in her dark
kitchen is contrasted with the necessity of saving money, which – strange
to say – helps the rich again.

Thought-images refer to real objects or situations that are produced
by man and shaped by society. There is no longer any metaphysical or
other emblematic truth hidden behind their appearance, yet they have
a social context that has to be explained. When the *flâneur*/collector
discovers these objects, they do not speak immediately; they have to be
arranged and interpreted. The problem is very similar to Brecht's
observation that a photograph of the AEG factories does not say much
about this industrial complex. Pictures say less than the proverb would
have it, or, as Benjamin noticed, photorealism can aestheticize even
slums and poverty.[19] As we have seen in the case of Brecht's *War Primer*,
the images have to be reconstructed, illuminated differently, or just
explained by a written commentary (*subscriptio*) to make them emblems
of our society that can be read and understood. Thought-images, in
contrast to traditional emblems, are concrete objects/situations of a
capitalistic society that criticize the social reality they reveal.

It is still not clear what happens between observation and commentary
in a thought-image. What mediates between image and thought? With
emblems, the mental activity stimulated by the image is contemplation
leading to an idea or a moral. With thought-images, readers have to
reflect on the true nature of an object or situation (not just accept the
appearance); we have to discover their contradictions and criticize
them. What we need is a critical theory that can explain why the simple
answer by a poor woman in a dark kitchen, "I am saving electricity," is

so shocking. A theory is necessary to relate the concrete image to a general concept or to understand the situation of the old woman in the larger context of economic laws (such as ownership of the means of production, working conditions, exploitation, surplus value). The theory that helps decipher the concrete images of capitalist society is called Marxism, and indeed most of the authors who used this prose form are Marxists, of many shades to be sure. This theory criticizes alienated and reified relationships and situations in society, showing that they are historically determined and can therefore be changed. Thought- images, we can now sum up, describe a modern experience, reflect upon it, and return to the experience that is now understood, as the commentary shows. In their best examples thought-images become "dialectical images,"[20] which present, analyze, and grasp a situation in order to change it. Thought-images are not just thought-provoking, they provoke action. Brecht's "Marxist emblems" and Benjamin's "dialectical images" can be considered operative forms that aim at practice. Bloch's *Spuren* belongs to the same genre, even if his stories are sometimes longer and more poetic. The following story (quoted in part) is an ideal example for summarizing the description of the genre:

Forms of Play, Alas

Today did not look as if it would amount to much.

With no money, even Paris seems smaller. Went to the old workingmen's pub, there are worse ones which are no cheaper.

But I saw someone there who was really letting himself go. So utterly, so innocently enjoying himself, just as it should be. The man opposite me had lobster in his work-worn fists, he bit and spat the red shell, spattering the floor. But he partook joyfully of the tender creature inside, when he finally had it, quietly and judiciously.

Here at last was something good which was no longer being sullied by the bourgeoisie enjoying themselves; this did not taste of the sweat of those who go without, the disgrace of capital gains. This was unusual enough in Paris, where as yet no bourgeois is ashamed about being one, and not only comfortably, but also proudly declares himself privately affluent. The worker with the lobster was also reminiscent of something else, of that great rapture, long ago. Moreover, a certain notion of later glimmered, when money no longer howls for goods or wags its tail in them. Where we will be spared having to make the extremely ridiculous choice between pure beliefs and pure sustenance.[21]

The situation in the workers' pub is simple enough: a man eats lobster and enjoys it – not much to that. Yet the intellectual who observes and describes him sees it all differently. His commentary not only brings the absent bourgeois into the picture, it also establishes a contradiction between the food of the bourgeoisie and the worker eating it here. The lobster in the stained hands of the worker is, for Bloch, a trace of great things to come. The idyllic moment in the pub becomes transparent for revolutionary history. The worker with the lobster, an emblematic image, reminds Bloch of past revolutions and anticipates a liberated humanity, when there will no longer be a class society based on commodities and money. A tender irony is hidden in the title and the exposition: the critical observer is a displaced intellectual who has to go to a workers' pub because he has no money. There he witnesses a utopian, mouth-watering moment that anticipates his liberation. But alas, this is only a *Spielform*, a form of play!

This story contains everything that is typical for a thought-image: an emblematic structure (title, description, reflection), image and thought mediated by critical theory, and a utopian vision; and yet one could ask whether this prose is representative of modernism at all. One finds in *Spuren* not only traditional prose forms and allegorical structures but also a conventional narrator and a pragmatic purpose – in short, a closed form with a clear function. What is so modern about it?

Modernism with Patina

If Bloch's modernism depended only on his theoretical writings, he could easily be defined as a modernist. His defense of expressionism against Lukács and Kurella, his interest in and writings about surrealism, and his cultural essays in *Heritage of Our Times* certainly qualify him as one of the leading theoreticians of the "experience of modernity" (Benjamin). But this approach will not do, since it uses the aura of theory to expect or demand modernist prose. As we all know, theorizing well does not guarantee good prose, not even thought-images.

Another approach to defining the modernity of Bloch's texts would be to use the bird's-eye view of the history of ideas. Starting with Schiller's analysis of modern disharmony and alienation, his projected reconciliation, and his theory of modern literature,[22] one could continue with Hegel's skepticism about the possibility of art in modernity: he criticizes the prose of modern life and its abstractness, which make it impossible for the artist to represent the totality of modern experience adequately in art. Philosophy and theory have replaced art, which has become prosaic and partial. But precisely what makes the traditional great art forms a thing of the past (except for the novel) works in favor of the thought-image. Indeed, from this perspective the thought-image can be viewed as the modern form *par excellence*. It demonstrates the abstractness of life in isolated images and partial situations, and to make sure that the realism of its narrative is properly understood, the theoretical commentary makes the surface of reality transparent by disclosing the underlying social truth. Image, prose, and theory form a dialectical image that makes the prose of life visible and readable. The dilemma of modern art is thus the virtue of the thought-image. But even this legitimation of the thought-image as a modern prose form sounds more convincing in its philosophical abstractness than the textual proof actually is. Therefore we have to go back to the text in order to establish its modernism as a textual quality.

So far we have defined the modernity of thought-images by their emblematic structure, their modern subject matter, and a critical method. But this characterization alone will not suffice to claim Bloch's *Spuren* as a modern text, and there is indeed more sophistication in Bloch's simple stories than meets the untrained eye. To uncover these qualities we have to consider another aspect of Bloch's theory of modernism. Bloch's concept of avant-garde has an aesthetic as well as a political dimension, because it combines new literary techniques with the political interest of the "broad masses." It is very similar to Benjamin's position in his lecture, "The Author as Producer" (1934), in which he advanced the radical thesis that "the proper political tendency of a work includes its literary quality."[23] Let us consider this literary quality.

"Truth is concrete." For no other aspect of modern prose does Hegel's *dictum* seem truer than for thought-images. They are based on reality, and their realism is based on theory. The unity of image and thought, the description of an object or situation and reflection about it, guarantees that the reality is interpreted and understood. Only theory and interpretation make reality transparent for truth. Bloch was no friend of documentary literature, be it naturalism or reportage, both of which rely on the immediacy of facts and life. Truly realistic art has to make visible tendencies hidden in reality. To recognize these tendencies, the artist needs what Bloch calls "exact phantasy."[24] Phantasy is the subjective factor that corresponds to the teleological nature of the objective world. The creative process brings out these tendencies; art is the *Vor-schein* (pre-appearance) of the real possibility.

These observations are still too general and belong more to the sphere of aesthetics than of poetics. I shall focus now on the modern techniques of which Benjamin speaks in his essay. I have already mentioned that Bloch is in most cases not the author but merely the narrator of found stories. Not unlike Brecht, he changes and transforms the text and material in order to accentuate a new meaning or to demonstrate the possibility of change. For this creative method Bloch coined two verbs, deconstruct and distort (*zerfällen* and *entstellen*). Modern art and literature distort reality until it is recognizable, which means that they help to understand the underlying truth of society and to discover tendencies that point beyond it.

To demonstrate modernist technique I have chosen a text from Robert Musil's *Literary Estate While Alive* (1936) that in structure and style comes very close to being a thought-image. *Triedere* (telescope),[25] as this essayistic narrative is called, describes what happens when we use a telescope to look at things we would not normally observe through a telescope. In this experiment we isolate buildings, things, and people and distort reality beyond recognition. The telescope becomes an "ideological instrument," and the corresponding theory is called "isolation." The normal attitude of looking at things is disrupted and reality loses its contours, its a priori totality. Exposed in this manner, things look strange, alien, and uncanny. We look at reality with new eyes and recognize that its normal, everyday appearance is only one possible side of it. The isolation of things and their distortion produce an alienating effect that is critical and prognostic at the same time. (Bloch may have had something similar in mind when he observed in the preface to *The Principle of Hope* that one needs the strongest telescope to penetrate the presence, the darkness of the lived now. Bloch wants nothing less than to "trieder" time.[26])

Isolation, fragmentation, and distortion of reality are only one side of modern art corresponding to another: montage. In the collages of Braque, Picasso, or Schwitters, fragments of authentic life are glued together and challenge the notion of a separation of art and life. Similarly the photomontages of John Heartfield and the "photograms" of Brecht combine picture and text in order to transform the picture and make it readable. Thought-images can be regarded as epic montages: they too combine image and thought in order to decipher the contradictions of reality. *Spuren* as a whole can be read as a montage that brings together things and situations that are far apart and often irreconcilable, as in "Forms of Play, Alas," where a lobster-eating worker, the hat of a bourgeois, and the explosion of a seltzer bottle are read as traces of a revolutionary history that connect the present with the past. One text even uses montage as the theme for a story and contemplates the artistic possibilities of this technique:

> The interplay of such an evening is montage, separating the close, bringing together the most distant, just as that appears in such a heightened way in the pictures of the sort drawn by Max Ernst or Chirico. That which is encoded in these things exists there quite objectively, even if the faculty for grasping it more or less accurately is only now awakening, mediated by the social earthquake. Painters, as mentioned, and poets have gone ahead in these lateral connections of things, very broadly spread.[27]

The cross-connections of things and the reading of traces, criss and cross, open up the hollow spaces of reality, discover possibilities and tendencies that otherwise would have been overlooked.

In an essay of 1931, "Poesie im Hohlraum" (Poetry in a Hollow Space), Bloch deals with the disintegration of bourgeois culture and its heritage, and he speaks about the necessary work of a "dialectical avant-garde" that uses this heritage and transforms it for its own purposes.[28] This could be "the birth of utopia out of the spirit of destruction."[29]

Among the forms that could be used and transformed, he includes the "subversive fairy tale," the revolutionary use of "pulp novels," "surrealism," and the utopian surplus of distorted masterworks. Of all these forms and techniques, which he used himself in *Spuren*, surrealism seems to be the most interesting, since this style uses the isolation of things (*objets trouvés*) and the montage of fragments as a creative method to disrupt the normal order of things and to take a fresh and critical look at reality. That which has a shocking effect in pictorial/figurative arts is difficult to imitate in literature, yet Bloch believes that there is something like surrealist thinking and writing. In his review of Walter Benjamin's *One-Way Street*, he characterizes the surrealistic perception of the world as consisting of interest in details and fragments, interruption, cross-connection, and improvisation. The whole book is a "montage of fragments," and correspondingly the philosophical interpretations are fragments, too. It lies outside the sphere of traditional, systematic philosophy, and Bloch characterizes it as philosophical "improvisation" and "revue." What is missing, he criticizes, is a "concrete intention": "Even one-way streets have a destination."[30] In contrast, Bloch's *Spuren* has a material tendency.

Bloch's concept of the avant-garde includes two elements easily forgotten in the discussion of advanced, highly cultivated modernism: popularity and tendentiousness. "Today the artist can be considered an avant-gardist," he writes, "only if he succeeds in making the new art forms useful for the life and the struggle of the broad masses; otherwise glittering alloy is nothing but old iron. It is wrong to think that the gap between the old avant-garde and the masses is insurmountable."[31] Both tendencies, however mediated, are present in *Spuren*. Bloch's narrative style may be confounded, but at the same time it is spontaneous and has the quality of oral story-telling. His narration leads to thinking, yet his philosophy is neither academic nor esoteric. The political tendency is not as strong as our selection of examples suggests, but the utopian vision is present in most of the stories, if one deciphers the traces correctly.

Finally, thought-images no longer adhere to the principle of autonomy in art. In contrast to poetic images and/or symbols that rest in themselves and stimulate contemplation, thought-images confront the reader with reality and provoke an answer, if not change. Their critical theory and didactic function render the question of disinterested pleasure superfluous.

The important question "Should one act or think?" that makes many practical philosophers blush receives from Bloch a tolerant answer that does not overburden theory:

One can also ask whether the thinker is doing anything at all. He lifts up something of that which exists by writing it. He seeks to make a few things brighter by showing where they're going.[32]

214 NOT YET

It is not up to philosophers and writers to change the world. To make things dance, nothing less than a revolution would be necessary. Until then, writers are critical observers who describe and interpret the world with the hope of changing it. "Thinking has to open this window," Bloch continues, and maybe this is the proper image for the philosophical observer who was once fascinated by a red window. "This secret window," Bloch concludes, "is the convex lens for the utopian material the earth is made of."[33]

Notes

I would like to thank my colleague Jim Steakley for translating the texts of Brecht, and those of Bloch not included in the translations from *Spuren* that follow this essay.

1. Bertolt Brecht, *Gesammelte Werke* (Frankfurt am Main: Suhrkamp, 1967), V, p. 377.
2. Ibid., V, p. 389.
3. Theodor W. Adorno, *Noten zur Literatur* (Frankfurt am Main: Suhrkamp, 1961), p. 131.
4. Gert Ueding, *Glanzvolles Elend* (Frankfurt am Main: Suhrkamp, 1973), p. 187.
5. Ernst Bloch, *Literarische Aufsätze* (Frankfurt am Main: Suhrkamp, 1965), p. 242.
6. Ernst Bloch, *Spuren* (Frankfurt am Main: Suhrkamp, 1965), p. 242.
7. Ibid., p. 16.
8. Siegfried Kracauer, "Zwei Deutungen in zwei Sprachen," in *Ernst Bloch zu ehren,* ed. Siegfried Unseld (Frankfurt am Main: Suhrkamp, 1965), p. 146.
9. Bloch, *Spuren*, p. 17.
10. Ibid., p. 21.
11. Hans Mayer, "Ernst Blochs poetische Sendung," in *Ernst Bloch zu ehren*, pp. 21–30.
12. Theodor W. Adorno, "Benjamin's 'Einbahnstrasse,'" *Über Walter Benjamin* (Frankfurt am Main: Suhrkamp, 1970), p. 55.
13. Albrecht Schone, *Emblematik und Drama im Zeitalter des Barock* (Munich: Beck, 1964), pp. 18–30. See also Heinz Schlaffer, "Denkbilder," in *Poesie und Politik*, ed. Wolfgang Kuttenkeuler (Bonn: Kohlhammer, 1973), pp. 137–54.
14. Walter Benjamin, "Theses on the Philosophy of History," *Illuminations*, ed. Hannah Arendt (New York: Schocken, 1969), p. 257 ff.
15. Bertolt Brecht, *Kriegsfibel* (Berlin: Aufbau, 1955).
16. Ibid., p. 44.
17. Ernst Bloch, "Erinnerung," in *Über Walter Benjamin: Mit Beiträgen von Th. W. Adorno, E. Bloch, et al.* (Frankfurt am Main: Suhrkamp, 1968), p. 17.
18. Bloch, *Spuren*, p. 16.
19. Walter Benjamin, "The Author as Producer," *Reflections*, ed. Peter Demetz (New York: Harcourt Brace Jovanovich, 1978), p. 229 ff.
20. Walter Benjamin, *Schriften I* (Frankfurt am Main: Suhrkamp, 1955), p. 489.
21. Bloch, *Spuren*, p. 22 ff.
22. Jürgen Habermas, *The Philosophical Discourse of Modernity* (Cambridge, Mass.: MIT Press, 1987), pp. 45–50.
23. Benjamin, "Author as Producer," p. 221.
24. Bloch, *Literarische Aufsätze*, p. 137.
25. Robert Musil, *Prosa, Dramen, späte Briefe*, ed. Adolf Frise (Reinbek: Rowohlt, 1957), p. 492 ff.
26. Ernst Bloch, *Das Prinzip Hoffnung* (Frankfurt am Main: Suhrkamp, 1973), I, p. 2.
27. Bloch, *Spuren*, p. 167.
28. Ibid., p. 133.
29. Ernst Bloch, *Erbschaft dieser Zeit* (Frankfurt am Main: Suhrkamp, [1962] 1973), p. 371.
30. Ernst Bloch, *Vom Hasard zur Katastrophe* (Frankfurt am Main: Suhrkamp, 1972), p. 324.
31. Bloch, *Spuren*, p. 202.
32. Ibid., p. 71 ff.
33. Ibid.

From *Spuren* by Ernst Bloch

Too Little

One is alone with oneself. In the company of others most people are alone even without themselves. One must break free from both of these conditions.

Sleeping

At first, in ourselves, we are empty. Thus we easily fall asleep if there are no external stimuli. Soft pillows, darkness, silence allows us to fall asleep, the body grows dark. If one lies awake at night this is by no means wakefulness but rather a sluggish, exhausting crawling around on the spot. It is then that one notices how uncomfortable it is to be with nothing other than oneself.

Long and Drawn-out

Waiting equally creates a sense of tedium. But it also makes one drunk. Anyone who stares for a long time at the door through which he expects someone, him or her, to come, can become intoxicated. As if by monotonous singing which draws and draws one. Where one is drawn is obscure, but it is probably into nothing good. If the man, the woman one was expecting does not come, the clear disappointment does not simply dispel the intoxication. It just mingles with its result, a particular kind of hangover, which is present here as well. Hoping is an antidote to waiting, which not only provides one with something to drink, but also with something which has to be cooked.

Always Therein

We cannot be alone for long. It is not enough, it is eerie in the little box which is too much one's own. Yet one carries this around everywhere one goes, particularly when one is young. It is then that many become strangely withdrawn into themselves, they make themselves silent. It rattles down like chains and buries those who are only withdrawn into themselves. Because they cannot let go of themselves, they are frightened in the very space in which they are. Into which they are driven, even without something else taking them there. There is only fear of what cannot be seen. That which afflicts us visibly is what we are frightened of, insofar as one is weaker, or one faces one's enemy. But all that helps combat the fear of loving ourselves, or forgetting ourselves, because this fear comes only out of ourselves, when we are alone. Whoever is not able to do this adequately becomes bored. Whoever can do this either considers himself important or accepts what he does outside himself exactly as it is. Neither of these two is so far removed from the other, and they even alternate in most people, allowing them to get up in the mornings, even if they don't have to. And during the day both disappear only halfway.

Blending In

Is it good? I asked. To a child everything tastes best somewhere else. But they quickly notice what is not right there as well. And if it were as nice at home, then they wouldn't be so glad to leave. They often sense early on that things could be very different here as well as there.

Sing-Song

Odd, how some people behave when not being watched. Some carve faces for themselves in the morning, some others dance themselves a face, most hum nonsensically to themselves. Even when they are having a break, perhaps making a payment, many hum something which cannot be understood, which they themselves don't hear, but within which there may lie a great deal. Here, masks fall off, or new ones are put on, it depends, the whole thing is mad enough. Alone, many people are slightly insane, they sing a piece of that which used to be wrong with them and has not yet been fixed. They are distorted and imagined puppets [*pupae*], because they have been forced to grow up even more distorted and desolate.

Slight Change

I knew someone who didn't make much of himself. As a child, he said, he had been quite proud, he had to be the first in any game. Whoever did not do what he told them was beaten up and for the most part the young gentleman retained the upper hand, probably because his opponent didn't punch very hard.

But later of course it came to an end, abruptly, as if it had been swallowed. We who had been in the lower classes with him still remembered: he had been a really pitiful boy during this period. When the others were in their wild years they took it out on the new coward, they dunked him in the bath, tied a rope around his leg on the playground and he had to hop. He took an exercise book from the boy who had done him least harm, and afterwards the boy was punished for it; in short, he had become a pathetic fellow, nasty and weak. But then something remarkable happened: when he was fourteen or a little older, around the first stages of puberty, the proud child actually came back, the wretched boy was discarded, his manner changed for a second time, he grew strong and soon became the leader in the very same class. He was brash with his words with a quite genuine sense of power, cheeky self-assurance, and little poise; he walked into public houses exclaiming: Hats off, Fritz Klein is coming. The good citizens had no hats on anyway. Another saying of his, which came later on, was: He who rejects me is condemned. Yet he need not have said such frivolous things, there was something about the boy now anyway, something very unusual and certainly difficult to explain, which he had in common with others whom I met later on and who, incidentally, were not always the best people: he radiated power, one could barely resist it.

And the same man continued in his story: many years later, naturally, he had established himself in a good position, had authority and respect, and he was furnishing his house; the workmen suddenly had a feeling about him, or an old, long-forgotten joke at his expense, which he simply cannot explain any better, but that side of his personality from earlier in his life was back, at least the fellows behaved as if it were, and grinned. In other words something in him, he thought, must not have been right, at least something must have remained unset from the bad old days. Like dogs smelling the sex of humans, so the workmen in the small town (and what fellows they were) had a different kind of sense, which was just as precise. A distant memory became fresh in his own mind, and he wanted to have learned from it that no grass grows over inner misdeeds, indeed that one can always become the coward that one was again and one can always do the bad things one did, if those who have come after him perceive his old times so clearly.

One of those among us, who simply did not believe in the individual self, sought a friendlier meaning. But it clearly depends on the situation in which the person finds himself; accordingly the wretched or benevolent airs, the weak or strong actions will come to light. If the honorable man had had no tracks to follow for this new, or rather childhood self, which had begun to approach again at the age of fourteen, then he would not have been able to narrate this didactic story. Instead, the workmen would have found him in the criminal register where the petty scoundrels go to the dogs or are hanged, particularly those who are weak and recidivist.

Lamp and Cupboard

Someone said that anything which is alive today can only be had in groups of two, or at most three people. He was thinking of love, friendship, conversation; he was a kind-hearted, despairing man, who felt cold at work and did not see what could come out of it in general. For all this, he did not care much for individualist or big-headed people, but rather he was firmly on the side of the masses, though admittedly the genuine, vital and now non-existent ones. So, as unbourgeois as possible, he withdrew to the small bourgeois side, not into the home, but to where there was still a lamp on the table.

But someone else told the following story: when I was furnishing a room for myself and thought it was really quite welcoming, something extraordinary happened. I had bought old furniture, yet when I had finished, I noticed, moreover women and friends of mine noticed, that, so to speak, all the chairs were missing. Along the walls there were cabinets, sideboards, medium-sized cupboards and mostly large ones, in the middle lay a carpet, which filled the room; yet clearly I had forgotten to provide the means for sitting, for conversing, which I thought I loved. Even the lamps, which were clearly not omitted, stood less ready for conversation, and less suited to reading and were rather just illuminative and protruding, like disconnected arms of the wall. A clever woman said that a man is what he sees moving along before him; but one should not be so much of a man, said the narrator, or so much of one that one simply has everything moving along or standing against the objective wall. The man in question was even lacking in objectivity to the extent, perhaps, that his room contained only beautiful, heavy, proud show-pieces, almost like a woman. It was a lesson to me, concluded the astonished furnisher, and he visited his friend, the very one about whom the first story was told, and who was so civilized, that he even still hated wide ties.

Becoming Well Accustomed

Those who are having a somewhat hard time already perceive this quite acutely. At least in their senses; in their judgement things look more hazy, here they let themselves be easily distracted. But just like their bodies, their senses mimic the pitching and swaying of the carriage, which takes them to the factory or the office in the mornings. At most, becoming accustomed helps a little, as a very mild intoxicant, which one barely recognizes as such. For the whole of bourgeois life is permeated by it and can be coped with only because of it. If, on the other hand, the situation becomes completely desperate, not only monotonous, but devastatingly bad, a much stronger antidote develops, one which comes from within ourselves. Even young children become strangely intoxicated if their school marks are worsening and they are in the midst of a streak of bad luck. Adults perceive it differently, but in a similar way: if someone has staked everything on one card and lost it all, now and again an utterly remarkable sense of joy about being at the end of one's tether like this manifests itself. A gentle happiness, which absorbs the blows, so that for a while, at least, they miss their target or land off-centre. No strength comes out of this, but whilst habit withdraws and numbs us, the small glimmering intoxication in the midst of bad luck is the pleasure of defiance. A defiance which it seems has no longer a need to defy, and which makes one peculiarly free, if only for a short while. A piece of something which has not come is hidden there, partly as a nest egg, partly as a lamp, and not only as an inner one.

Take Note

More and more is appearing among us in the margins. It is the small things one should pay attention to, pursue. A matter which is simple and unusual will often take one the furthest. One hears for example a story like the one about the soldier, who came late to roll call. He does not position himself in rank and file, but rather beside the officer, who "as a result" does not notice. Apart from the entertainment this story provides, yet another impression is at work here: what was going on here; there was indeed something going on, going on in its own right. An impression which does not come to rest once it has been heard. An impression on the surface of life, so that it cracks, possibly.

In short, it is good also to fantasize. For there is really so much which is not concluded when it happens, even when it is beautifully told. Rather, strangely enough, there is more going on, there is more to the event, in that it shows or suggests something. Stories of this kind are not simply told, one also looks for their significance, or at least pricks up one's ears and wonders what was going on there. From the occurrences there emerges an ability to take note, which would otherwise not be like this, or an ability to take note which already exists and uses minor events as traces and examples. They indicate something less or more, which upon being told should be considered, and upon consideration should be retold; something which is not quite right in these stories, because it is not quite right with us and in general. Some things only become comprehensible in the form of such stories and not in more elaborate or elevated forms, or at least they are comprehended differently in these forms. An attempt will now be made to tell and to note how some of these ideas came to one's attention, this will be in the manner of a dedicated amateur, noting whilst telling, and whilst noting, meaning what is being told. But the more ancient desire to listen to stories still existed, good and humble ones, stories in differing tones, from different years, peculiar ones, which when they come to an end really do end, having moved the listener. It is a random pursual of traces, put together in sections which simply divide up the framework. For everything one encounters and notices is the same after all.

Situation

The Poor Woman

What are you doing? I asked. I am saving, said the poor woman. She had already been sitting in the dark kitchen for a long time. It was easier than saving food, after all. Since there is not enough for everyone, the poor come to the rescue. They work for the big shots even when they are at rest and left alone.

The Filth

How far one can sink. I heard that yesterday, and all the rest that goes along with it.

A drunken woman lay in the rue Blondel. The policeman seizes her. *Je suis pauvre*, says the woman. That is no reason for puking all over the street, bellows the policeman. *Que voulez vous, monsieur, la pauvreté, c'est déjà à moitié la saleté*, says the woman and takes another swig. Thus she had described, explained, and transcended herself, all at once. Whom or what should the policeman arrest now?

The Gift

One can have anything for money, they say. Just not happiness; on the contrary, children begin early on to get exactly this. An eight-year-old girl recently saved a boy from drowning. Or rather she screamed for so long when she saw the blue-faced lad, that people came and pulled him out. For her screaming the child got twenty marks from Santa Claus, a lot of money, but not too much, as we will hear. For, another time when the girl is looking out of the window, something long and thin is floating on the water, and she hurries out of the house. "Sir, there are another twenty marks drifting past!" (It was really only a tree trunk.) If one considers the consequences connected with this event (the sight of drowned corpses and so on), the trauma was strangely lessened, indeed prevented, by money. A double dose of evil was relieved. The angel in the girl came to rest. It is the lowest form of bad luck to be poor. Santa

Claus, who rarely comes, does not relieve it, but puts it at least into proper perspective.

Differing Needs

A story is told about a horse and dog who were friends. The dog saved the best bones for the horse, and the horse gave the dog the most fragrant bundles of hay, and thus each wanted to do what was kindest for the other, and thus neither of the two ate their fill. Just such misfortune can still be found among even the closest of people, especially of different sexes, when they are not able to get out of what they have built for themselves, but also between people who are less intimate. A modest demand for what is generally given, mostly well-meaningly, certainly helps a lot. For if one sees the bundles of hay, in other words most people's evenings, or Sundays, one cannot comprehend how they can carry on living.

Forms of Play, Alas

I

Today did not look as if it would amount to much.

With no money, even Paris seems smaller. Went to the old working-men's pub, there are worse ones which are no cheaper.

But I saw someone there who was really letting himself go. So utterly, so innocently enjoying himself, just as it should be. The man opposite me had lobster in his work-worn fists, he bit and spat the red shell, spattering the floor. But he partook joyfully of the tender creature inside, when he finally had it, quietly and judiciously. Here at last was something good which was no longer being sullied by the bourgeoisie enjoying themselves; this did not taste of the sweat of those who go without, the disgrace of capital gains. This was unusual enough in Paris, where as yet no bourgeois is ashamed about being one, and not only comfortably, but also proudly declares himself privately affluent. The worker with the lobster was also reminiscent of something else, of that great rapture, long ago. Moreover, a certain notion of later glimmered, where money no longer howls for goods or wags its tail in them. Where we will be spared having to make the extremely ridiculous choice between pure beliefs and pure sustenance.

II

One set out quite differently from usual this evening. Did not guard oneself from the street, its center, on which the vehicles roared up and down, to the left and to the right, fiercely and toward us.

Instead this center was at last alive, indeed, something was growing on it. The occupying traffic laid aside its artillery, withdrew into the distance or to the outskirts, the wonderful asphalt was inhabited. Colorful paper lanterns stretched diagonally across it, formed a low space in which people danced. Houses were now its walls, the luminous windows all around shone like new lamps, like self-illuminated mirrors, also with people inside. And the most beautiful thing was that the space for dancing was only closed off at the sides, and otherwise had the length of the street to itself, including the side streets. On the next corner music was also being played, and couples strolled through the shining quartier.

This is a Paris street on the 14th of July, the great day. When the Bastille was being stormed people danced as well, on the ground where the prison had been leveled. It represented the meadow of the blessed, and it has remained so; naturally in those days one danced in a different manner. But even if the revolutionaries have become calm, a distant memory rushes through the "national festival" again, every so often. Not entirely belonging to the nation, for there is no peace for the bourgeois gentilhomme who came afterwards. Because, when on the 14th of July 1928 a car, driven by a man with a straw hat, wanted to push its way through one of the dance streets, the people did not make way, even though no one was dancing at that moment and droves of taxis had already passed through. It was probably the straw hat which provoked them; ordinarily this would have meant nothing in particular, but here, curiously, it was a symbol of the ruling class, perhaps because of its light color and because machines are otherwise not usually operated by people wearing straw hats. The provocative straw hat did not retreat, but instead accelerated on through the crowd. But twenty fists had already seized hold of the car from behind and were pulling it back down the street, in spite of the raging exhaust pipe, back and forth to the taciturn rhythm of the spontaneous tiltyard; the proprietor himself behaved calmly, with a certain sinister enjoyment of the sport of this reaction. Only once could he almost have succeeded in pushing through, but then came the second thing to bring joy to one's heart: a young girl suddenly leapt in front of the car and danced, smiling and fearless, with flower in her hand, then in her mouth, she dictated the movements of the gentleman, who was stopping, and when the car came to a halt, she bowed with great and graceful mockery. Here the driver really should have let himself be pulled back, but the ruling classes still capitulate awkwardly, abstractly and undialectically – in short, instead of taking stock of the situation and conceding himself to it, the provocateur reversed the force of his acceleration forward into a no less arrogant acceleration in retreat, turned around, and through this difficult and wrong maneuver now really did drive into the crowd. Several women were pinned against the wall, the men no longer had any space behind the turning machine, and the air began to ripple briskly, invectives began to fly, the car was seized at its sides as it might have been during an insurrection and would have been overturned had its proprietor not brought the steering wheel into the right position and the car flown from the scene. But at least the straw hat experienced what befits the fleur-de-lys, whichever form it takes. A young fellow had knocked it off the bourgeois's head, thrown it up high into the air, and others caught hold of it, the music was playing again and couples were dancing, and not just with their feet and bodies. Now their hands had something to do as well, they could reach for the straw hat as it was tossed through the air by one couple to the next until it finally lay on the ground, degraded and crushed, a very modest, very allegorically trampled representative of the Bastille. Unsuspecting taxi drivers who now approached and wanted to cross to the nearby boulevard turned around right away; commercial interests don't participate in civil wars. And even the rebel streets soon forgot again that they had been the only ones in Paris to dance a little on the 14th of July. Thus the straw hat never made it into a police report, let alone into history, but instead only into this minor, anticipatory narrative.

Translated by Jamie Owen Daniel

A Small Reflection on a Dream Thrice Removed of Hope from a Refugee Camp

Mary N. Layoun

> It is in Jabal Amman
> that you should look for resurrection
> it is in the Wahdat Camp
> that you should look for spring
> it is on the bones of Abou Sliman
> that you should write koranic verses
> Etel Adnan, "The Beirut–Hell Express"[1]

Thomas More designated utopia as a place, an island in the distant South Seas. This designation underwent changes later so that it left space and entered time. Indeed, the utopians, especially those of the 18th and 19th centuries, transposed the wishland more into the future. In other words, there is a transformation of the topos from space into time. With Thomas More the wishland was still ready, on a distant island, but I am not there. On the other hand, when it is transposed into the future, not only am I not there, but utopia itself is also not with itself. This island does not even exist. But it is not something like nonsense or absolute fancy; rather it is not *yet* in the sense of a possibility; *that* it could be there if we could only do something for it. Not only if we travel there, but *in that* we travel there the island utopia arises out of the sea of the possible – utopia, but with new contents.

Ernst Bloch, "Something's Missing"[2]

In the high-ceilinged room of glass and steel, the mechanically regulated metal window louvers opened and closed to a rhythm of their own. Around the huge table in the center of the room, the discussion was of "the internalization of systems of domination." By way of illustration, one of the men present, a distinguished writer and critic, told the story of his participation in a film project for which Palestinian children in refugee camps in Lebanon had been asked about their dreams of return to Palestine. One young boy told the distinguished writer and critic his dream of riding with his fellow refugee-camp residents on a bus back to Palestine:

> The bus from the Lebanese refugee camp reaches Palestine; it stops at a central square in a large town. The people on the bus from Lebanon are called one by one to board the other buses waiting in the square for the trip back to the various villages, towns, and cities from which they were forced some fifty years earlier. The Palestinian boy is distressed as he sees the friends, neighbors, and acquaintances of a young lifetime leave the bus. Why do we have to leave each other? Why can't we live together as we did in Lebanon?

In the huge room with the mechanically louvered windows, heads nodded somberly. The poor young boy preferred the community of a refugee camp to returning home? Prisoners get used to – even don't want to leave – their prisons; the young boy was used to the refugee camp. More nodding. Solemn smiles. The young boy's dream was not the only one in the room.

In the very last section ("Certainty, unfinished world, homeland") of the concluding chapter of *The Principle of Hope*, Ernst Bloch's massive compilation of hope's traces in the world as he knew it, and in which he "returns" to the figure of Karl Marx ("Karl Marx and Humanity"), Bloch reiterates: "The tomorrow in today is alive; people are always asking about it. The faces which turned in the utopian direction have of course been different in every age ... but all are set up around that which speaks for itself by still remaining silent." Bloch's attempt to trace "hope" – as, in its various manifestations, insistently if still silently pointing to a better or "right" world – ranges famously through a diverse, even disparate, collection of textual and visual traces. His attempt is most interesting, not for its pursuit of the telos of hope – for Bloch resolutely holds that it is resistant to prediction. Rather, Bloch's tracing of hope(s) suggestively points to the constantly multiple, fluid, and symptomatic flashes (the "anticipatory illumination," in Jack Zipes's felicitous translation of *Vorschein*)[3] of a "not-yet." But that not-yet is one that speaks for itself by not speaking – or, by not *exactly* speaking. For its silent abiding is almost but not quite visible, almost but not quite audible. Thus (in something resembling a poststructuralist reading *avant la lettre*), *The Principle of Hope* points to what is *not* utterable or audible as just as significant and as demanding of a reader/listener as that which is spoken, heard, seen. This insistence on the importance of the unspoken or unperformed suggests, then, a virtual imperative for an implied reader who listens, watches, notices.[4] This charge of the "not-yet" for an implicit audience itself underscores what Fredric Jameson indicates as the necessary differentiation of Bloch's "*philosophical* system" from its "*hermeneutic* use."[5] For the former, Jameson reminds us, "there is a right and wrong way of presenting human reality," "the judgements of truth and falsehood still exist as valid conceptual categories."[6] But, for the latter, those judgements of truth and falsehood and "right and wrong" presentation (and representation) are conceptual distinctions intimately implicated in one another. The "wrong" is a distorted or masked attempt to configure the "right." Within the "false" is an attempt to answer "truly." Parenthetically, this postulation need not necessarily predicate itself on a single and monolithic "true" or "right" – even though, for Bloch, it can sometimes seem to do so. And also, the "wrong" way of telling a story or the systemic judgement of something as "false" carries a charge, then, to a careful reader/listener/participant to attend to the flashes within it of the "right" or "true." In this scheme of things, the careful reader/listener is a postulated necessity. And, there is no easy dismissal of low or popular culture, of the unorthodox, of the politically incorrect, of the false.[7] And so the text – whether a daydream, a fascist propaganda sheet, a fairy tale, an advertisement, or an expressionist painting – can function (for its audience and/or its producer) as a figure of desire for something beyond itself, a something else that looks not back to a past but forward (the "*Vor*" of *Vorschein*) to a not quite foreseeable future.

Now, at first, the story of the young Palestinian boy's distant dream and its retelling as "the internalization of systems of domination" might seem far from the critical reconsideration of the work of Ernst Bloch in the present volume. For a young refugee boy's imaginary return to Palestine is an instance of personal narrative quite distinct from those favorite literary and philosophical texts which so often constitute the touchstones for Bloch's massive philosophical and hermeneutic effort. But the young boy's dream is not so far from Bloch's citation of the *Vorschein* of daydreams, of stories, of tales. Nor is it any less significant a participant in the imagining of a future. It is perhaps a tiny refraction of, or trope for, a million texts in this one fragile one – a young boy's dream of return to Palestine.

And then again, the opening citation of Ernst Bloch from a dialogue between him and Theodor Adorno might seem to abruptly shift the ground of the young Palestinian boy's dream from the particular and historically rooted to the general and abstract. But, if Bloch's work counsels anything, it is the workings of the (more) general in the detail of the particular. The specific historical dream of the young boy for a return to Palestine is, without negating or sublimating his specific dream, simultaneously the longing for a return home. It is that place toward which Bloch points in the closing of his *Principle of Hope* as a home and childhood where no one has yet been.

True genesis is not at the beginning but at the end, and it starts to begin only when society and existence become radical, i.e. grasp their roots. But the root of history is the working, creating human being who reshapes and overhauls the given facts. Once he has grasped himself and established what is his, without expropriation and alienation, in real democracy, there arises in the world something which shines into the childhood of all and in which no one has yet been: homeland. [1,375–6]

That that home is one the young boy never knew, could not know given the circumstances of his life (and the lives of many like him) in a refugee camp in Lebanon, does not mitigate his yearning. (The camps are literally mapped by that yearning with place names from Palestine.) In fact, the young boy's dream represents in a particular fashion that longing of which Bloch writes. In an arguably small and particular way, the specific dilemma and promise – the hope – of the young boy's dream and its retellings suggest something of what seems most pertinent in Bloch's notion of utopia and hope. And it suggests the necessity of "re-utilizing" Bloch's own keen insistence that the future toward which "hope" points is precisely that which is not a mappable space or a regulatable time. It is there, latent – not yet conscious (as opposed to *unconscious*), awaiting recognition not as itself – the "future(s)" – but as *Vorschein.* In fact the "new" of the "not-yet" will be precisely that which we did not – indeed, could not possibly – foresee.[8]

Even though we might well not concur with Bloch's insistence that "in the long run, everything that meets us, everything we notice particularly, is one and the same,"[9] his resolute insistence on pointing to the anticipatory flashes of hope in the present is an important notion. And, in theory at least, there is no necessary or irrevocable link between the totalization of everything as "one and the same" and the insistence on the fluid, multiple, and symptomatic flashes of the not-yet. Precisely in the spirit of Bloch's own notion of "re-utilization" (*Umfunktionierung*), his theorizing of the workings of hope is scarcely exempt from – in fact could lend itself to – some such "re-utilization." So then, for all the biographical and intellectual contradictions of Bloch and his work,[10] for all the overwhelming weight of his insistence on a totality working its way toward an (unforeseeable) end, for all the sometimes slow and burdensome pace of his argumentative prose, juxtaposing the young Palestinian boy's thrice removed dream to Bloch's "principle of hope" is a startling reminder of the disruptive and illuminative power of imagining the future. It is also a startling reminder of the rich potential of a "re-utilization" of Bloch's work – if one not necessarily only on his own terms.

The notion of "homeland" obviously has particular poignancy and concrete meaning for any diaspora. The historical circumstances of the

Palestinians for at least the last forty-five years as exiles, some in their own land; as a forcibly displaced people; as refugees in other countries; and, as potential returnees – makes the call of the "homeland" especially compelling. So too, it makes compelling the specificity of a spatially and temporally *locatable* return. This rather literal notion of a locatable "homeland" is not foreign to Bloch's "principle of hope."[11] But what is interesting in the simultaneous consideration of Bloch's work and the young boy's dream and its retelling is the presence of two different and opposed homeland communities in that dream and the extent to which their mutual presence in the boy's dream suggests "that which speaks for itself by remaining silent." And what is silent is only noticeable in the interstices of what is spoken.

The two kinds of community-in-the-homeland in the young Palestinian boy's dream point to what is left unquestioned at its second retelling. Spatially, both communities are somewhere on the ground of historic Palestine. Temporally, they are in a future where we are not (yet). But the organization of homeland and community in the distant time and nearby place is a strikingly contested one in the boy's dream. The second context in which the dream was recounted (perhaps even the first) was one which would seem to privilege return to the "homeland" as return to the community organization of a pre-exilic past. In the boy's dream, this is accounted for in the return of each rider on the bus from the Lebanese refugee camp to their original village or town or city. The years of the refugee camps are bracketted to return to "home" as and where it was. But the second version of the homeland – the young boy's "childish" and plaintive question of what happens to the community of the refugee camp – is one in which the years of diaspora and refugee camps are figured into rather than rendered extraneous to or excess for the "homeland." The privilege of (chronological) precedence is not automatically assumed. The more and less distant pasts coexist uneasily in relation to a dream of the future. But from that future, the years of the refugee camp are not foreclosed; they are there in the young boy's plaintive question, in his distress as the occupants of the bus from the refugee camp in Lebanon leave one by one to go elsewhere, to return home.

Of course, the young boy, in his recounting of the dream to the distinguished writer and critic who visits the refugee camp, is too young to possibly know first hand the village or town of his family. His life in the refugee camp is, obviously enough, his only experience of community. To that extent, the writer who solicits his dream and the others in the high-ceilinged room who listen to the writer retelling the young boy's dream are at least partly accurate in their assertion that the young boy is attached to his "prison." For he knows nothing else; he is "attached" to what he knows and catches dream-glimpses of the future through that which he already knows. As do we all. But the glimpses of the future afforded in his dream are actually neither in that of the re-establishment of pre-exile communities nor in that of the preservation of refugee-camp communities. They are, instead, in the silence between those two futures or "homes." They are in that which neither the second nor the first retelling of the dream can seem to accommodate. That is a future community of which the dimensions are not ascertainable but which cannot afford to abandon *either* kind (or time) of community – neither that of pre-1948 (or 1967) Palestine *nor* that of the intervening years of exile and diaspora, and not those other communities which are not figured here.

The discussion around the huge table in the high-ceilinged room, in contrast to and framing (at least in that retelling) the dreams of the young boy, was more world-weary and vastly (and painfully) more battle-weary. Mostly men, and a few women, mostly eye-witness survivors of the 1982 battle of Beirut and of the camps, mostly committed and distinguished spokesmen for their people(s), the discussion in the high-ceilinged room – like the young Palestinian boy's dream – suggested other "anticipatory illuminations" of possible futures, not in the characterization of the young boy's dream as "the internalization of systems of domination," nor in the implicit projection of pre-1948 (or 1967) communities as the authoritative ones. In the young boy's dream at its first and second (here, third) recounting, in the other stories told around the table in the high-ceilinged room, the possible futures hold on in their silence. The overwhelming, vociferous weight of multiple pasts – of 1936–39, 1948, 1967, 1973, 1982, 1987, 1988 – compels attention. Indeed, to ignore those pasts and their tragedies is, as Marx *pace* Hegel reminds us, to witness their "return" (as farce). But in the fervent attempts to imagine the future, in the discussions of necessary pragmatism, of very real past and present injustice, of constitutive law and the state (and, sometimes at least, of society), the young Palestinian boy's dream seems a trenchant if fragile reminder of the extent to which we can imagine or catch glimpses of but not know the future – or predict its outline.

Bloch's work, like the young boy's dream, is a reminder, too, to attend to the "anticipatory illuminations" of the futures, not only in what we feel "certain" will be the case, though sometimes figured there too, but also imbricated in the complex configurations of daydreams and literary imaginings, in declarations of independence and bulletins of the uprising, in the banners and graffiti, in the organization of social movements and popular committees. Not that these are "open books" waiting to be read and marshaled in the calculation of an equation. *This* equals, or will be made to equal, *that*. As the massive compilation of readings and theorizing in *The Principle of Hope* suggests, "reading" or listening is no such uncomplicated endeavor of constructing equivalencies. For to forget the silence of the future(s) for which the young

Palestinian boy's dream – like much of Bloch's work – struggles to hold open a space veers toward the valorization of what Jacques Rancière has, in another context, called "the legal, the necessary, and the legitimate," the contraction of utopia and hope to the "utopia of absolute guarantee;" or, to reiterate the trope used above, to treat the careful reading/listening/watching which Bloch's work encourages as the simple calculation of equivalencies. That is Rancière's notion of the lethal construction he calls "overlegitimated power." And the utter violence wrought in the name of those equivalencies, that overlegitimation, that uncomplicated and uncontradictory "reading" of an "open book," is what paved the way for the young Palestinian boy to the refugee camp in the first place. If the homeland (as resonant in the Arabic "*watan*" as in the German "*Heimat*") is not just an uncomplicated return to communities of the past, neither is it the "internalization of systems of domination" or the perpetuation of present communities. In that we attempt to travel there rather than only to construct it as Rancière's "utopia of absolute guarantee," it "arises out of the sea of the possible . . . but with new contents." The young Palestinian boy's dream, in the future toward which it turns but of which it cannot directly speak, suggests something perhaps not so dissimilar from the "hope" of Ernst Bloch: *True genesis is not at the beginning but at the end.*

Notes

1. Etel Adnan, "The Beirut–Hell Express," *Women of the Fertile Crescent: Modern Poetry by Arab Women*, ed. Kamal Boullata (Washington, DC: Three Continents Press, 1981).

2. Ernst Bloch, "Something's Missing: A Discussion between Ernst Bloch and Theodor W. Adorno on the Contradictions of Utopian Longing," in *The Utopian Function of Art and Literature: Selected Essays*, trans. Jack Zipes and Frank Mecklenburg (Cambridge, Mass.: MIT Press, 1988, pp. 1–17).

3. Cf. his "Introduction" to Bloch's *The Utopian Function of Art and Literature*, esp. pp. xxxv–vi.

4. This is one of the instances – in Bloch's insistence on the necessity of a critical hermeneutical process for more than the analyst – in which his debt to and substantial revision of the work of Freud are striking.

5. See his "Ernst Bloch and the Future," in *Marxism and Form* (Princeton, NJ: Princeton University Press, 1971), pp. 116–60, and esp. pp. 124–5. But also Jameson's resonant discussion of utopia and ideology – in *The Political Unconscious: Narrative as a Socially Symbolic Act* (Ithaca, NY: Cornell University Press, 1981), for example – as well as his critical readings of popular culture elsewhere seem substantially informed by his earlier work on Bloch.

6. *Marxism and Form*, p. 125.

7. This is, perhaps, one reason why Bloch's work is so encyclopedic.

8. Fredric Jameson's parallel of the future in Proust's *A la recherche du temps perdu* to that of Bloch's *The Principle of Hope*, and his work in general, is instructive here. In a wonderful commentary, Jameson cites Proust's Marcel endlessly composing to himself the letter he wants to receive from his beloved Gilberte until, suddenly, he realizes that he can never receive the letter that he is composing precisely because he is composing it. And so he gives up composing letters altogether so as not to foreclose the possibility of actually receiving one. According to Jameson, "As in Bloch, the future always turns out in Proust to be that which is more, or other, than what was expected, even if what had been expected was . . . dissatisfaction itself" (*Marxism and Form*, p. 151). See Bloch's *The Principle*

of Hope (II, p. 621) for one of the many instances in which he points out, here in a discussion of Marx, that "actual descriptions of the future are deliberately missing" in a "keeping open" of future possibilities.

9. *Spuren* (16); quoted in Fredric Jameson, *Marxism and Form*, p. 125.

10. For a discussion of Ernst Bloch as "scandal and embarrassment to most of his contemporaries in both heterodox and orthodox Marxist circles" (p. 174), as "a fossilized remnant of Western Marxism's earlier years" (p. 194), which is nonetheless an astute reading of Bloch's work in many ways, see Martin Jay's "Ernst Bloch and the Extension of Marxist Holism to Nature" in his *Marxism and Totality* (Berkeley: University of California Press, 1984).

11. For a most explicit example, see his discussion of Zionism in *The Principle of Hope*, II, pp. 598–610, where he focuses on the Zionist construction of the Israeli nation-state-as-homeland. But there is a suggestive tension throughout the work as a whole between the metaphoric and the literal homeland – though Bloch clearly comes down on the side of an as yet unrealized socialist "homeland" predicated on an end to exploitation and alienation.

Bibliography

Adamson, W. *Marx and the Disillusionment of Marxism.* Berkeley: University of California Press, 1985.

Adnan, Etel. "The Beirut–Hell Express." *Women of the Fertile Crescent: Modern Poetry by Arab Women.* Ed. Kamal Boullata. Washington, D.C.: Three Continents Press, 1981, pp. 72–84.

Adorno, Theodor W. *Notes to Literature.* Trans. Shierry Weber Nicholsen. New York: Columbia University Press, 1991. 2 vols. German edn.: *Noten zur Literatur.* Frankfurt am Main: Suhrkamp, 1961.

—— "Benjamin's 'Einbahnstrasse.'" *Über Walter Benjamin.* Frankfurt am Main: Suhrkamp, 1970.

—— "A Portrait of Walter Benjamin." *Prisms.* Trans. Samuel and Shierry Weber. Cambridge, Mass.: MIT Press, 1984.

Al-Azmeh, Aziz. *Islams and Modernities.* London and New York: Verso, 1993.

Applegate, Celia. "The Question of Heimat in the Weimar Republic." *New Formations,* 17 (Summer 1992), pp. 64–74.

Aristotle. *The Basic Works of Aristotle.* New York: Random House, 1941.

Arnold, Matthew. *Culture and Anarchy. Poetry and Criticism of Matthew Arnold.* Ed. A. Dwight Culler. Boston: Houghton Mifflin, 1961.

Arnot, Robin Page. *William Morris: A Vindication.* London: Martin Lawrence, 1934.

—— *William Morris: The Man and the Myth.* London: Lawrence & Wishart, 1964.

Aronowitz, Stanley. "Technology and Culture." *Canadian Journal of Political and Social Theory,* 9: 3 (1985), pp. 126–33.

—— and Henry A. Giroux. *Education under Siege.* South Hadley, Mass.: Bergin & Garvey, 1985.

—— and Henry A. Giroux. *Postmodern Education.* Minneapolis: University of Minnesota Press, 1991.

Augustine, Saint. *Confessions.* Harmondsworth: Penguin, 1961.

Ayer, Alfred J. *Bertrand Russell.* Chicago: University of Chicago Press, 1988.

Baddeley, Alan D. *Your Memory: A User's Guide.* Harmondsworth: Penguin, 1983.

Bakhtin, M.M. *The Dialogic Imagination: Four Essays.* Ed. Michael Holquist. Trans. Caryl Emerson and Michael Holquist. Austin: University of Texas Press, 1981.

—— see Vološinov, V.N.

Barrett, B. "Words and Things." In *Destabilizing Theory.* Ed. Michele Barrett and Anne Phillips. Stanford: Stanford University Press, 1992.

Barthes, Roland. *Mythologies.* Paris: Seuil, 1957.

Baumann, Zygmunt. *Socialism, the Active Utopia.* London: Allen & Unwin, 1976.

Benjamin, Andrew, ed. *The Lyotard Reader.* Oxford: Basil Blackwell, 1989.

Benjamin, Walter. *Briefe.* Frankfurt am Main: Suhrkamp, 1966. 2 vols.

—— *Illuminations.* Trans. Harry Zohn. New York: Schocken, 1968. London: Collins, 1973.

—— *The Origin of German Tragic Drama.* Trans. John Osborne. London: New Left Books, 1977.

—— *Schriften I.* Frankfurt am Main: Suhrkamp, 1955.

—— "The Author as Producer." *Reflections.* Ed. Peter Demetz. New York: Harcourt Brace Jovanovich, 1978.

—— "Central Park." *New German Critique,* 34 (1985), pp. 48–55.

—— "Theses on the Philosophy of History." In *Illuminations.* Trans. Harry Zohn. New York: Schocken, 1969.

Bentley, James. *Between Marx and Christ.* London: Verso, 1982.

Bernal, Martin. *Black Athena: The Afroasiatic Roots of Classical Civilization.* Vol. I: *The Fabrication of Ancient Greece 1975–1985.* London: Free Assocation Books, 1987.

Bernstein, Richard J. "Dewey, Democracy: The Task Ahead of Us." In *Post-Analytic Philosophy.* Ed. John Rajchman and Cornell West. New York: Columbia University Press, 1985, pp. 48–58.

—— "One Step Forward, Two Steps Backward: Richard Rorty on Liberal Democracy and Philosophy." *Political Theory,* 15: 4 (1987), pp. 538–63.

Berryman, Philip. *Liberation Theology: Essential Facts about the Revolutionary Movement in Latin America and Beyond.* New York: Pantheon, 1987.

Beverley, John. "The Margin at the Center: On *Testimonio* (Testimonial Narrative)." *Modern Fiction Studies,* 35: 1 (Spring 1989), pp. 3–11.

Bloch, Ernst. *Abschied von der Utopie.* Ed. Hanna Gekle. Frankfurt am Main: Suhrkamp, 1959.

—— *Atheismus im Christentum.* Frankfurt am Main: Suhrkamp, 1968.

—— *Erbschaft dieser Zeit.* Frankfurt am Main: Suhrkamp, 1962, pb 1973.

—— *Heritage of Our Times.* Trans. Neville and Stephen Plaice. Cambridge: Polity Press. Berkeley and Los Angeles: University of California Press, 1990.

—— *Geist der Utopie*. Frankfurt am Main: Suhrkamp, 1973. 3 vols.

—— *Vom Hasard zur Katastrophe*. Frankfurt am Main: Suhrkamp, 1972.

—— *On Karl Marx*. Trans. John Maxwell. New York: Herder & Herder, 1971.

—— *Die Kunst, Schiller zu Sprechen*. Frankfurt am Main: Suhrkamp, 1969.

—— *Literarische Aufsätze*. Frankfurt am Main: Suhrkamp, 1965.

—— *Natural Law and Human Dignity*. Trans. Dennis J. Schmidt. Cambridge, Mass.: MIT Press, 1986.

—— *Das Prinzip Hoffnung*. Frankfurt am Main: Suhrkamp, 1959.

—— *The Principle of Hope*. Trans. Stephen Plaice, Neville Plaice, and Paul Knight. Cambridge, Mass.: MIT Press. Oxford: Basil Blackwell, 1986. 3 vols.

—— *Spuren*. Frankfurt am Main: Suhrkamp, 1969.

—— *Subjekt–Objekt: Erläuterungen zu Hegel*. Frankfurt am Main: Suhrkamp, 1962.

—— *Thomas Münzer als Theologe der Revolution*. Frankfurt am Main: Suhrkamp, 1969.

—— *Tübinger Einteitung in die Philosophie*. Frankfurt am Main: Suhrkamp, 1970.

—— *The Utopian Function of Art and Literature: Selected Essays*. Trans. Jack Zipes and Frank Mecklenburg. Cambridge, Mass.: MIT Press, 1988.

—— "Bilder des Deja Vu." *Verfremdungen I*. Frankfurt am Main: Suhrkamp, 1962, pp. 24–36.

—— "Dialectic and Hope." Trans. Mark Ritter. *New German Critique*, 9 (Fall 1976), pp. 3–11.

—— "Erinnerung." In *Über Walter Benjamin: Mit Beiträgen von Th. W. Adorno, E. Bloch, et al*. Frankfurt am Main: Suhrkamp, 1968.

—— "Herausbringen, unverfälschtes Ordnen: Über die Möglichkeit eines Systems, aber eines Offenen." *Der Mensch als geschichtliches Wesen: Festschrift für M. Landmann*. Ed. Klaus-Jürgen Grundner. Stuttgart: Klett, 1974.

—— "A Jubilee for Renegades." Trans. David Bathrick and Nancy Vedaer Shults. *New German Critique*, 4 (Winter 1975), pp. 17–26.

—— "Nonsynchronism and the Obligation to its Dialectics." Trans. Mark Ritter. *New German Critique*, 11 (Spring 1977), pp. 22–39.

—— "A Philosophical View of the Detective Novel." In *The Utopian Function of Art and Literature*. Trans. Jack Zipes and Frank Mecklenburg. Cambridge, Mass.: MIT Press, 1988, pp. 245–64.

—— "Zur Ontologie des Noch-nicht-Seins." *Tübinger Einteitung in die Philosophie*. Frankfurt am Main: Suhrkamp, 1970.

—— "Recollections of Walter Benjamin." In *On Walter Benjamin*. Ed. Gary Smith. Cambridge, Mass.: MIT Press, 1988, pp. 338–45.

—— "Religious Truth." *Man on his Own: Essays in the Philosophy of Religion.* Trans. John Cumming. New York: Herder & Herder, 1971.

—— "Something's Missing: A Discussion between Ernst Bloch and Theodor W. Adorno on the Contradictions of Utopian Longing." In *The Utopian Function of Art and Literature: Selected Essays.* Trans. Jack Zipes and Frank Mecklenburg. Cambridge, Mass.: MIT Press, 1988, pp. 1–17.

—— "Upright Carriage, Concrete Utopia." *On Karl Marx.* Trans. John Maxwell. New York: Herder & Herder, 1971.

Bloch, Jan Robert. "How can We understand the Bends in the Upright Gait?" *New German Critique,* 45 (Fall 1988), pp. 9–41.

Bockris, Victor. *Warhol: The Biography.* London: Frederick Muller, 1989.

Borge, Tomás. *Christianity and Revolution: Tomás Borge's Theology of Life.* Ed. and trans. Andrew Reading. Maryknoll, NY: Orbis, 1987.

Borges, Jorge L. *Labyrinths.* London: Penguin, 1970.

Brecht, Bertolt. *Gesammelte Werke.* Vols. 2 and 18. Frankfurt am Main: Suhrkamp, 1973.

—— *Kriegsfibel.* Berlin: Aufbau, 1955.

Buck-Morss, Susan. *The Dialectics of Seeing.* Cambridge, Mass.: MIT Press, 1989.

Butler, Judith. *Gender Trouble: Feminism and the Subversion of Identity.* New York: Routledge, 1990.

Cabet, Etienne. *Voyage en Icarie.* Paris and Geneva: Ressources, 1979.

Calvino, Italo. *Una pietra sopra.* Turin: Einaudi, 1980.

Cawelti, John. *Adventure, Mystery and Romance: Formula Stories as Art and Popular Culture.* Chicago: University of Chicago Press, 1976.

Connerton, Paul. *How Societies Remember.* Cambridge: Cambridge University Press, 1989.

Cox, Harvey. "Ernst Bloch and 'The Pull of the Future.'" *New Theology No. 5.* Ed. Martin Marty and Dean G. Peerman. New York: Macmillan, 1968, pp. 191–203.

Cunha, D.A. *As Utopias da Educaco: Ensaios Sobre as Propostas de Paulo Freire.* Rio de Janeiro: Paz e Terra, 1985.

Cunningham, Adrian et al. *"Slant Manifesto": Catholics and the Left.* London and Melbourne: Sheed & Ward, 1966.

Dallmayr, Fred. *Margins of Political Discourse.* Albany, NY: SUNY Press, 1989.

Denning, Michael. *Mechanic Accents: Dime Novels and Working-Class Culture in America.* London: Verso, 1987.

Doyle, Arthur Conan. *Sherlock Holmes: The Complete Novels and Stories.* New York: Bantam, 1986.

Eagleton, Terry. *Literary Theory.* Minneapolis: University of Minnesota Press, 1983.

—— *The New Left Church.* Baltimore: Helicon, 1966.

Ebert, Teresa. "Political Semiosis in/of American Cultural Studies." *American Journal of Semiotics*, 8: 1–2 (1991), pp. 113–35.
—— "Writing in the Political: Resistance (Post) Modernism." *Legal Studies Forum*, 15: 4 (1991), pp. 291–303.
Eco, Umberto. *The Role of the Reader*. Bloomington: Indiana University Press, 1979.
—— "Quattro forme di enciclopedia..." *Quaderni d'italianistica*, 2: 2 (1981), pp. 105–22.
Ellis, Marc H. *Towards a Jewish Theology of Liberation*. Maryknoll, NY: Orbis, 1987.
Foster, Hal, ed. *The Anti-Aesthetic: Essays on Postmodern Culture*. Port Townsend, Washington: Bay Press, 1983.
Foucault, Michel. *Foucault Live*. New York: Semiotext(e), 1989.
Fraser, Nancy and Linda Nicholson. "Social Criticism without Philosophy: An Encounter between Feminism and Postmodernism." *Theory, Culture and Society*, 5: 2–3 (June 1988), pp. 373–94.
Freire, Paulo. *Conscientization*. Bogota: Association of Education Publication, 1973.
—— *Education: The Practice of Freedom*. London: Writers & Readers Press, 1976.
—— *The Politics of Education: Culture, Power and Liberation*. South Hadley, Mass.: Bergin & Garvey, 1985.
—— "Reading the World and Reading the Word: An Interview with Paulo Freire." *Language Arts*, 62: 1 (1985), pp. 15–21.
—— and Donaldo Macedo. "A Dialogue with Paulo Freire." In *Paulo Freire: A Critical Encounter*. Ed. Peter McLaren and Peter Leonard. London: Routledge, 1993.
Freud, Sigmund. *Civilization. Society and Religion: Group Psychology. Civilization and its Discontents and Other Works*, Harmondsworth: Penguin, 1985.
—— *Three Case Histories*. New York: Macmillan, 1963.
Gadamer, Hans-Georg. *Truth and Method*. 2nd. rev. edn. New York: Crossroad, 1990.
Gadotti, M. *Reading Paulo Freire: Life and Work*. Albany, NY: SUNY Press, forthcoming.
Garaudy, Roger. *From Anathema to Dialogue: A Marxist Challenge to the Christian Churches*. Trans. Luke O'Neill. New York: Herder & Herder, 1966.
Gekle, Hanna. "The Phenomenology of the Wish in *The Principle of Hope*." *New German Critique*, 45 (1988).
Geoghegan, Vincent. *Reason and Eros: The Social Theory of Herbert Marcuse*. London: Pluto Press, 1981.
—— *Utopianism and Marxism*. London: Methuen, 1987.
—— "Ernst Bloch and the Ubiquity of Utopia." *Utopianism and Marxism*. London and New York: Methuen, 1987.

Giddens, Anthony. The *Constitution of Society*. Berkeley and Los Angeles: University of Calfornia Press, 1984.

Giroux, Henry A. *Border Crossing*. New York: Routledge, 1992.

—— *Postmodern Education*. Minneapolis: University of Minnesota Press, 1991.

—— "Introduction." *The Politics of Education: Culture, Power and Liberation*. South Hadley, Mass.: Bergin & Garvey, 1985, pp. xi–xxv.

Goode, John. "William Morris and the Dream of Revolution." In *Literature and Politics in the Nineteenth Century*. Ed. J. Lucas. London: Methuen, 1971.

Green, Ronald M. "Ernst Bloch's Revision of Atheism." *Journal of Religion*, 49 (1969), pp. 128–35.

Gross, David. "Bloch's Philosophy of Hope." *Telos*, 75 (Spring 1988), pp. 189–98.

Grossberg, Larry. *We Gotta Get Out of This Place: Popular Conservatism and Postmodern Culture*. New York: Routledge, 1992.

Gutiérrez, Gustavo. *A Theology of Liberation: History, Politics, Salvation*. Ed. and trans. Sister Caridad Inda and John Eagleson. Maryknoll, NY: Orbis, 1973.

Habermas, Jürgen. *The Philosophical Discourse of Modernity*. Cambridge, Mass.: MIT Press, 1987.

—— *Philosophical-Political Profiles*. Trans. Frederick G. Lawrence. Cambridge, Mass.: MIT Press, 1983.

—— *Theory and Practice*. Trans. John Viertel. Boston: Beacon Press, 1974.

—— "Conservative Politics, Work, Socialism and Utopia Today." In *Habermas: Autonomy and Solidarity*. Ed. Peter Dews. London: Verso, 1986, pp. 131–47.

—— ed. *Observations on "The Spiritual Situation of the Age"*. Trans. Andrew Buchwalter. Cambridge, Mass.: MIT Press, 1987.

—— "Philosophical-Political Profile." *New Left Review*, 151 (May/June 1985), pp. 75–105.

Hammett, Dashiell. *Red Harvest* [1929]. New York: Vintage, 1982.

Heinitz, Kenneth. "The Theology of Hope according to Ernst Bloch." *Dialog*, 7 (1968), pp. 34–41.

Heym, Stefan. "Ash Wednesday in the GDR." *New German Critique*, 52 (Winter 1991), pp. 31–5.

Higbee, Kenneth. *Your Memory*. London: Piatkus, 1989.

Hinkelammert, Franz J. *The Ideological Weapons of Death: A Theological Critique of Capitalism*. Trans. Phillip Berryman. Maryknoll, NY: Orbis, 1986.

Hobbes, Thomas. *Leviathan*. Oxford: Basil Blackwell, 1960.

Horkheimer, Max. *Critical Theory*. New York: Seabury Press, 1972.

Hudson, Wayne. *The Marxist Philosophy of Ernst Bloch*. New York: St. Martin's Press. London: Macmillan, 1982.

—— "Ernst Bloch: 'Ideology' and Postmodern Social Philosophy." *Canadian Journal of Political and Social Theory*, 7: 1–2 (Winter 1983).

Hume, David. *A Treatise of Human Nature.* Harmondsworth: Penguin, 1969.

Huyssen, Andreas. "Mapping the Postmodern." *New German Critique*, 33 (Fall 1984), pp. 5–52.

Jameson, Fredric. *Marxism and Form: Twentieth-Century Dialectical Theories of Literature.* Princeton, NJ: Princeton University Press, 1971.

—— *The Political Unconscious: Narrative as a Socially Symbolic Art.* Ithaca: Cornell University Press, 1981.

—— "Of Islands and Trenches." *Diacritics,* June 1977, pp. 2–21.

—— "Reification and Utopia in Mass Culture." *Social Text,* 1 (Winter 1979), pp. 130–48.

Jay, Martin. *Marxism and Totality.* Berkeley: University of California Press. Oxford: Polity Press, 1984.

Joyce, Clyde. "Disco Fascism?" *Europe Express.* Channel 4, London, 17 February 1990.

Kaes, Anton. *From Hitler to Heimat: The Return of History as Film.* Cambridge, Mass. and London: Harvard University Press, 1989.

—— "Ideology, Marxism, and Advanced Capitalism." *Socialist Review,* 42 (Nov.-Dec. 1978), pp. 37–65.

Kellner, Douglas. "Postmodernism as Social Theory: Some Challenges and Problems." *Theory, Culture and Society,* 5: 2–3 (June 1988), pp. 239–69.

—— "Film, Politics, and Ideology: Reflections on Hollywood Film in the Age of Reagan." *The Velvet Light Trap,* 27 (Spring 1991), pp. 9–24.

—— "Toward a Multi-perspectival Cultural Studies." *Centennial Review,* 20: 446.

—— and Harry O'Hara. "Utopia and Marxism in Ernst Bloch." *New German Critique,* 9 (Fall 1976), pp. 11–34.

—— "Introduction to Ernst Bloch, 'The Dialectical Method.'" *Man and World,* 16 (1983), pp. 281–4.

Kirby, Peadar. *Lessons in Liberation: The Church in Latin America.* Dublin, Ireland: Dominican Publications, 1981.

Knight, Stephen. *Form and Ideology in Crime Fiction.* London: Macmillan, 1980.

Kracauer, Siegfried. "Zwei Deutungen in zwei Sprachen." In *Ernst Bloch zu ehren.* Ed. Siegfried Unseld. Frankfurt am Main: Suhrkamp, 1965.

Kundera, Milan. *The Book of Laughter and Forgetting.* New York: Viking/ Penguin, 1981.

Laclau, Ernesto and Chantal Mouffe. *Hegemony and Socialist Strategy: Towards a Radical Democratic Politics.* Trans. Winston Moore and Paul Cammack. London: Verso, 1985.

Laibach. *Opus Dei.* Mute Records, 1987.

Landmann, Michael. "Talking with Ernst Bloch: Korcula, 1968." *Telos*, 25 (Fall 1975), pp. 165–85.

Laplanche, J. and J.-B. Pontalis. *The Language of Psychoanalysis*. Trans. Donald Nicholson-Smith. New York: Norton, 1973.

Lears, T.J.J. "The Concept of Cultural Hegemony: Problems and Possibilities." *American Historical Review*, 90: 3 (1985), pp. 567–93.

Lenhardt, Christian. "Anamnestic Solidarity: The Proletariat and its *Manes*." *Telos*, 25 (Fall 1975), pp. 133–54.

Lenin, V.I. *What is to be Done?* Peking: Foreign Languages Press, 1975.

Lernoux, Penny. *Cry of the People: The Struggle for Human Rights in Latin America: The Catholic Church in Conflict with U.S. Policy*. Harmondsworth: Penguin, 1982.

Levitas, Ruth. *The Concept of Utopia*. Oxford: Phillip Allen. Syracuse: Syracuse University Press, 1990.

—— "Marxism, Romanticism and Utopia: Ernst Bloch and William Morris." *Radical Philosophy*, 51 (1989), pp. 27–36.

Lowenthal, Leo. *An Unmastered Past: The Autobiographical Reflections of Leo Lowenthal*. Berkeley: University of California Press, 1987.

Lukács, Georg. *The Destruction of Reason*. London: Merlin, 1980.

Lyotard, Jean-François. *The Postmodern Condition: A Report of Knowledge*. Trans. G. Bennington and B. Massumi. Minneapolis: University of Minnesota Press, 1984.

MacIntyre, Alasdair. "Practical Rationalities as Forms of Social Structure." Irish Philosophical Journal, 4: 1–2 (1987), pp. 3–19.

McLaren, Peter and R. Hammer. "Critical Pedagogy and the Postmodern Challenge." *Educational Foundations*, 3: 3 (1989), pp. 29–62.

Maier, Charles. *The Unmasterable Past: History, Holocaust, and German National Identity*. Cambridge, Mass. and London: Harvard University Press, 1988.

Mandel, Ernest. *Delightful Murder: A Social History of the Crime Story*. Minneapolis: University of Minnesota Press, 1985.

Mannheim, Karl. *Ideology and Utopia*. London: Routledge & Kegan Paul, 1979.

Marcuse, Herbert. *Counter-Revolution and Revolt*. London: Alan Lane, 1972.

—— *Eros and Civilization*. London: Sphere, 1972.

—— *Negations*. Harmondsworth: Penguin, 1972.

—— *One-Dimensional Man*. London: Sphere, 1972.

Marin, Louis. "Pour une théorie du texte parabolique." In Le Récit évangélique. Ed. Claude Chabrol et al. [Paris:] Aubier Montaigne, 1974.

—— *Utopiques, jeux d'espaces*. Paris: Minuit, 1973.

Maron, Monika. "Writers and the People." *New German Critique*, 52 (Winter 1991), pp. 36–41.

Marx, Karl. *Early Writings*. Trans. T.B. Bottomore. New York: McGraw-Hill, 1964.

—— and Friedrich Engels. *Collected Works*. London: Lawrence & Wishart, 1975–.

—— and Friedrich Engels. *Die Deutsche Ideologie*. Werke 3. Berlin: Dietz, 1956.

Mayer, Hans. "Ernst Blochs poetische Sendung." In *Ernst Bloch zu ehren*. Ed. Siegfried Unseld. Frankfurt am Main: Suhrkamp, 1965.

Meier, Paul. *William Morris: The Marxist Dreamer*. Brighton: Harvester, 1978.

Menchú, Rigoberta. *I, Rigoberta Menchú. An Indian Woman in Guatemala*. Ed. and intr. Elisabeth Burgos-Debray; trans. Ann Wright. London: Verso, 1984.

Merleau-Ponty, M[aurice]. *Phénoménologie de la Perception*. Paris: nrf, 1945.

Metz, Johannes B. *Theology of the World*. Trans. William Glen-Doepel. New York: Herder & Herder, 1969.

Middleton, David and Derek Edwards, eds. *Collective Remembering*. London: Sage, 1990.

Moltmann, Jürgen. *The Theology of Hope: On the Ground and Implications of a Christian Eschatology*. Trans. James W. Leitch. New York and Evanston: Harper & Row, 1967.

—— "Hope and Confidence: a Conversation with Ernst Bloch." *Dialog*, 7 (1968), pp. 42–55.

Moretti, Franco. "Clues." Trans. Susan Fischer. In *Signs Taken for Wonders: Essays in the Sociology of Literary Forms*. London: Verso, 1983.

Morris, William. *News from Nowhere* [1890]. London: Longmans, Green, 1905.

Morton, A.L. *The English Utopia*. London: Lawrence & Wishart, 1952.

Moylan, Tom. *Demand the Impossible: Science Fiction and the Utopian Imagination*. London and New York: Methuen, 1986.

—— "Anticipatory Fiction: *Bread and Wine* and Liberation Theology." *Modern Fiction Studies*, 35: 1 (Spring 1989), pp. 103–21.

—— "Bloch against Bloch: The Theological Reception of *Das Prinzip Hoffnung* and the Liberation of the Utopian Function." *Utopian Studies*, 1: 2 (Fall 1990), pp. 27–52. (Reprinted as ch. 7 in the present volume.)

—— "Mission Impossible: Liberation Theology and Utopian Praxis." *Utopian Studies III*. Ed. Michael Cummings and Nicholas D. Smith. Lanham, NY: University Press of America, 1990, pp. 33–65.

—— "Rereading Religion: Ernst Bloch, Gustavo Gutiérrez and the Post-Modern Strategy of Liberation Theology." *Center for Twentieth Century Studies Working Papers*, 2 (Fall 1988).

Murphy, Peter. "Postmodern Perspectives and Justice." *Thesis Eleven*, 30 (1990), pp. 117–32.

Musil, Robert. *Der Mann ohne Eigenschaften*. Hamburg: Rowohlt, 1972.

—— *Prosa, Dramen, späte Briefe*. Ed. Adolf Frise. Reinbek: Rowohlt, 1957.

Nägele, Rainer. *Theater, Theory, Speculation: Walter Benjamin and the Scenes of Modernity*. Baltimore: Johns Hopkins University Press, 1991.

Negt, Oskar. "Ernst Bloch – The German Philosopher of the October Revolution." Trans. Jack Zipes. *New German Critique*, 4 (Winter 1975), 3–17.

Ollman, Bertel. *Alienation*. Cambridge and New York: Cambridge University Press, 1976.

Orwell, George. *Nineteen Eighty-Four*. London: Penguin, 1989.

Peck, Jeffrey M. "Rac(e)ing the Nation: Is There a German 'Home'?" *New Formations*, 17 (Summer 1992), pp. 75–84.

Petrov, Krinka P. "Memory and Oral Tradition." *Memory: History, Culture and the Mind*. Ed. Thomas Butler. Oxford: Basil Blackwell, 1989.

Plato. *Protagoras and Meno*. Harmondsworth: Penguin, 1956.

—— *Theaetetus*. Oxford: Clarendon Press, 1973.

Porter, Dennis. *The Pursuit of Crime: Art and Ideology in Detective Fiction*. New Haven, Conn.: Yale University Press, 1981.

Poster, Mark. *Existential Marxism in Postwar France*. Princeton, NJ: Princeton University Press.

Proust, Marcel. *Remembrance of Things Past*. Vol. 1. London: Penguin, 1989.

Puiggros, Adriana. "Prologue to Freire, Paulo and Betto, Frei." *This School Called Life*. Buenos Aires: Legasa, 1988.

Rabinbach, Anson. "Between Enlightenment and Apocalypse: Benjamin, Bloch and Modern German Jewish Messianism." *New German Critique*, 34 (Winter 1983), pp. 78–125.

—— "Unclaimed Heritage: Ernst Bloch's *Heritage of Our Times* and the Theory of Fascism." *New German Critique*, 11 (Spring 1977), pp. 5–21.

.Rancière, Jacques. "Overlegitimation." Trans. Kristin Ross. *Social Text*, 31–2. Durham, NC: Duke University Press, 1992, pp. 252–8.

Raulet, Gerard. "Critique of Religion and Religion as Critique: The Secularized Hope of Ernst Bloch." *New German Critique*, 9 (Fall 1976), 71–87.

Reich, Wilhelm. *Sex-Pol*. New York: Vintage, 1972.

Roberts, R.H. *Hope and its Hieroglyph*. Atlanta: Scholars Press, 1990.

Rorty, Richard. *Consequences of Pragmatism*. Brighton: Harvester, 1982.

—— *Philosophy and the Mirror of Nature*. Oxford: Basil Blackwell, 1980.

Rosen, Charles. "The Ruins of Walter Benjamin." In *On Walter Benjamin*. Ed. Gary Smith. Cambridge, Mass.: MIT Press, 1988, pp. 152–60.

Rosenzweig, Franz. *Franz Rosenzweig: His Life and Thought*. Ed. Nahum Glatzer. New York: Schocken, 1961.

Ruppert, Peter. *Reader in a Strange Land*. Athens: University of Georgia Press, 1986.

Sacks, Oliver. *The Man Who Mistook His Wife for a Hat*. New York: Harper & Row, 1987.

Said, Edward W. "Opponents, Audiences, Constituencies, and Community." *Critical Inquiry*, 9: 1 (Sept. 1982), pp. 1–26.

Santner, Eric L. *Stranded Objects: Mourning, Memory, and Film in Postwar Germany*. Ithaca and London: Cornell University Press, 1990.

Schlaffer, Heinz. "Denkbilder." In *Poesie und Politik*. Ed. Wolfgang Kuttenkeuler. Bonn: Kohlhammer, 1973, pp. 137–54.

Scholem, Gershom. *Walter Benjamin: The Story of a Friendship*. Trans. Harry Zohn. New York: Schocken, 1981.

Schone, Albrecht. *Emblematik und Drama im Zeitalter des Barock*. Munich: Beck, 1964.

Smith, Gary, ed. *On Walter Benjamin*. Cambridge, Mass.: MIT Press, 1988.

Somay, Bülent. "Towards an Open-ended Utopia." *Science-Fiction Studies*, 11: 1 (1984), pp. 25–8.

Spillane, Mickey. *I, the Jury* [1947]. New York: NAL, 1968.

Strategies Collective. "Building a New Left: An Interview with Ernesto Laclau." *Strategies*, 1 (Fall 1988), pp. 5–28.

Striedter, Jurij. "Journeys through Utopia." *Poetics Today*, 3: 1 (1982), pp. 35–60.

Suvin, Darko. *Metamorphoses of Science Fiction*. New Haven: Yale University Press, 1979.

—— *Positions and Presuppositions in Science Fiction*. London: Macmillan. Kent, Ohio: Kent State University Press, 1988.

—— "Can People be re(presented) in Fiction?" In *Marxism and the Interpretation of Culture*. Ed. Cary Nelson and Lawrence Grossberg. Urbana: University of Illinois Press, 1987, pp. 663–96.

—— "The Performance Text as Audience–Stage Dialog Inducing a Possible World." *Versus*, 42 (1985), pp. 3–20.

Tager, Florence. "The Relation between Politics and Culture in the Teaching of Working Class Students." *Curriculum Inquiry*, 12: 2 (1982), pp. 209–19.

Taussig, Michael T. *Shamanism, Colonialism, and the Wild Man: A Study in Terror and Healing*. Chicago and London: University of Chicago Press, 1987.

Terdiman, Richard. *Discourse/Counter-Discourse: The Theory and Practice of Symbolic Resistance in Nineteenth-century France*. Ithaca: Cornell University Press, 1985.

Theweleit, Klaus. *Male Fantasies I: Women, Floods, Bodies, History*. Cambridge: Polity Press, 1987.

Thompson, E.P. *William Morris: Romantic to Revolutionary*. London: Merlin, 1977.

Thompson, Jim. *A Hell of a Woman* [1954]. Berkeley, Cal.: Black Lizard/ Creative Arts, 1984.

Tiedemann, Rolf. "Historical Materialism or Political Messianism."

Benjamin: Philosophy, Aesthetics, History. Ed. Gary Smith. Chicago: University of Chicago Press, 1989.

Ueding, Gert. *Glanzvolles Elend.* Frankfurt am Main: Suhrkamp, 1973.

Vansina, J. *Oral Tradition: A Study in Historical Methodology.* London: Routledge & Kegan Paul, 1965.

Vassiliev, Dimitri. "Interview." *Bookmark.* BBC2, London, 21 June 1989.

Vološinov, V.N. [= M.M. Bakhtin]. *Marxism and the Philosophy of Language.* New York: Seminar Press, 1973.

Weiler, K. "Freire and a Feminist Pedagogy of Difference." In *The Politics of Liberation.* Ed. Peter McLaren and Colin Lankshear. London: Routledge, 1994.

Welch, Sharon. *Communities of Resistance and Solidarity: A Feminist Theology of Liberation.* New York: Orbis, 1985.

Whittington, Harry. *The Woman is Mine.* Greenwich, Conn.: Gold Medal, 1954.

Williams, Raymond. *Culture and Society 1780–1950.* London: Penguin, 1958. Garden City, NY: Anchor, 1960.

—— *Problems in Materialism and Culture.* London: Verso, 1980.

Wohlfarth, Irving. "On the Messianic Structure of Walter Benjamin's Last Reflections." *Glyph,* 3 (1978).

—— "On Some Jewish Motifs in Benjamin." In *The Problem of Modernity.* Ed. Andrew Benjamin. New York: Routledge, 1989.

Wright, Partrick. "Heritage and Danger: The English Past in the Era of the Welfare State." In *Memory: History, Culture and the Mind.* Ed. Thomas Butler. Oxford: Basil Blackwell, 1989.

—— *On Living in an Old Country: The National Past in Contemporary Britain.* London: Verso, 1985.

Yates, Frances. *The Art of Memory.* London: Ark, 1984.

Yúdice, George. "Marginality and the Ethics of Survival." In *Universal Abandon? The Politics of Postmodernism.* Ed. Andrew Ross. Minneapolis: University of Minnesota Press, 1988, pp. 214–37.

Zavarzadeh, Mas'ud and Donald Morton. "Signs of Knowledge in the Contemporary Academy." *American Journal of Semiotics,* 7: 4 (1990), pp. 149–60.

Zipes, Jack. "Introduction: Ernst Bloch and the Obscenity of Hope." *New German Critique,* 45 (Fall 1988), pp. 3–9.

—— "Introduction: Toward a Realization of Anticipatory Illumination." *The Utopian Function of Art and Literature: Selected Essays of Ernst Bloch.* Trans. Jack Zipes and Frank Mecklenburg. London and Cambridge, Mass.: MIT Press, 1988, pp. xi–xliii.

Notes on Contributors

Klaus L. Berghahn is Professor of German at the University of Wisconsin, Madison. He is a contributor to the *History of German Literary Criticism* edited by Peter Uwe Hohendahl (1988) and the author of several books, including *Schiller, Ansichten eines Idealisten* (1986).

Stephen Eric Bronner is Professor of Political Science and Comparative Literature at Rutgers University. His many publications include *Of Critical Theory and its Theorists* (1994) and *Moments of Decision: Political History and the Crises of Radicalism* (1992).

Jamie Owen Daniel is Assistant Professor of English at the University of Illinois at Chicago. She has published essays on Bloch, Adorno, and concepts of the public sphere, and is the co-translator of Oskar Negt and Alexander Kluge's *Public Sphere and Experience* (1993).

Tim Dayton is Associate Professor of English at Kansas State University. His most recent work is on Muriel Rukeyser's *The Book of the Dead.*

Vincent Geoghegan is Professor of Political Theory at Queen's University, Belfast, Northern Ireland. His latest books are *Ernst Bloch* (1996) and *Utopianism and Marxism* (1987).

Henry A. Giroux is the Waterbury Professor of Education at Penn State University. His most recent books include *Fugitive Cultures: Race, Violence, and Youth* (1996) and *Channel Surfing: Race Talk and the Destruction of American Youth* (1997).

David Kaufmann is Associate Professor of English and Cultural Studies at George Mason University in Fairfax, Virginia. He is the author of *The Business of Common Life: Novels and Classical Economics between Revolution and Reform* (1995) and more recently of several articles on Adorno.

245

Douglas Kellner is Professor of Philosophy at the University of Texas, and is the author of many books and articles on philosophy, social theory and cultural criticism, including *Media Culture: Cultural Studies, Identity and Politics Between the Modern and the Postmodern* (1995) and the forthcoming *The Postmodern Turn*, co-edited with Steven Best.

Mary N. Layoun is an Associate Professor of Comparative Literature at the University of Wisconsin, Madison. Her most recent publications include essays in *Mistrusting Refugees*, ed. Daniel and Knudsen (1995), and *Between Languages and Cultures: Translation and Cross-cultural Texts*, ed. Dingwaney and Maier (1995). She is presently completing a book, *Boundary Fixation?: The Rhetoric of National Culture in Crisis*.

Ruth Levitas is Senior Lecturer in Sociology at the University of Bristol, England. She is the author of *The Concept of Utopia* (1990), and is currently working on concepts of social exclusion and inclusion in contemporary political discourse.

Ze'ev Levy is Professor of Philosophy and Jewish Thought at the University of Haifa, Israel. His recent publications in English include *David Baumgardt and Ethical Hedonism* (1989) and *Baruch or Benedict: On Some Jewish Aspects of Spinoza's Philosophy* (1989).

Peter McLaren teaches at the School of Education and Information Studies at the University of California, Los Angeles. His most recent books include *Critical Pedagogy and Predatory Culture* (1995) and *Revolutionary Multiculturalism: Pedagogies of Dissent for the New Millennium* (1997).

Tom Moylan is Associate Professor of English and Cultural Studies at George Mason University in Fairfax, Virginia. He is the author of *Demand the Impossible: Science Fiction and the Utopian Imagination* (1986), and has published essays on science fiction, utopianism, and cultural and political theory.

Darko Suvin is Professor of English and Comparative Literature at McGill University in Montreal, Canada. He has published widely on utopia and science fiction, and his recent publications include *Positions and Presuppositions in Science Fiction* (1988) and *Lessons of Japan* (1996).

Jack Zipes is Professor of German at the University of Minnesota. He has written extensively on Ernst Bloch and critical theory. His most recent books are *Happily Ever After: Fairy Tales, Children and the Culture Industry* (1997) and *The Yale Companion to Jewish Writing and Thought in German Culture, 1096–1996* (1997), edited with Sander Gilman.